CRITICAL ACCLAIM FOR
The Best Travelers' Tales

"This book will grace my bedside for years to come."
—Simon Winchester, from the Introduction to
The Best Travelers' Tales 2004

"Travelers' Tales books are a sweet relief indeed. These titles luxuriate in that complicated beautiful, shadowy place where the best stories begin, and the most compelling characters roam free. *The Best Travelers' Tales 2004* is a collection of memories from travelers who visit both the exotic and the familiar, and come away with rich stories."
—*ForeWord Magazine*

"Every book I've seen in the 10 years that Travelers' Tales has been publishing, has included top writing of the sort that makes me feel as if I'm with the traveler—and in many cases I must say I'm very happy I'm not. Some are funny, some sad, some thought provoking. This is exactly what people mean when they refer to excellent 'armchair travel.' Go—without having to actually climb Mount Kalaish in Tibet or get robbed in Dar es Salaam."
—*The Times-Picayune*

"Any guidebook can inform globetrotters about their destination's lodging, restaurants, and attractions. But only someone who's been there can spin stories about the day to day life of faraway lands. Travelers' Tales editors choose the cream of the crop."
—*SF Weekly*

"Of course, we all love Travelers' Tales and were happy to see them put together *The Best Travelers' Tales 2004*, a wonderful collection of wonderful tales from around the world."
—*Transitions Abroad*

TRAVELERS' TALES BOOKS

Country and Regional Guides
America, Australia, Brazil, Central America, China, Cuba, France,
Greece, India, Ireland, Italy, Japan, Mexico, Nepal, Spain, Thailand,
Tibet, Turkey; Alaska, American Southwest, Grand Canyon,
Hawai'i, Hong Kong, Paris, Provence, San Francisco, Tuscany

Women's Travel
Her Fork in the Road, A Woman's Path, A Woman's
Passion for Travel, A Woman's World, Women in the Wild,
A Mother's World, Safety and Security for Women Who
Travel, Gutsy Women, Gutsy Mamas

Body & Soul
The Spiritual Gifts of Travel, The Road Within, Love & Romance,
Adventures in Wine, Food, How to Eat Around the World,
The Adventure of Food, The Ultimate Journey, Pilgrimage

Special Interest
Not So Funny When It Happened, The Gift of Rivers,
Shitting Pretty, Testosterone Planet, Danger!, The Fearless
Shopper, The Penny Pincher's Passport to Luxury Travel, The Gift
of Birds, Family Travel, It's a Dog's World, There's No Toilet Paper
on the Road Less Traveled, The Gift of Travel, 365 Travel, Sand in
My Bra, Hyenas Laughed at Me, Whose Panties Are These?

Travel Literature
A Sense of Place, Kite Strings of the Southern Cross,
The Sword of Heaven, Storm, Take Me With You, Last Trout
in Venice, The Way of the Wanderer, One Year Off, The Fire
Never Dies, The Royal Road to Romance, Unbeaten Tracks in
Japan, The Rivers Ran East, Coast to Coast, Trader Horn

TRAVELERS' TALES

THE
BEST
TRAVEL
WRITING
2005

TRUE STORIES
FROM AROUND THE WORLD

TRAVELERS' TALES

THE BEST
TRAVEL WRITING
2005

TRUE STORIES
FROM AROUND THE WORLD

Edited by
JAMES O'REILLY, LARRY HABEGGER,
AND SEAN O'REILLY

Travelers' Tales
San Francisco

Art Direction: Michele Wetherbee/Stefan Gutermuth
Interior design and page layout: Melanie Haage using the fonts
Nicholas Cochin and Granjon.

Distributed by: Publishers Group West, 1700 Fourth Street,
Berkeley, California 94710.

ISBN 1-932361-16-2
ISSN 1548-0224

First Edition
Printed in the United States
10 9 8 7 6 5 4 3 2 1

One cannot divine nor forecast the conditions
that will make happiness; one only stumbles
upon them by chance, in a lucky hour, at the
world's end somewhere...

— WILLA CATHER (1873–1947)

Table of Contents

Publisher's Preface

I STOOD AT THE FRONT DESK OF THE BADRUTT'S PALACE Hotel in St. Moritz, Switzerland, waiting for the clerk to hand me the stamps I'd just bought. Instead, he plucked postcards from my hand, licked the stamps, and began to place them precisely. The last stamp, however, tore at the corner when he was removing it from the main sheet, but instead of leaving well enough alone, he tore off the tiny, orphaned piece and reunited it with the rest of the stamp, which he'd already affixed. When he was finished, he gave me a huge smile and put my postcards in the outgoing mail.

I laughed as I went out the door—a laugh of surprise at such care. To say it was good service wouldn't do it justice, because it bore much more the mark of a warm heart.

Most of us travel to connect with this mystery of the other, the strange land, the incomprehensible tongue, and the inner vistas of a different way of life. And if we manage to come away physically unscathed, we never come away without the tire marks of human contact, whether we're crossing a border, trusting a guide in the bush, getting directions from a taxi driver, or being touched by the spirit of a hotel clerk.

Paul Harper, author of "Waiting to Arrive," a story in this collection about a journey to the Nigerian frontier, wrote in a different piece about his stint as a bicycle mechanic in Ghana:

When I hear the clink of hammer on screwdriver
in any West African City—something as steady and
eternal as time—it means many things. It is a sound
of defiance, a sound of reassurance that, yes, people
are still riding bikes, and above all a comfort that
I will not be missed. But there somewhere in the
ringing space between beats is a pang, a reminder of
an alliance that never happened, of all the other things
I meant to do, of what I left behind and what can still
be done.

You too are that stranger, who may pass through
town like a ghost or leave as a friend who has earned
the regard of those he's met. It's worth asking yourself,
when you travel, are you a parasite, neutral agent, or
catalyst?

Recently I was running at the Stanford stadium, when
an old guy going the opposite way passed me saying,
"How you doing, bro?" His greeting was the best thing
that happened to me that day, as I was still digesting
the news of the tsunami in Southeast Asia. His words
were like a light shining on me, and I left the stadium
thinking the obvious: "Why yes! He is my brother."
And so were those who'd just died in the disaster, and
so are those who survived. As are the billions of people
out there waiting to meet you, just as some of them met
the travelers in this book, who brought home the things
that happened to them, and the ways they were marked
abroad, in tragedy, in happiness, in farce, in anger, and
in love.

Be generous with yourself this year—go out and connect, spread yourself around. Travel more, not less. And

then come home and tell a story to your friends about what it's like just over the horizon, where your brothers and sisters live.

James O'Reilly
Palo Alto, California

Introduction

Tom Miller

GREAT TRAVEL WRITING CONSISTS OF EQUAL PARTS curiosity, vulnerability, and vocabulary. It is not a terrain for know-it-alls or the indecisive. The best of the genre can simply be an elegant natural history essay, a nicely writ sports piece, or a well-turned profile of a bar band and its music. A well-grounded sense of place is the challenge for the writer. We observe, we calculate, we inquire, we look for a link between what we already know and what we're about to learn. The finest travel writing describes what's going on when nobody's looking.

Moritz Thomsen (1915-1991) was one of the great American expatriate writers of the twentieth century. Period. A soft-hearted cuss, a man of almost insufferable integrity, a lousy farmer and a terrific writer, his books have long since been smothered by the avalanche from megapublishers (yet remarkably, three of his titles remain in print). Although all his works could be considered travel memoirs imbued with a sense of place, his third book, *The Saddest Pleasure*, embodies some of the very finest elements of the genre: constant doubt, a meddlesome nature, and a disregard for nationalism. (The book's title comes from a line in Paul Theroux's novel, *Picture Palace*: "Travel is the saddest of the pleasures.") Thomsen, who stayed in Ecuador following his mid-nineteen-sixties Peace Corps stint, pledged allegiance to nothing except his station as an expatriate. And as an expat he was free to judge us all, an undertaking he finessed with acute observations, self-deprecation, and a flavorful frame of reference that ranged from a Tchaikovsky symphony to a Sealy Posturpedic mattress.

Inquisitiveness. Yes. In *The Art of Travel*, a book worth staying home for, Alain de Botton quotes Alexander von Humboldt's childhood curiosity: "Why don't the same things grow everywhere?" And as children we might also ask, "Why doesn't everyone look the same?" "Why don't we all speak the same language?" Or, to quote Rodney King's adult exasperation, "Can't we all just get along?" It is these pure and simple questions of innocence that should accompany travel writers, not iPods, Palm Pilots, cell phones, or laptops. Travel with paper and pen, a book, maybe a bilingual dictionary. Ask the questions a child might.

In the late nineteen-seventies I advanced a notion that the U.S.-Mexico frontier was really a third country, two thousand miles long and twenty miles wide, and went about testing it. I had little awareness of travel writing, but when my book about the borderland came out in 1981, reviews invariably referred to it as travel literature, a category I had never really considered.

Reviewers anointed me a travel writer; I didn't choose the label. Others have recoiled at the identity. "I detest the term," Jonathan Raban told the *Chicago Tribune*. Eddy L. Harris insisted to the same newspaper: "I'm not a travel writer. Absolutely not." Although I've openly embraced it, the name sometimes makes me uncomfortable, too. It's as if travel writing was considered a second-tier calling—"non-fiction lite."

Yet surely as buses plunge off Peruvian mountainsides and Norwegian freighters collide with Liberian tankers,

the basic ingredients of formula travel writing will endure. Henry Miller succumbed. When he lived in Paris,
Miller wrote the odd travel piece for a friend's publica-
tion. "They were easy to do, because I had only to consult
the back issues and revamp the old articles," he wrote in
Tropic of Cancer. "The principal thing was to keep the adjectives well-furbished." Be skeptical of writers who talk
of snow-capped peaks, bustling marketplaces where the
beadwork is always intricate, and shy but friendly natives.
(You'd shy away, too, if foreigners constantly accosted you,
cameras, notepads, and tape recorders at the ready.) The
essayist who calls a town quaint, the plaza charming, or
the streets teeming, has no literary imagination. Distrust
any writing that opens with a quote from a cabby or closes
with one from a bartender.

What the writers in the following pages so elegantly
accomplish is first-person sociology, economics, anthro-
pology, history, geography, politics, biology, cultural studies, even criminology. Their fulsome stories tell of near-
suicide in Mayan country, a Laotian fortune-teller, and
a Paris bistro. The contributors here use Odysseus as a
guide, consider that Balinese canoes carry culture as well
as cargo, and navigate corruption and highways to reach
Bucharest. They are not prone to niceties, either. Their
refreshing honesty reveals a world of surprising love and
disappointing fools, unforeseen circumstance and invigo-
rating challenges.

My favorite travel accounts all have an unspoken sub-
text. They are full of polemic, prejudice, adversity; revelation, conquest, triumph, and there is plenty of those quali-
ties in these stories, too. Leilani Marie Labong, frustrated
from teaching English in Japan, found herself "cursing
its backwards ways." Dustin W. Leavitt learned to say he

was a scholar, not a writer, in a country where the former is respected and the latter suspect. Suz Redfearn met her literary mentor and idol, the late Spalding Gray, on a nude beach in California. For other writers in this book, such as Murad Kalam peregrinating to Mecca or Mark Jenkins slipping into Burma, annoying hosts and global boundaries just get in the way. "Somebody must trespass on the taboos of modern nationalism," wrote Robert Byron in *The Road to Oxiana*, defending travelers whose writings insult their hosts. "Business can't. Diplomacy won't. It has to be people like us."

The finest travel writing gets under the skin of a locale to sense its rhythm, to probe its contours, to divine a genuine understanding. We shed pre-, mal-, and misconceptions about a land, then sneak up on it and develop our own prejudices. Pico Iyer, appraising Dharamsala, pauses to allow that the point of travel "is to journey into complication, even contradiction." Sally Shivnan, in her piece set in Spain, writes of approaching the Alhambra with "the best kind of naïveté"—knowing just enough to want to know more. It's difficult to parachute into a setting for just a few days and emerge with confident, intelligent writing. I am often envious and always bewildered by writers such as Joan Didion who spent two weeks in El Salvador and emerged with a most respectable book about that country at war, or Andrei Codrescu who did a fly-by over Cuba and crash-landed with *Ay, Cuba!*

Travel literature, including many of the examples in this fine collection, usually consists of writers from industrial countries visiting far less developed lands. (For a memorable variation to this regrettable state of affairs, read *An African In Greenland*, by Tête-Michel Kpomassie from the 1980s; or, from a century earlier, read the Cuban

José Martí's essays on life in the States.) Not surprisingly, there is little tradition of homegrown travel literature in Namibia, Belize, or the Ukraine. Many countries publish anthologies of outsiders looking in at them, curious visitors who never quite unpacked their bags. In *Notes of a Villager*, the Mexican author José Rubén Romero laments, "Our country is like a cow fallen over a cliff, rich in spoils for the crows of other nationalities."

As unrepentant crows from other nationalities, the contributors to *The Best Travel Writing 2005* have enthusiastically picked at the rich spoils the world has lain bare. And we always go back, all of us, because somewhere in the world another cow is always falling over another cliff.

✄ ✄ ✄

Tom Miller has been bringing us extraordinary stories of ordinary people for more than thirty years. His highly acclaimed travel books include The Panama Hat Trail, *about South America,* On the Border, *an account of his adventures in the U.S.-Mexico frontier,* Trading with the Enemy, *which takes readers on his journeys through Cuba, and, about the American Southwest,* Jack Ruby's Kitchen Sink, *winner of the Lowell Thomas Award for Best Travel Book of 2000. Additionally, he has edited two collections,* Travelers' Tales Cuba, *and* Writing on the Edge: A Borderlands Reader. *His articles have appeared in* Smithsonian, The New Yorker, The New York Times, LIFE, Natural History, *and many other publications. He lives in Arizona, and can be reached at tommillerbooks.com.*

For more of Tom Miller's thoughts on writing, see his interview with Michael Shapiro in A Sense of Place: Great Travel Writers Talk About Their Craft, Lives, and Inspiration.

~~~~ ~~~~ ~~~~

Cause for Alarm

Is it wise to trust in the kindness of strangers?

In the shadow of fabled Timbuktu lies the medieval town of Djenné, and every child's fantasy: here the most colossal mud pie in the world rises from the desert. The Djenné Mosque is 12,000 square feet and built entirely of sand and sticks. Its tan minarets reach for the clouds like arms outstretched in prayer. Six steps, symbolizing the transition from profane to sacred, lead into the mosque. Centuries of monsoons have somehow spared this house of Allah. As I am admiring the holy sandcastle, a teenager with a crutch approaches. In flawless English he announces, "My name is Toka. I would like to show you around. May I?" I haven't heard a word of English in two weeks. "Follow me," he offers, his bright smile illuminating his dark face like a crescent moon.

Although Toka has a discernible limp, he hops over the

river of raw sewage running in the middle of the street and capers up six flights of stairs like a mountain goat to show me an unparalleled view of the city. I can barely keep up. He points to what looks like a Walt Disney castle surrounded by a moat off in the distance. "That's where my family lives," he waves proudly. "Sirimou. Would you like to see a traditional Malian village?"

The path to Sirimou winds through a floodplain so hot and dry that three cows have keeled over like jack-knifed semis. Their corpses are already covered with a dusting of sand. Their ribs protrude, bleached white as piano keys. "When I was six years old, I got sick with the flu," Toka begins. "I remember being delirious with a high fever, and then I couldn't use my legs." A procession of villagers on their way to market shares the road with us: barefooted women with newborns strapped to their backs balance wooden bowls brimming with millet or firewood on their heads. A man on a bicycle with a freshly butchered sheep tied behind his seat with a vine goes by. "My family didn't know what was the matter with me, but they couldn't afford to find out," Toka relates, matter-of-factly. "For years, I walked on my fists, dragging my legs behind me like a seal. Then my parents built me a wheelchair so I could roll through the alleys with my friends."

We pause under a baobab tree, which offers the only respite from the heat. Its trunk looks like an elephant's leg, wrinkled at the knees. Its bare branches pierce the cloudless blue satin of the sky. Toka's gaze is drawn heavenward. "Three years ago, when I was fifteen, I was playing in front of the mosque where I met you, when an American woman spotted me. The next thing I knew, she was taking me to the doctor in Bamako and they told me I had polio. But that's not the most amazing thing." His brown eyes fix on my green ones like magnets. "She was an angel. She flew me home with her to Chicago. Even though she already had seven kids. And she paid for three reconstructive surgeries for my legs." Toka plants his crutch in the sand emphatically. "When I returned to Mali, six months later, I walked off the plane by myself. It's a miracle. How can I ever repay what they did for me?" He looks to the sky again. The sun glints off the whites of his eyes. "That's why I want to help whenever I can."

Sirimou is built on a hill, so when the Bani River floods, the town becomes an island accessible only by dugout canoe or rickety bridge. We go for the bridge. The call to prayer floats over the rooftops. A throng of screaming children greets us. The older siblings are carrying the younger ones, adorned with fetishes to ward off evil spirits: braided leather thongs gird their waists and ankles, bone talismans encircle their necks. The babies shriek in terror when they see me, but the brave toddlers fight over my hands. "*Tobabou!*" they shout (white person). "*Bonjour. Ça va?*" They tap my pockets eagerly, patting me down for candy or ballpoint pens. "Bonbon? Bic?" a dozen ever-hopeful voices giggle.

"Ignore them," Toka shoos them away with his crutch. The children scatter, but soon we are surrounded by the village mothers and teenage daughters wearing hammered gold crescents as big as bananas in their noses and ears. The tallest woman taps her jaw and moans. Her front teeth are missing. I can see she needs aspirin. I pour two Advil into her palm and offer my bottled water. She refuses the water but grabs the pills. Now women are pawing at me from all sides, yelling, grabbing, pushing, shoving. I don't think they will hurt me, but I am being crushed as they press in on me. I start dispensing all the Advil I have left, but Toka orders me to stop. "They get medicine from everyone who comes here. There is nothing wrong with them. They just see you as an opportunity to get something." He speaks to them harshly and they glide back into their doorless houses, like snails retreating into their shells.

Toka leads me through narrow, convoluted streets. I try to notice where we are going, but the streets are really just packed earth between the houses, which all look the same anyway, and I realize that without my guide I am completely lost. Somewhere in the middle of the labyrinth is a mosque, and beside it, a husband and wife have set up shop: neat mounds of white rice, peanuts in the shell, and metal containers of milk. The husband, sitting on sheepskin, is transforming foliage into fishing line by twisting the leaves between his fingers and thumbs as though rolling a cigarette. His wife, on a straw mat beside him, is equally dexterous, spinning creamy clouds of fleece into yarn using her toes as the spindle. With her free hand, she cracks a peanut between her teeth and offers me the prize.

Five men who have been leaning against the side of the mosque in the shade watching me now step forward into the bright sunlight, saying something that sounds guttural and harsh. "They are complaining their eyes hurt because they have been studying the Koran so much," Toka translates. "They want your sunglasses." One of them tries to grab them from the top of my head, but Toka fends them off with his crutch. "They're lying. They do this to everyone. Pay no attention to them." Toka has been emphatic that I ignore the children, the women, and the religious students of the village. But next, the imam comes out of the mosque, gesticulating angrily. "What does he want?" I ask. "That's the imam," Toka replies. "You can't ignore him. He wants you to come with him."

The imam wears a heavy white cotton robe that grazes his ankles, a white crocheted prayer cap, and plastic sandals. His skin is as dark and shiny as an oil slick. He's in a hurry. I follow a few paces behind. The imam leads me into his house. Wooden prayer tablets with Arabic verses scrawled on them are strewn about the dirt courtyard. Wicker fish traps hang on the walls. A small boy is untangling a fishing net so voluminous he seems caught in it. His sister, perched on an oil drum, is braiding straw mats. They watch me with wide saucer eyes, but their hands never leave their work.

The imam leads me deeper into the courtyard, past a blackened fire pit with calabashes, pottery sieves, and stacks of animal hides, past two women threshing millet cobs in a wooden pail playing a musical game while they work. They alternate their pestles...thud...thwack...thud...thwack.... and between downbeats, they clap their hands in counter rhythms. Their sweat drips into the grain. They giggle. They pretend not to notice me. The imam is focused and intent. He steps over the threshold into his house. The walls are made of straw and mud. There are no windows.

Where is the imam taking me and just what exactly does he plan to do with me once we get there? My mind is racing. Who can help me if his intentions are less than honorable? The kids mending the nets and mats? The wives who are busy threshing tonight's dinner? It is not that long after September 11th and all I can think about is Daniel Pearl. I try to slow my breathing down. I look at Toka for reassurance, but he just pushes me forward with his crutch. The imam is waiting. The imam means business.

I haven't seen another white person in the two weeks I have been here. My arms and legs are covered, but my head is unveiled. Can they tell by my face that I am a Jew? I am carrying a camera. I am carrying an American passport. I am a target. And I am afraid. If they decide to do something to me, no one will ever know. There are no telephones in this village, no radios, no cell phones. There is nowhere to run, nowhere to hide. The imam pulls aside the braided straw mat that serves as the door to his bedroom.

I hesitate. Toka whispers, "He wants to show you something," and he nudges me into the room. There is a bare double mattress on the floor. The imam's clothes are hanging from a wire over the bed. I hear the rhythm of the threshing in the courtyard, but what could the women and children do? I hold back still.

I shouldn't have allowed myself to get into this situation. I should have used better judgment. But I wanted to trust because I believe it's important to make connections with people different from me, to learn about other cultures, to make eye contact and trade smiles. This is how we make peace. By trusting each other. By making leaps of faith. By stepping out of ourselves into others' lives and beliefs and honoring them. But now my heart is in my mouth and I don't have time to think anymore. I can taste my fear, metallic and cold as iron.

The imam kneels on the bed and reaches for something. There. He has it in his hands. He turns around and inches slowly towards me. He is concealing it in the folds of his robe. He has some gray whiskers in his beard, his toenails need trimming. I shrink back, but Toka is right behind me. The imam puts one hand on my shoulder, and I finally see that in his other hand he is clenching…a clock. The clock face is analog. It is 11:20. The ticking is so loud, I wonder if it's a bomb. Why is he showing me his clock? Does this mean my time has come? The imam forces the clock into my hands. He is getting more and more impatient, jabbing at the dial, poking my arm. From the growling sounds exploding in his throat, it seems his agitation is about to come to a head.

Now it is 11:21. I am holding my breath. My heart-beat matches the sweep of the second hand. As time slows down to seconds and fractions of seconds, I focus on every detail of the clock. It is made of white molded plastic in the shape of the Taj Mahal. The hands are gold. The numbers have curly tails. The clock takes two AA batteries. There are five buttons with Arabic writing on them. The imam is pointing at some other buttons, beneath the Arabic ones, with words in English: ON OFF SET ALARM. "He doesn't speak English," Toka says. "He wants you to set his prayer clock." The imam's palms are pressed together in front of his chest and a beseeching smile quivers in the bird's nest that is his beard. Relief blows through me, hot as a desert wind. An ear-to-ear grin cracks my face. I can breathe again. The sky has never looked so blue.

In this dusty, fairy tale village of mud and straw, perched on a hill overlooking a floodplain, where there is no medicine, no electricity, no running water, and no telephone, everything takes time, and time is everything. There is a time for fishing and a time for mending the nets, a time for sowing the millet seeds and a time to let the fields lie fallow, a time for shearing the sheep and a time for slaughter. Time is as precious as the river that brings the fish, the clouds that bring the rain, and the sun that nourishes the crops, dries the fish, bakes the mud bricks of the tiny houses that hold so many lives. And prayer is the golden thread that runs through the necklace of moments that make up whole lifetimes here in Sirimou. I set the imam's clock with gratitude and hand it back to him. He cradles it with the gentleness of a new mother. He thanks me with his eyes, and shows us to the door. The millet-threshing wives look up from their pails and bid Allah to be with us as we leave their house. "My family is just around the corner," says Toka. "Let's go." He skips through the dusty streets on his gimpy leg and crutch with all the exuberance of a pony nearing its barn. A herd of curious goats trots after us bleating, and the imam's voice, calling *"Allah Akbar,* God is great," drifts over the rooftops like snow.

✼ ✼ ✼

Deborah Fryer is a freelancer who has won numerous awards for her writing, including 1ˢᵗ place in the Moondance Film Festival Short Story Contest. She lives in Boulder, Colorado.

ᖷᖷᖷ

Part Lao, Part *Falang*

A culinary adventure leads to unexpected places.

FOR SIX MONTHS, I ATE EVERYTHING OFFERED TO ME in Laos. Mostly that meant noodle soup, sticky rice, ground chicken, and spicy papaya salad. But at a picnic outside Vientiane, I let my friend Phet spoon blood pudding into my mouth, and at the That Luang Festival, I tasted blackened frog. On the bus to Pakse I even nibbled roasted bat, though the sight of it, a crisp winged rodent, made me think, *plague, black plague.*

I thought it rude to decline food in a country where the average annual income was $300, to disparage the nourishment of people who'd welcomed me into their villages and homes. But it was deeper than that; while some people eat to feel love, in my family you ate to show love. If you didn't eat the green beans and the cheesecake it was like saying, "Grandma, I don't really love you, and you don't have to love me back."

So one Friday in Vientiane I chewed and swallowed three *luk phet*, duck embryos, straight from the eggs. I'd taught four classes that day, then went for drinks with Langsy, Nisith, and Patrick: two Lao officials and the reigning Belgian bureaucrat on my U.N. project.

The threesome raised their glasses.

"We hope you stay another year," Langsy said.

"We move classes to beer shop," Nisith said. "Drink beer, English come."

As they joked about adding Beerlao to my English-teaching budget, I wondered if they knew of my struggles in the Intermediate Class, how the students used my discussion exercises to impersonate ancient stone Buddhas.

This beer shop overlooked the Mekong. An orange sun blazed over the flat brown river and threw columns of light across the wood floors and bamboo walls of the room. Nisith and Langsy wore gray cadre uniforms, and Patrick his usual pastel Don Johnson ensemble with a thin gold chain around his neck. The waitress placed a plate of small, barely blue eggs in the center of our plastic table.

Langsy explained, in a mixture of English and Lao, that these eggs were *luk phet*, types one through five. A "one" was a gooey zygote; a "five" would have wings, a beak, eyes.

Patrick grinned at me, but I wouldn't meet his gaze. I rolled up my sleeves. I was wearing a blue and black Lao silk skirt that fell to my ankles and a white button-up shirt. My hair was pinned neatly in a bun. In my role as teacher I'd conformed to Lao standards of femininity, but for Patrick, I refused to play the squeamish girl.

As instructed, I cracked the first two eggs to find a glutinous mass of yolk in the white—ones or twos. I stared at the nearly finished plate and reached for a third. *Trade it in*, I thought, as soon as I picked one. But I wiped my mind clean, cleared it like a blackboard, and cracked the thin blue casing.

"A number five," Langsy said, stating the obvious.

It looked no different from a newly hatched bird, only more vulnerable, moist. I glanced at the table to see if I might sequester it in the mounting rubble of shells. I considered losing it up the sleeve of my blouse, but Nisith and Langsy were watching my hands, my face. So I opened my jaw and inserted the embryo, broke its body enough to wash it down with the beer. It tasted like flesh, feathers, and salt.

I smiled.

"Do you like?" Langsy asked, genuinely curious.

"*Sep lai.*" Delicious, I lied, barely controlling my face. I'd trained myself to believe "delicious" meant thank you, thank you for your kindness.

They smiled.

I felt the duck lodged inside. It seemed to have grazed a tube in my chest. My throat felt scratched and I chugged a half glass of beer. Then I finished it, trying to erase the sense memory. I felt queasy, though I didn't know whether from the actual baby bird or because I'd pushed my body too far.

When I stepped out of Patrick's Land Rover an hour later, the ground seemed to lurch upwards in a crooked slant. I waved goodbye, hoping he hadn't noticed me stagger. Inside my house I collapsed beneath the gauzy tower of my mosquito net. The sound of frogs by the river, usually soothing, sounded like a demonic chant.

Hours later I bolted upright, drenched in sweat, struck by *tuk thong,* exploding stomach. I made it to the bathroom before the first wave of nausea crashed and crouched there all night, intermittently sleeping on the cool tile floor. In a book called *Staying Healthy in Southeast Asia*, I'd read about everything that could go wrong with a human body, starting with roundworms, pinworms, threadworms, and tapeworms. After a while, the afflictions blurred together: typhoid typhus malaria yellow fever dengue fever. Japanese encephalitis meningococcal meningitis plague fever flu. Tetanus. Blood flukes. Liver flukes. The symptoms for "river blindness" formed a perfect haiku:

skin can become thick,
dark, scaly redness and tears,
finally, blindness

Anthrax, not to be confused with ailments like fungus, lice, and scabies, lurked in goatskin products. I'd even read up on drowning and electric shock. It seemed the more I knew about these things, the less likely they were to happen.

I tried to remember what the book had said of enduring *tuk thong,* and its possibly fatal effects. In a moment of digestive detente, I plucked it from the shelf. After forty-eight hours, when I couldn't keep water down, I decided to visit Mahasot.

Phet had said of Mahasot Hospital, "It is better to go there *never.*" Her sister once set her broken arm at home. Her father healed his malaria with a tall glass of dog's blood. Barring dire emergency, many Lao preferred to first visit a shaman or a monk.

Mahasot Hospital was on the river road near my house, past the Temple That Khao and the local market. Pavement had been stripped from this road and there was a giant gash in the dirt around the building with the sign "Foreigner Clinic." I scaled the far side of the ditch on all fours. My hands looked like someone else's, and the night seemed too bright.

Mahasot was considered the best hospital in Laos. Still, you had to bring your own anesthetic, toilet paper, and food. The rural hospitals were worse. An Australian friend in Oudomxay had once stitched up his own hand. There were stories of provincial hospitals that borrowed tools for amputations, after accidents with unexploded American bombs. People traveled by foot and cart for days to reach Mahasot. I had only to walk three blocks.

The waiting room was fluorescent lit, greenish, empty. A layer of dust coated the linoleum floor. A nurse wearing a mismatched white uniform and flip-flops leaned her push mop against a row of metal chairs and greeted me with a *wai*, hands in prayer position. With a broken pencil she recorded my name. She peered into my face with a mixture of compassion and the raw curiosity provoked by *falang*, foreigners—even a sick one at 2 A.M. This nurse, soft-voiced, sweet-faced, could not have been older than twenty.

She fetched a Lao doctor in a white lab coat who spoke to me in what sounded like fluent French. I replied in Lao. We ruled out English. I told him I couldn't keep down water. Since my Lao didn't convey the violence of the symptoms, I embellished with my hands. The nurse laughed out loud, and suddenly I laughed, too. The doctor scowled.

"*Bo penn nyang*," the nurse said. Don't worry. This was the Lao national motto.

Right then I suspected there was nothing to be done. Perhaps I'd come to the hospital to feel less alone. The Lao said all sickness was loss of soul; your spirit left your body. I didn't feel nauseated anymore, but I felt a searing heat beneath my sternum and a sour taste in my mouth.

The nurse led me to another brightly lit room, gestured for me to lie on a narrow stretcher. She looked down at me, smiling. "You can sleep here," she said in Lao.

The doctor came in, holding something I couldn't see. He had the haunted look of a man who knew exactly how shoddy the hospital was and still wanted to do his job. Lipstick marks stained the pillowcase and one beige curtain. Two mosquitoes circled overhead, so fat they wobbled in flight.

The doctor seemed disappointed that I didn't speak French, because he started again in that language, "something something something IV."

He held up a bag of fluid, a line, and a needle.

"No, no thanks. *Merci. Bo penn nyang.*"

He went over to the trash and pulled out crumpled white paper to show that the needle had been wrapped, was clean. He made a very French noise, a little clicking sound that might soothe a horse.

"I can't. *Bo die.* No."

His mouth trembled, his lips pursed. The doctor turned his back, left the room as if propelled by a gust of wind. I exhaled. I looked again at the marks on the curtain: a dark reddish brown, too large to be lipstick. I turned on my side, though I couldn't curl up on the narrow space.

The nurse ambled back to my narrow cot.

"*Mi fen bo?*" Do you have a boyfriend?

"Are you in love?" was an everyday question in Laos, similar to how people at home asked, "What do you do?" As if your job were the defining feature of your humanity.

The closest I had to a romance in Laos was a crush on one of my young students, Viengphet, whom I tried not to call on too much despite his wicked grin, his well-pressed sea-green shirts, his cumbersome and distracting hands. I'd secretly named one of my goldfish after him. If I were feeling extremely risqué I'd park my bike right up close to his, peddle to peddle.

"*Bo mi*," I told the nurse. Don't have. "How about you?"

"*Nyang*." Not yet.

She waited by my stretcher, sighed, stood vigil. She brought me water and I drank it.

"A bill?" I asked in Lao, as I rose from the cot.

"*Bo penn nyang*," she waved her hand.

As I walked home, I thought how the doctor had shown anger, how un-Lao that was. How un-Lao I'd been for saying no, even to a needle. I was sure it had been clean, yet I'd made him lose face after seeking his help. I'd lost face myself. I stopped at an intersection to stare at the Mekong, to listen to its flat insistent whisper. I turned toward home, wanting the sanctuary of bed before the first temple bell.

Forty-eight hours of *tuk thong* left me five pounds lighter and unsteady in my flip-flops. I called in sick to work on Monday. In addition to low-grade narcolepsy, I felt an acute dread of leaving the house. I figured this was culture shock, round two. Supposedly it was inevitable, and it came in bouts, though the syndrome was missing from the "c" topics—chilblains, choking, cholera, condoms, constipation, convulsions—indexed in my book.

"Kathryn," Phet chimed into the phone, "I come to visit. After work."

"No, no, *bo penn nyang*, I'm fine." I tried to sound firm, sick, and polite all at once.

"I come," she said, "Patrick says you are sick."

After another nap and several hours of reading, I decided to tidy the most disgraceful aspects of my kitchen, sweeping up the tracks of dust left by my bike, and the flattened, paper-thin frog, the size of a quarter, that had appeared there a week before. I'd let it remain; the mystery of its arrival was a symbol of everything I didn't understand about Laos.

Soon after, Phet appeared at my screen door, kicking her shoes off on the porch.

"At my house I will make you *feu*." Noodle soup.

"I can't eat."

"Segetdao, you have to eat."

I couldn't help but smile at my Lao name.

"Just come." She handed me the extra helmet.

I wasn't too surprised when Phet stopped her motorbike, and I opened my eyes beneath the clear helmet plate, we were in a remote industrial outpost of Vientiane rather than in Phet's front yard.

"First, we go to the *mau-du*."

In Laos the shortest distance between two points was never a straight line. I'd learned that the night we set out for a party but ended up, with no explanation, attending a birth. Or the day Old Buffalo was supposed to take me to a library but stranded me at the Polish Embassy instead.

There was no explanation. It was like the flattened frog appearing on my kitchen floor, something to simply accept. And I knew, or suspected, that Phet thought my malaise best addressed by a *mau-du*, a fortuneteller. The fading light cast a mood like the edges of a painting. Only a peeling water tower interrupted the darkening plains of sky. We waited in front of the *mau-du's* house, which was gray wood and corrugated tin, unscreened and indistinguishable from the others. These tenuous structures jostled shoulder-to-shoulder on the narrow road. Six months earlier I might have called these hovels; I thought of them now as homes. From around stone ovens in other yards, shapeless talk, tufts of smoke, and the scent of steamed corn and barbecued meat mingled in the air. Nothing stood quite up and down, as if poverty were a small daily earthquake that disrupted the architecture. Children of all heights ran in shrieking packs, bare feet pounding the dirt.

Phet inched over on the bench and tucked her arm in mine, propping me up.

"*Sabaidi.*" The *mau-du* appeared in the doorway—doll sized, with black eyes that seemed particularly large in the recesses of her creased face. Her voice was tiny, her smile wide. More skeleton than flesh, she tilted to one side, but walked evenly, lightly. Her hair was gray and sparse and no longer conformed to gravity.

We followed her into a home with cement floors, entirely empty of furniture. The air smelled of bleach and a thick animal scent, like the woodchips in a hamster pen.

Walking behind the *mau-du* and Phet in the dim hallway, I felt huge, white, silly, and fragile: Humpty Dumpty in Asia. We reached a small room at the corridor's end. It was also empty, except for a bamboo mat

on a tiled floor, and a tattered blanket swaddling five
still-blind puppies nestled against a nursing mutt. Once
seated, my eyes adjusted to the dark.

"Put 2,000 kip," Phet whispered.

I put two brown bills on a plate beside a deck of cards
and a short white candle. Phet extracted two more bills
from her yellow backpack. The *mau-du* struck a match
from a small pack, held it above the candle's wick. Her
hand quavered and the flame couldn't catch. Finally
Phet cupped her own hands over the woman's shaking
fingers, and the candle flicked on. Their eyes met, and
they flashed smiles.

"Mix," Phet pointed to the cards.

I shuffled the deck, which was floppy as napkins. As
directed, I turned two cards over, a jack of diamonds
and an eight of clubs. The *mau-du*'s voice was a waver-
ing soprano.

Phet translated, "It's good that you used your right
hand—it is much more lucky to reach out in this way,
reaching for the future."

The *mau-du* spread the rest of the cards around the
two that I'd chosen. With one finger, she tapped each
number and face, concentrating.

"Two men love you," she crooned in Lao, in a voice that
shook like her hands, "a tall man, and a short man."

I flipped through a mental Rolodex of men, categoriz-
ing them by height. The *mau-du* paused for affirmation.
I thought about my last lover, now a Peace Corps volunteer in Africa. He was short, by Western standards.
I nodded. As for the tall one, that was anyone's guess.
Viengphet was tall, relative to most Lao. I let my head
move vertically, and she moved to another part of the
constellation.

"You will have great success in your work. That is what the cards say. Whatever you choose, you will have success."

Though I mostly understood, Phet followed with the English. I curled my shoulders in modesty, though secretly I felt relief, a glimmer of hope for even my Intermediate Class.

"Ayah," the *mau-du* sighed. She prodded one cluster and said three times, and with grave intensity, "*Pen huang lai pod.*"

Phet didn't translate this, but grinned so that her pointed incisors showed on each side of her mouth. She knew I understood. It was apparent without supernatural intercession: *You worry too much.*

"This is your biggest problem," the *mau-du* continued, "You must not worry so much." She exhaled, looked at me with her black eyes, and having made her point, focused on the last part of the wheel. "There are two people who will help you a lot. You will soon hear from someone far away."

"What do you want to know about the future?" Phet asked me.

"Will I go home or stay another year?"

The *mau-du* tapped the cards again, muttered to herself, then looked up.

"You will go home to your country and come back to Laos."

Phet smiled, dropped her eyes to conceal the spark of *ha*. This was her prediction, too.

"Another?" the *mau-du* said.

The sparse light of the candle flickered over their faces, widened shadows beneath their eyes. This half-light obscured the *mau-du's* age, and maybe even my foreignness. They didn't seem hurried for me to speak, but stared at the shivering flame. The three of us sat on the bamboo mat, legs off to the side. One puppy squirmed and disrupted the whole slumbering pile. The room was so still I could hear its fur rubbing the blanket, and the softest animal sigh.

I felt purged, as I used to in psychotherapy, though 2,000 kip would not have paid my therapist for sixty seconds. Really, weren't those the basic things? You are loved. You are not forgotten. Things will turn out well. People will help you. Don't worry so much. *Don't worry.*

The *mau-du's* wrist looked as if it could easily snap, though it somehow propped her up. There was the architecture of bodies, too, weighed by poverty, weighed by worry. But I'd begun to feel lighter in that room, bare except for life, three humans, five newborn puppies, a candle, and a deck of cards.

I shook my head. "Thank you. No questions."

When it was Phet's turn she shuffled the cards deftly, turned two upward. It was clear that the two women had a regular date. They spoke about the jack of spades as if he were a common friend.

After a few minutes, we stood, and returned with squinting eyes through the fluorescent-lit hall. Phet and I bowed a *wai* goodbye to the *mau-du*, and stepped into the now complete night. The streets had emptied and it was dark, the dark of no streetlights anywhere, only stars and the round glowing rock of a moon.

"I think—maybe some foreigners don't believe so much in the *mau-du,*" Phet mused before she flipped the plastic mask of her helmet over her face.

"Well I'm part Lao, part *falang.*"

"We go to my house for noodles, *na?*"

⚡ ⚡ ⚡

Kathryn Kefauver recently completed an MFA from the University of San Francisco. Her stories have appeared in The Gettysburg Review, The Journal, The South Florida Sun-Sentinel, The Christian Science Monitor, *and* Going Alone: Women's Adventures in the Wilderness. *She received an Associated Writing Programs Intro to Journals First Prize for Nonfiction in 2003, and a MacDowell Fellowship in 2004.*

❧ ❧ ❧

The Concorde, R.I.P.

Sometimes the good old days really were.

"THE PAST," WROTE L. P. HARTLEY IN ONE OF THE finest first lines of any novel (*The Go-Between*), beloved of high-school essayists and seasoned magazine journalists alike, "is a foreign country: they do things differently there."

Differently and—let's be honest—a little bit stupidly. It's a rarely acknowledged fact that however much we may respect the people who have lived before us on this earth, we feel a sense of quiet superiority to all previous generations, flowing from the undeniable fact that we know things They didn't know, and can do things They never could. Sure, I admire Isaac Newton for having single-handedly figured out most of the laws that govern the physical universe—I doubt that in his shoes I could have managed it—but when I reflect on the countless

hours he spent slaving in his basement over a hot cauldron, convinced it was possible to turn lead into gold,
well...I pity the deluded fellow. That's a mistake I don't
see myself ever making. All else being equal, I would
prefer to live in the Future than the Past, less because
the joy and convenience of the Future's technological ad-
vances so appeal to me than because the ignorance of the
Past seems, in a quiet, irrational way, so undignified.

As of October 2003, however, that sense of superiority met a unique and unprecedented challenge. The
Concorde, the universe's first and only faster-than-
sound airliner, was retired from service, thereby plunging the world back into the pre-1969 dark ages when
the minimum theoretical travel time across the Atlantic
for civilians was six hours, rather than three. Next to
Isaac Newton, we will still—technologically speaking—look like gods. But next to Halston, the Beatles,
Princess Diana, Joan Collins, Oscar de la Renta, Naomi
Campbell, and every other lucky soul who had the
money and the foresight to fly the Concorde while it was
still around, we are going to look a little...quaint. For
the first time in history, the zenith of human progress is
behind us, winking grotesquely in the rearview mirror,
and what that's going to feel like one can only imagine—though one supposes, as L. P. Hartley might have
put it, it's going to feel rather foreign, and bad.

It was in this spirit of grim apprehension that I traveled in July of that fateful year to London's Heathrow
Airport, where I had an appointment to be shown
around the Concorde in its hangar. On top of my mis-
givings about the retirement of the plane, I was coping
with a substantial degree of personal disappointment.
I had been born in the year of the Concorde's first

flight, grown up in leafy southwest London not far
from Heathrow, and over the years come to regard the
prospect of flying through the sky at twice the speed of
sound, cocktail on my armrest, while contemplating the
hazy blue curve of Earth, the purple-back edge of Space,
and the back of Sting's head, as a birthright, a sort of
droit du seigneur. I had never had any clear picture of
the circumstances—whether a rich friend would char-
ter a Concorde and fly us all to see the fashion shows
in Milan, or I'd become very rich myself, or I'd find
myself being extradited from somewhere in shackles at
extremely high speed to beat an expiring statute of limitations. I just knew that one day It Would Happen. The
announcement on April 10, 2003 that, barring a miracle,
no, It Would Not Happen, was a bitter, roughly plum-
sized pill to swallow, Visiting the Concorde in its hangar,
I assumed, would swell the pill to roughly the size of a
grapefruit—and this I was braced for.

I was not, however, braced for a pill the size of a wa-
termelon.

The beauty of the Concorde, I realize immediately
upon entering the hangar, is visible in photographs, but
what does not show up on film is how little that beauty
has to do with human aesthetics, and how much it has
to do with the pure math of aerodynamics. In photos
the Concorde looks "designed"; you could imagine that
once the engineers had finished the hard part, building
whatever incredible, super-powered engines were going
to take the plane through the sound barrier, they passed
the project on to Philippe Starck, or someone like him,
to come up with a fittingly elegant, aerodynamic fuse-
lage. In person, though, watching it interact with actual
light and actual air, you realize that everything—every

slow curve and taper, every needle-thin point—is the way it is for a single, simple reason that anything else would be slower. This is more than someone's great idea of a sexy-looking plane; this is what planes are supposed to look like. I had known that the Concorde was "beautiful" and "good," and that to see it go would be "sad." Standing beneath it, gawking up, I feel I'm in the presence of something "true" and "right," and that to see it go will be "wrong." As I'm given a tour of the plane's exterior by Claud Freeman, the burly South African who has been the chief engineer of British Airways' fleet of seven Concordes for the last sixteen years, I begin to moan with genuine sorrow.

And Claud really isn't helping. He keeps using the phrase "unlike on a normal, subsonic aircraft" and gesturing through the hangar door at a group of fat, slow, ugly seven-something-sevens squatting on the tarmac like warthogs guarding a fragment of a Snickers bar. If anything should be retired it is surely *them*, the "blunties," as they were pityingly known in the Concorde hangar. We should be turning on the news this month and watching retro-enthusiasts tearfully boarding the last 747, everyone dressed to the nines in thrombosis stockings and clutching copies of *War and Peace* to their chests. Not the last flight of the Concorde. It just isn't right.

Worse, Claud insists on stopping every eighteen inches or so, as we tour the plane's underside from nose to tail, to point out yet another impossibly elegant design feature that in thirty-four years even *military* aviation hasn't replicated. For example, because its engines can accept only air traveling at less than the speed of sound, even when the plane itself is at Mach 2, the Concorde has revolutionary computerized air intakes mounted beneath its wings to decelerate the air. When

the Concordes were retired to museums, the computers
were removed. Why? For fear that a gang of teenagers
might hot-wire the plane and fly off? No. For fear that
someone might *steal the design*. If the fact that we're
worried our enemies might steal our secrets by *visiting a
museum* isn't evidence of something going badly wrong
in the natural sequence of events then I don't know what
would be.

Claud takes me on board and lets me sit in one of the
seats—and suddenly it's too much to bear. Here I am. I
have finally made it onto the Concorde. I'm actually sitting in one of the seats, but rather than rocketing off into
the stratosphere as is my destiny, I am now expected to
get up and leave the plane. This is the end of a dream.
For the Concorde and me, this is it.

Not far from tears, I start bargaining pathetically
with Claud. Can this *really* be the end? The Concordes
aren't being dismantled, actually, they're only being sent
to museums, so surely in a few years' time…when the
economy picks up again…there's nothing to stop some
Larry Ellison-type billionaire from blowing a few hundred million on putting them back in service? Maybe
Richard Branson will relaunch his failed campaign to
acquire a Concorde for Virgin?

No, apparently. Now that Airbus is withdrawing
its technical support—trashing all the molds it used to
make spare parts, et cetera—Concorde could never get
"recertified."

Well…but eventually there'd be another supersonic
airliner, would there not? Some cash-rich government
somewhere looking to put itself on the map?

Extremely doubtful. The Concorde was flying before
every hundred-millionaire had his own private jet, and

even then it found barely enough market share to scrape by. Anyone who tried to start the whole program again from scratch would need his head examined.

But surely, one can never say never. One can *famously* never say never.

One can never say never, Claud concedes, but in a way that, coming from a man who has given so much of his life to the Concorde and would presumably like nothing more than a shred of hope to cling to, sounds an awful lot like "never."

But you know what? I'm O.K. now. It was many moons ago—or at least many suns—that emotional day in the hangar at Heathrow, and though I know now as a cold hard fact that I will go to my grave having never flown on the Concorde, I have discovered—to my joy— that I can live like this. It actually isn't so bad. I look in my rearview mirror, I see the Concorde, and, frankly, it fits in just fine with all the other relics of the past. There's a penny-farthing bicycle with its comically mis- matched wheels...there's the Concorde, pointy-nosed icon of late-twentieth-century glamour...there's the *Normandie*...No problem at all. I have adjusted.

Part of it is that, on the train back from Heathrow that day, scribbling on a legal pad, I came up with the theory. "Glamour is the first casualty of Progress" is the theory's tagline. While the end of the Concorde might look like a backward step for Homo sapiens, that's just an optical illu- sion. The fact is that we have e-mail now, and broadband videoconferencing. The fatal problem for the Concorde— deeper than the grubby, prosaic issues of revenue streams and the bursting of the dot-com bubble—is surely that no one really needs to fly that fast anymore. The days of a CEO having to streak through the sky at twice the speed of sound, exploding through conference-room doors on far-flung continents to pant, "No. No. My vote is No," are behind us. We aren't slowing down at all. In fact we've accelerated to such a ridiculous speed that, just as we once broke the sound barrier, we have now broken the geography barrier. We aren't only faster than sound these days, we're faster than *travel*.

It actually feels rather pleasant to have the Concorde there in the rearview mirror. It's a comfort. The thirty-four years that will now presumably come to be known as the Concorde Era will be remembered for their unbridled exuberance and optimism. In our anxious present, that spare-no-expense decadence feels an awful lot like innocence, lost but not forgotten.

❧ ❧ ❧

Bruno Maddox was born in 1969 and raised in London. He attended Harvard, where he managed to compensate for four years of middling grades with a prizewinning, hastily-typed thesis on the use of adjectives in restaurant menus. A former book reviewer for The New York Times *and* The Washington Post, *Maddox took over the editorship of* SPY Magazine *in 1996, elevated it to within spitting distance of its former glory, then accidentally bankrupted it after two short years. He lives in London and New York, and is the author of* My Little Blue Dress.

❦ ❦ ❦

The Passenger

Can anyone tell him who she was?

S HE STOOD IN SHIMMERING HEAT WAVES ALONG QUEEN
Ka'ahumanu Highway on a hot October day.
I couldn't believe anybody would be standing in the
sun at high noon on what seemed like the hottest day
of the year. I thought at first the woman in the white
dress might be a mirage. Dark skin, the color of coffee,
Caribbean maybe; black hair in dreadlocks, she looked
real as a rainbow. She stuck out her thumb and I
stopped.

My day full of strange encounters began in Honolulu at
the airport. A security guard wanted to inspect my carry-on.

"Oh, I love your books," she said, finding only spooky
books in my bag.

I gave her one. She gave me a *mahalo*, and waved me
through.

In line for coffee a Charles Manson look-a-like, one of the terminal's homeless denizens, hit me up for $3. He wanted "a wet, double tall French vanilla latte." His outrageous request made me laugh. I gave him a buck. While waiting for my coffee I was paged repeatedly: "...please return to the Security Gate." I finally got my coffee and went back to find I'd dropped my ticket to Kona during the security check. I ran to the gate only to find my plane was late. By the time I got to the Big Island the Budget rental car outfit was out of cars.

"We have a ten-passenger van you can have for the same price as an economy sedan."

"It's just me," I said.

"It's all we have," the clerk said. She handed me the keys to what looked like a Roberts Overnighter tour bus.

That's how I came to be all alone driving an air-conditioned van big enough for ten people on Queen Ka'ahumanu Highway on the Big Island of Hawai'i on a hot October day.

My destination was Waimea School where I'd been invited to read from my books to the children as part of Waikoloa Beach Marriott's annual spooky "talk story" event. I saw the hitchhiker just after leaving the airport. With an empty ten-passenger van, I decided to give her a lift.

I stopped, she got in, and I immediately felt something was wrong but didn't know what. The chilled van seemed warmer with her aboard.

"Where're you going?"

"Waimea," she said.

"Me, too," I said. "Do you live there?"

"No," she said, "just visiting."

She was neither young nor old, but somewhere in between, with caramel skin, charcoal hair, bright, clear eyes and a soft voice that sounded like music. She carried neither suitcase nor backpack but a white canvas bag stuffed with newspapers and magazines, and handwritten notes on yellow legal pads. She had a musty aroma of sweat and something flammable. I thought the rental van had a gas leak.

Queen Ka'ahumanu Highway is unique in Hawai'i. The two-lane black asphalt not only runs through twenty miles of black lava landscape, it crosses over several layers of historic lava flows and under four of the island's five volcanoes—Kohala, Hualalei, Mauna Loa, and Mauna Kea. Pele-land if there ever was, Pele of course being the goddess of fire.

Most passersby see only a bleak black expanse but my passenger knew and identified each and every lava flow with evident pride as if each flow were an object of art in her private collection.

"Ka'upulehu flowed to the sea in 1801," she said as we passed under Hualalai volcano. "It filled Kiholo Bay...

"...and the 1859 Mauna Loa flow ran from 9,000 feet near the summit to the sea...

"...the Kaniku flow covered Waikoloa and ran into the fish ponds at Anaeho'omalu..."

Although I had no way to verify the truth of her words, her keen recitation startled me.

"How do you know all this?" I asked.

"Just do," she said. "It's my hobby."

We rode in silence for a mile or so. I half expected her to ask for a cigarette—a common request of Pele.

"Don't you want to ask me for a cigarette?"

"I don't smoke," she said, smiling.

We rode on in silence.

"Are you sure you're not Madame Pele?" I finally asked. I couldn't help it.

"Oh no," she said. "I'm not Madame Pele."

"How do I know?"

"Believe me," she laughed.

"I'm not sure I do," I said.

In misty rain, we approached Waimea town. She said good-bye and thanks at the T-intersection.

"I'll get out here," she said at the stoplight, opened the door and jumped out.

She cut across the corner gas station; I half expected the gas pumps to burst into flames. That never happened. Something just as startling did. As I watched her walk away, she disappeared. Vanished in thin air. One minute she was there, the next she was gone, like that. I asked the gas station attendant if he'd seen the woman in white.

"No, brah, see nothing."

I found Waimea School library full of kids waiting to hear spooky tales that Friday afternoon. The library was cool and quiet, I was hot and sweaty.

"Are you O.K.?" one of the librarians asked. "You look like you've seen a ghost."

"I'm not really sure but I think I just gave a ride to a woman who may have been Madame Pele."

The librarian had a sympathetic smile. "I know," she said. "It happens a lot here."

That night at a dinner party hosted by Patti Cook, who knows everybody in Waimea, I told my story to the other guests and asked if they had ever seen the woman hitchhiking along the Queen's highway or walking in their town. Now, Waimea's a small town, and surely someone

would have seen a woman in a white dress with dread-
locks who knew a lot about old volcanoes but nobody ever
had, at least that's what they told me.

⤝ ⤝ ⤝

Rick Carroll is the co-editor of Travelers' Tales Hawai'i *and the*
author of numerous books, including Huahine: Island of the Lost
Canoe, Chicken Skin: True Spooky Stories of Hawai'i, *a best*
seller in the Islands, and Madame Pele: True Encounters with
Hawai'i's Fire Goddess,*" from which this story was excerpted.*

❧ ❧ ❧

Just Chicken

A small place in Paris provided far more than good food.

O N A RECENT TRIP TO PARIS, A PEEK AT MY DINING guide confirmed the Restaurant du Midi was still there. As I read on, however, my heart sank, realizing my friend was gone.

> With the departure of Claude Menard, new talent arrives from Southwest France to re-adorn this adorable bistro, its copper moldings intact and still weathered by time, with the panache that it never would have lost had it not changed hands. The menu is more expensive with duck in luscious berry sauces and a solid, debonair wine list. But if there's a dish that really must be ordered in this tiny corner of a largely forgotten part of the 15th *arrondissement*, it's the chicken, miraculously endowed with simplicity and justice.

In spite of the review, I knew that without Monsieur Menard, the place could never be the same. Instead of going out for dinner, I settled back in my chair.

The man arose in my memory, his rosy face and snowy hair, those rugged arms, his pot belly smartly tucked—as the French will—under his t-shirt, and roving, twinkling, mischievous eyes ready for me each time I entered his establishment.

We met over fifteen years ago, when I was moving to the city and temporarily set up at the Holiday Inn in the 15th *arrondissement*. Near train stations and exits to major highways, the quarter idled between the dingy outskirts and the intimacy and glamour commonly appreciated as Paris. Dog shit stuck longer to sidewalks, migrants with wooden teeth and unsavory regards passed on the street, and at night cats furiously mated while drunks shouted. To awaken to the sounds of someone throwing up outside my window wasn't unusual in the wee hours of a Saturday morning. On occasion from above low-lying fog and largely decrepit buildings, the Eiffel Tower's pointy top helped me remember what city I lived in.

Starving one night after a day-long meeting without breaks, I alighted from the Métro and swore to myself I'd find a decent place to eat rather than submit to hotel cuisine. Wandering without regard, I followed a boulevard that turned into an alley which swung around to a cul de sac. Sore feet from walking on three-inch heels stopped me at an unassuming green façade with oversized windows and neatly tucked-aside interior lace curtains. The voice of a long-time friend whispered, "It's the little out-of-the-way places you will fall for. Do not overlook them."

By the time I swung open the door, briefcase weighing me down, hair flattened and sticking out in all the wrong ways, clothes smelling of the day's energies, and eyes maniacal from hunger, the man behind the bar had checked me out. With an abrupt, obnoxiously Gallic shrug, he turned his back on me.

"Damn French," I thought, tending to my feet by lifting one set of toes and then the other. At 7 P.M.—too early for "real dining" according to the haughtier side of the culture—his wordless message was clear: I was way out of line. He continued washing glasses but, each time his head rose to the smoked mirror in front of him, his eyes darted my way.

I couldn't help but stall over the tables for two and four, each decorated with white cloth, candle, and fresh pink rose. Empty green bottles lined two walls, labels from fine Bordeaux and Burgundy vintages organized alongside lesser-known Côte du Rhônes. The garlic and butter smells so seduced my appetite in the cheery place, that I decided to hold out on this French man. His rude shrug, I had learned from similar encounters, was best served by ignoring. Two could play his game.

"We do not serve until 7:30."

"I can wait," I said, my gaze roving his walls rather than him.

"Suit yourself." He returned to his glasses. As he rubbed them dry, they squeaked happily. Afterward, he placed them gently on shelving behind the bar while humming a throaty version of "*Je ne regrette rien*" ("No Regrets"), a song made famous by France's wartime crooner, Edith Piaf.

After a minute or two, he looked up. "Well, have a seat anyway, *rousse* (redhead)."

This reference to my hair drew a smile from me. I

nodded to a table that would place me dead center, able
to study his bar walls containing the magnificent labels,
selections that, if they remain at all today, lie carefully
guarded in the *caves* of the wealthy and wine aficionados.
From here I could also attract his wandering attentions
once the place filled, which I knew it would, for it bore all
the signs of a local hangout—no menus, no chalkboards,
little in the way of luxury with its hardwood chairs and
everyday silverware. I suspected, however, that anything
required to dine well would appear at one's fingertips. He
nodded back and I settled.

"Apéritif?"

"*Un petit Ambassadeur* (a sweet-sour drink), *s'il vous
plaît*," I said.

"Ah, then you need nuts, too," he said, his voice more
melodic than when we started out.

The nuts arrived in a tiny dish. I waited until he
disappeared behind curtains to check out the bottom.
Limoges. Simple and white, but Limoges nonetheless. I
began to relax, and the Ambassadeur sank to my empty
stomach and then heated my sore toes, a massage without hands.

He waited until I finished my drink before returning
to the table. "You are going to start with something."

"What do you have?" I asked with as much noncha-
lance as I could muster. I would have downed a napkin
flavored with salt and pepper.

"Pumpkin soup."

"Anything else?"

"Take the soup. It's fresh."

"O.K."

"Tonight. Chicken for the main course," he said,
scratching the back of his head. Free of any notepad

to take orders, his other hand clutched the back of my chair for support. He studied a passing car, as though its driver might be someone he knew. His fingernails were clean, the only soil was on his apron.

"Just chicken?" I asked.

"Where are you from? The accent is lightly Swiss. Geneva?"

"Boston. That's in the United States."

From behind white eyelashes that made him look sleepy, his huge black eyes penetrated mine. He was either going to make love to me or kill me. I held my gaze and he let one bushy brow lower, then lower still.

"Red hair like that is Irish," he said.

"I'll take the chicken. And a half carafe of your house wine." I continued to gaze at him. From the back room, music began to play. More Edith.

He made a sweeping gesture with his arm, then wound around my table. Before disappearing again, he called to whoever was in the back that "We have a pumpkin and a chicken."

Served in a simple white bowl, the gourd this dish started out as was transformed to thick buttery swirls with a dollop of heavy cream in the middle. With smooth consistency touched with pepper and sea salt, its exact warm temperature invited immediate consumption. The owner did a double-take when he noted how rapidly it disappeared.

"You starve. Eat more in life," he said. "You won't be so frazzled like when you walked in here." He removed my bowl and poured me wine from a small handmade ceramic pitcher.

He allowed no time for a response because a foursome arrived, with whom he continued a debate likely started the day before about the status of mushrooms for the upcoming season. In short order, the place filled with elderly couples, families of three and four, lovers, a nun. Everyone knew the owner, who wound around tables just as he had my own, barely missing chairs and patrons, removing coats, offering seating, and advising them of the soup and the chicken. Over the murmur of diners debating other selections—yesterday's beef bourguignon, duck confit—he joked about the latest foibles at the Elysée Palace and the additional fast trains to support the upcoming Alpine winter holiday exodus. With a trailing, sweet ring, his words threaded every table's conversation. When not chatting, he hummed along with Edith. At times, voices lowered as did his massive body, to discuss the redhead in the center of the room. At one point I heard the word "*Americaine,*" and the couple to whom he spoke darted glances that I caught, which I think threw them off as they never looked again my way.

Chicken is chicken is chicken, they say. In my family, we were discouraged from ordering something as banal as chicken when dining out. So when he brought the meal, my expectations were set and I was unprepared for the deciding moment that it would become.

Indeed, chicken lay on the plate, a leg and small breast sitting contentedly in its own shining pale yellow juices, speckles of pepper on top, a sprig of parsley to the side. To look at, simple, fresh, inviting.

To eat, a journey through all that has made the French known for their cooking, yet more subtle and sublime than the world-renowned "book three months in advance" restaurants most tourists tend to seek out. Bites of perfectly roasted bird accompanied by the peppery, black currant flavors of the wine proved opera to my senses, and filled me aptly in spite of the conservative portion. He had to bring me extra bread so I could sop up the sauce.

I finished the wine and bypassed dessert, wishing instead to appreciate the meal's lingering pleasures, even as fatigue started warning me I had to walk home before hitting the sack. I paid and went to the counter.

However highbrow, a Parisian restaurant owner wants dearly to know one thing before you walk out, and this owner was no different.

"So, *rousse*, did you enjoy?" he asked.

I leaned into his bar, waiting for him to stop rubbing a glass. When he looked up, I got close enough so he could smell the garlic and wine on my breath.

"That was the best chicken I have ever, ever had in my entire life."

His eyes, clearly twinkling at my response as well as the contents of what had been a full wine glass within his reach all evening, devoured me along with his now gregarious smile. An aura as effervescent as his chicken took over. "Well, when you come back, ask for the chicken. I will have it for you."

"What is your name?" I asked.

"Menard," he said, reaching his hand to shake mine with a clutch that was fixed and whole.

"Kathleen," I said.

"*Rousse* is better."

During my years in Paris, I returned time and again, with friends, with executives from my company, most often alone. The word got out at my place of work, all the way across the Atlantic. "Go with Kathy to the chicken man." The marketing vice president I worked for, a wealthy, flamboyant traveler who only ate at the name places in Paris, became the biggest advertiser of the Restaurant du Midi. So enamored was he of the chicken place, he told everyone, describing over and over with delight his first encounter with Menard in this unassuming part of the city. "He kept calling me BEEEG BOSS!"

When I dined by myself I always showed up at seven and so had time to linger afterwards while Menard served meals. I would sit at the bar and there we learned about one another. He told me of Simone de Beauvoir who, before she died several years prior, took a table in the corner most Thursday nights. I talked of how the mauve dunes of Cape Cod spill into the Atlantic, of Boston and Back Bay and New England fall colors.

He served meals to German military during the war.

"Didn't that just kill you to have to do that?" I asked. That night I had stayed for another glass of wine and leaned over his bar, comfortable in our ever-reversing roles of listener and storyteller. (He never charged for the wine those nights.)

For a moment, he stopped stroking the bar with his towel and gave me a sleepy, mirthful look. "There are ways of getting even, *rousse*. The soup is made with multiple ingredients."

We laughed, joked, and I always ordered chicken. Prior to my return to the States after a stay of three years, I went to say good-bye.

"You won't return," he said, wrapping up a bottle of Burgundy as gift for me, a 1985 and one of his choicest.

"I will. You wait."

"You will marry a rich American who wears a cow-boy hat. You will have babies, a house with a pool in Hollywood or New York. Three times divorced, you will end up in Florida, white-haired and plump. You Americans are all alike."

Thus we concluded with our routine banter, he about stereotyped Americans and I about the irascible French.

"Three-quarters of you French will not go to Heaven when you die. You will go to the Other Place, subjected for eternity to the tutelage of Miss Manners! You will sink in your own sewage because you do not make plumbing a priority in this country. You will fart to death from eating rich food. You will miss me when I'm gone!"

That night, I walked home, as I had so many nights, satiated by food and the richly succulent, ruefully attractive Monsieur Menard. Whom I never did see again.

☙ ☙ ☙

Kathleen Comstock lived in Paris for three years where she developed her love for fine dining and travel. She is the author of the novel The Orchid House*, and she now divides her time between a home in central Massachusetts and one on Cape Cod with her family and two dogs.*

❧ ❧ ❧

Waiting to Arrive

Travels on the wrong side of Nigeria.

"I T IS NOT ENOUGH TO RUN, ONE MUST ARRIVE AND know when one has arrived." Nigerian proverb.

There is a Nigeria embedded in minds, steeped in a science of hearsay, denuded of history and dressed in front page rags, a caustic calamity nobody wants to touch. It is a Nigeria of bloody pagan rites, vein-bulging screams on congested motorways, Sharia law lashings and amputations, unruly soldiers, babies named after Osama bin Laden, internet scams, ethnic and religious strife, cheap fluorescent plastic-ware, pretension, noise and naught else. It has been erected on a foundation of established enmity with neighbors and Western powers, the bricks and mortar supplied by newspaper headlines.

It only takes a storyteller to elaborate and embellish for the fable to acquire elephantine proportions and in Africa storytellers are in no short supply. Vibrant narratives weave together the threads of peoples' lives; story is central. The tsunami of Nigerian videos that crashes upon the shores of neighboring countries each year only furnishes the legend. Videos with names like *Kill My Wife* and *Final Burial* and almost always involving a human sacrifice in the pursuit of lucre in between episodic screaming and wide shots of chaotic Lagos overpasses. The triumphal Christian moral is almost an afterthought and certainly considered such by outsiders.

To dare to have abundant oil wealth and successful football teams on top of all this is considered by many Africans as taking things a little too far. Such gifts combined with a renowned tendency towards ostentatious outbursts seem to do the caretaking—the legend is in safe hands. It is a myopic picture seen from afar, like appraising a Rembrandt through an unfocused microscope. It is the Nigeria of outsiders, its borders gape across continents. It is, of course, a fiction—Nigeria is far stranger than this.

I found this fiction gently lapping the shores of reality in neighboring Benin. I noticed him as soon as I entered the room. Dressed in a dazzling *buba*, he brandished his flowing attire like a weapon, a device of intimidation. I was in the downstairs restaurant of a cheap Cotonou hotel, an immense dilapidation draped in rickety bamboo scaffolding. I wasn't sure if it was in the midst of construction or demolition. It looked like an English prison hulk moored 200 years and 2,000 miles out of time and place.

He lounged gloriously, greedily, across several pieces of furniture unidentifiable under the curtains of flesh and shimmering cloth hanging over them. Comfortable and elegant in his obesity, he had a striking resemblance to the reclining golden Buddha at Wat Pho in Bangkok. Two companions floundered at his table, one looked in random directions around the room with great disdain, while the other seemed comatose beneath impenetrable mirror shades. I sat alone at a nearby table. Almost immediately, he summoned me.

"What is your mission here?" his tone was, part scowl and part intimidation. I proffered an almost apologetic outline of my plans to cycle through the southwest of Nigeria and to this he launched batteries of biting, suspicion-fueled questions at me. It wasn't long before it emerged that I had used the same mode of transport to reach West Africa from Australia.

"You lie," he shuffled uncomfortably across his furniture. "Only a baby would believe you." This made a refreshing change from the usual embarrassed smiles and meek inquiries about my sincerity (or sanity) from people in Africa whenever this topic came up. The man behind the mirror shades perked up and showed some interest.

Buddha informed me that he was a doctor. "Of what?" I inquired. He seemed caught out for a moment but quickly recomposed himself and carefully weighed up his options, "mmmm . . . animals." He was in town to sort out some troublesome business regarding the claiming of $120 million in a Beninois bank account. He needn't have gone any further.

In Nigeria there is an entity known as 419. It is one of the country's largest earners of foreign exchange. 419 also refers to a section of the Nigerian criminal code dealing with fraud. Each year, good numbers of seemingly sane foreigners gleefully plunge lemming-like over the edge of reason and into the abyss of account overdrafts chasing money that doesn't exist.

Victims are offered generous dividends in return for their cooperation in clearing large sums of money into their account. Of course there are a series of complications, officials to be bribed, fees and commissions which need to be cleared up first. The loot never comes and as the gullible invest more money in the project they often become more obstinate in their belief in its veracity. It is a scam that preys beautifully on human frailties such as racial superiority (faxes and letters are couched in simple language with deliberate spelling mistakes), the pig-headed nature of the ego, and, of course, good old-fashioned greed and stupidity.

When the line was cast I didn't bite but asked for a cool million if I could prove that I'd cycled to West Africa. He nodded his assent and I soon returned from my room clutching newspaper articles from various countries detailing my bicycle trip. He twitched a little and the furniture in turn twitched in obedient aftershocks. Finally he retracted and agreed that what I had claimed was true. I considered referring to his baby remark but decided to leave it for the sake of the furniture.

He excused himself from the table as my food was served. Just before departing he told me that he was Nigerian; I feigned surprise. Here was all of Nigeria's onerous reputation invested in one man. The bellicose egotism, the daunting volume (decibels and cubic feet), the scam, even the clothes were cocky. These were myths I had come to dispel.

I wanted to paint a different picture, to prove friends wrong, Ghanaian friends who had responded with horror

to my travel plans: "Nigeria? Why? They will kill you."
"They chop people there." Surely with an estimated 120
million people (one quarter of the population of Africa),
Nigeria is entitled to a large slice of the headlines without being demonized. But among the other 360 million
Africans, Nigeria has few advocates. The legend is inscribed, as intractable as the Nigerian people, and in some
apparent act of self-flagellation, the people even relish it,
perpetuate it. It feeds on hyperbole, and in Nigeria there
is no shortage of this.

Any thoughts of a quiet meal were quashed by the
catatonic guy in the mirror shades who rose from the
dead and made his move. He started on the familiar
preliminary verses of the same scam with an exotic
twist—Sierra Leonean diamond wealth. He claimed to
be an international financier. I asked if he knew George
Soros. He said yes. He also claimed to be a member of
the G8. I asked which of the eight he was. He didn't
know but promised to find out.

Bored with the prospect of politely submitting to
another scam attempt, I took on the role of radical
revolutionary hero to detour or derail the conversation.
I asked him as a member of the G8 to use his vast wealth
to fund the debt cancellation of Africa. He wasn't sure
how to go about this. "Call Kofi Annan," I told him. He
said he wanted to get in on this debt relief game, the big
numbers seemed to excite him.

I tried to guide him on the righteous path. "Wear
the people's badge on your sleeve and bring down your
oppressors." He seemed doubtful, and talked about a
commission.

"Forget profits and returns," I told him, "step outside
the system and free your mind." He started talking about

some friend in Nigeria, a member of the G77 with $100 billion who had promised him money for a car.

"Buy a bicycle, go forth and preach the message on the street, foment disquiet and revolt." He didn't seem convinced.

Suddenly a shifty comrade entered with news. Their whispers were fearful and sprinkled with brief but frantic outbursts. I heard only scattered pieces of their conversation, I believe tossed aside expressly for my consumption. Persecution of Nigerians, targeting of Hausa and Yoruba speakers, how rich countries like Nigeria are free and poor countries like Benin are suspicious of outsiders because they are jealous of other's wealth.

Having lost all faith in humanity somewhere in the fetid depths of my last two conversations, I assumed that this was all staged and soon they would run out in the confusion of some mock police raid or lynching and I'd have to pay for the drinks. The Nigerian Buddha returned to make an appointment with me for the next day so that we could discuss the million dollars and where to invest it. I told him that I just wanted to spend it on beer. He left twitching. I quietly made my escape wondering if this was the level of intelligence of the scammers what could be said of the scammed?

The next day I was on my bicycle heading for Nigeria as planned. A crowd ahead seemed like the brand of mayhem common to any Cotonou intersection. There was an initial rush of movement then people surged in desperate tributaries filling the spaces between cars, trucks, and the ubiquitous spluttering mopeds. But as I pedaled on I could see it was far more than a dash for safety during a rare reprieve for pedestrians at the traffic lights.

I rolled into the center of a confused maelstrom of bodies.

Blood-spattered faces blared warnings at me to turn back. Alarm and agitation erupted at random and with worrying ease in pockets of the crowd—I didn't know who was chasing and who was being chased. Riot police preferred to remain stationary, only putting any energy into lunging with batons at anyone who came within range. Fear and violence swirled in the air and mixed with the suffocating moped emissions to form a giddying cocktail. People were feeding on it. It didn't seem a good time to ask someone what was going on. I was glad to ride through unscathed, a glaring white irrelevance.

I gathered only scraps over the following days as I approached the Nigerian border; mobs had been attacking people accused of using juju to steal the penises of others. Those thought to be foreigners (especially Nigerians who have some renown for this particular stunt) were targeted and many fled Cotonou. My thoughts went back to the Nigerians I had met the night before and I felt pangs of guilt. I had a cruel picture of Buddha being held down and searched for surplus penises while screaming offers of generous portions of his $120 million fortune to anyone who would furnish him with their bank account details. It was only later that I discovered that five people had been killed in the violence, hacked to death or necklaced, a procedure in which a tire is jammed over your torso, pinning your arms, and you are set on fire.

There is something to be said for soothsayers, gut feelings, and portentous signs, and when traveling it seems they acquire even more gravity. Perhaps the alarm bells should have been ringing. That Nigeria of many a fearful mind had reared before me incarnate in the form of Buddha. A thousand rumors, jokes and clichés had found a gracious host. I had endured two 419 scam attempts and plunged into a riot which was widely believed to be the result of Nigerian juju-men snatching other folk's penises. All of this before I had even crossed the border.

The messages had been neither subtle nor promising on a previous brush with Nigeria—a much feared one-day stopover in Lagos on a flight to Kinshasa some years earlier. While scrutinizing my plane ticket I shuddered at the realization that I would land in Lagos on Friday the 13th. Unfortunately I was already in the air by that stage. Two days earlier I had dreamt of Lagos: I was shot in the chest by a gangster brandishing a sawn off shotgun. I felt the heat of the lead tear through my sternum and then I became engulfed in white light—it is the only time I have died in a dream. It was a relief to be turned back at immigration and I joyfully acquiesced to nearly 36 hours of captivity inside Murtala Muhammed airport. I had been misinformed by a Togolese travel agent that I didn't require a visa to enter Nigeria and I felt deeply thankful to him.

Arriving at the threshold of the Nigerian immigration post, I knew that this time no such fortuitous bungling could save me—this time I had a visa. The officer was only half way into the task of getting into uniform. Moustachioed and bristling with bristles, he had the look of a tequila-swilling Mexican bandido in a spaghetti western. Behind him, a thinner version in singlet and khaki trousers wrestled with a chewing stick in his mouth.

He approached and asked me a question, a question I had heard before—a masterpiece of intimidation: "What is your mission?" Before I knew it there was Buddha before me, rising Phoenix-like from the ashes with a grin that said "Don't say I didn't warn you." I wondered how many times he could return to me like this during my time in Nigeria. How many times would a shameless boast, a sledgehammer putdown, or a theatrical flourish of clothes bring his face before me? How many ghostly visitations would it take before he proved to be the harbinger of doom I feared he was?

There was only one thing to do. I'd had enough of scams, penis snatchers, and doomsayers. I had seen and heard too much of that fearsome country described to me by so many concerned friends—I was in it, I was living it—I knew it was time to escape the nightmare.

The question hung in the air. My reply came, "I want to see Nigeria." I handed over my passport; I had arrived at last.

❧ ❧ ❧

Paul Harper's curiosity about Africa was roused in the fourth grade while staring at a world map when he saw the continent with names like Chad, Angola, Sierra Leone. He made his first trip there in 1995 after quitting psychology studies in Perth. His second visit was as a part of a round-the-world bicycle trip for debt cancellation from 1999 to 2001. He currently lives in Ghana working on bicycle and organic farming projects. He harbors dreams of riding his faithful bicycle, Charlotte, just about everywhere. When he is not poring over maps, he likes to ponder acts of subversion against the internal combustion engine, such as digging up the freeways of the world and transforming them into six-laned veggie patches.

꙳Ꙍ ꙳Ꙍ ꙳Ꙍ

The Tipping Point at Tikal

A heart to heart confrontation takes place in the
Guatemalan jungle.

"**H**I," SHE SAID.

Her red bandana was saturated from sweat, and my
hair, under straw hat, was soaked, too. We both stank
to high heaven. Conversation happens easily on the road,
easier even than in line at the supermarket. It must be the
backpacks. They proclaim we are both strangers here and
neither of us have any turf to defend or local image that
needs propping up. As backpackers, we have nothing to
offer but ourselves, no story to tell but our own.

We sat on opposite ends of a ten-foot-long granite stone
chiseled to the shape and angled precision of a stick of
butter by someone 2,000 years ago using…what? A piece
of flint? Banana leaves? This stone, which must have

weighed two tons, may have been the entire life's work of the carver. The edges were worn rounded now and the surface was a pitted moonscape as you would expect from having sat out in the rain all this time, the last half century of which was laced with acid.

The stone was alongside a courtyard near a pyramid-like temple rising 200 feet above the rainforest floor. Between the big bang and sometime in the 1800s this tower was the tallest man-made structure in the Americas. We had just climbed up and down it, a rite of passage for visitors to this Mayan city in the jungle of northern Guatemala, abandoned and entombed by Mother Nature for a thousand years except for a few acres that have been restored to near-original grandeur. Before "Hi," we hadn't spoken or met. We had climbed the steep narrow steps with a half dozen others, gripping the chain handrail that ran up the middle. We stood in an anonymous group at the top, transfixed by a view that sent our imaginations out across a never-ending carpet of treetops.

At the moment, both of us were keeping an eye on an inch-long ant, black as obsidian, crawling over and around the irregularities of the rock's surface. My interest was based on not wanting it to sneak up on my hand and take a chunk out of it. Beverly's interest stemmed from being an entomology grad student from the University of Florida. "Pre-working on my pre-dissertation," she said. A master's degree freshly under her belt, she was in the process of deciding if she wanted to jump back on the treadmill for the long journey to a doctorate. If you're a bugologist, the high-canopy rainforest of Guatemala will probably have what you're looking for. And if you need some space to just get your head together, well, there's plenty of that here, too.

But right now Beverly was baking in a palm's half shade like me, chugging bottled water. She was early twenties, perky and earnest, wearing the uniform of the day: t-shirt, jeans, hiking boots. She carried a daypack with water and a couple of those health bars made from factory-second dog biscuits. Her passport and money would be in there, too. Nobody leaves that stuff at their campsite. She met the world through eyes of an indistinct brownish-blue that seemed to be trying to observe everything in case there would be a quiz later. As we talked, she did my eyes and then checked out my hat, upper body, shoes, belt, hands, then a surreptitious check of the perimeter around us, and back again, all the while making the most casual conversation—a survival trait of women who travel alone—I've seen it a lot. I wonder if they even know they're doing it.

Her face was more angular than round, with a strong jaw and chin her best features. Too many nights sitting in the grad school library and scarfing down student union chili dogs had not helped her hips. But they weren't too bad at this point and she was young enough to effect whatever lifestyle disciplines she cared to in order to stay fit. She was nice-looking, and cleaned up would be even more so. And, of course, she was blithely immortal as she spoke of her studies and the future, as though her life would always be as it is now. No one in their twenties ever says "Thank God I have my health."

"Cockroaches," she replied when I asked about the nature of her research. She was doing a comparison between two variations, one in Florida and one in Guatemala, of the same basic brand of roach.

"Really? What kinds?" As if I would have a clue. Getting her to open up about roaches was easier than

getting pupae to pupate. She was looking at similari-
ties between the genus *Latinword latinword,* which are
all over the place in Florida, and *Latinword latinword*
which you can find under every other leaf in this part of
Central America. Her dissertation title would easily fill
three lines in print and seemed to imply some kind of
theory about twins being separated at birth and evolving
into separate cockroach armies. It had "parallel evolu-
tion" and morpho-something in the name.

Did you know there are thousands of species of cockroaches? Beverly knows. Did you know that the flying
cockroaches infesting South Florida originally came over
from Vietnam in fruit shipments and, in fact, the merchant
marine is the cockroaches' global transport system? They
get on with bell peppers in California and get off in Japan.
On with mutton in Australia and off in South Africa. We
spray and fumigate and stomp the little buggers but cockroaches are tenacious clingers to life. Hearing her describe
her crunchy little friends made me feel like things were
crawling on me. It must be interesting having an avoca-
tion that gives people the creeps. I wanted to ask her what's
a nice girl like you doing in a field of study like this, but
didn't yet know her well enough.

"So what is this?" I pointed, figuring here's where
I learn the Latin word for ant, *Eatibus anythingibus* or
some such.

"It's an ant."

"Ah." An entomologist outside her specialty is as Joe
Sixpack as the rest of us.

"Look." She pulled a small magnifying glass from her
pack and held it over the ant for me to see through. I
bent down close. On the other side of the glass it tripled
in length and had pincers the size of hedge clippers. As

calmly as if she were marking her place in a book, she placed her finger in front of the ant and wiggled it to see if it would latch onto her fingernail. It did so with a vengeance, lunging into the attack.

"Atta girl," she said, and dragged it forward an inch or so. The monster ant wrestled fearlessly with the fingernail. I was impressed that she had the wherewithal to get so personal with one of nature's most voracious eaters and that she would risk it shooting over the nail and onto the finger's tender flesh. O.K., so she was not Joe Sixpack.

She asked what I did and I mentally weighed two options. I could say I was a writer, which impresses people for some reason, especially young women, but really wasn't true since I probably spent 90 percent of my waking life on administrative work in an office, completely unrelated to actual writing. On the other hand, saying I was a paper-pusher would have zero charisma, but it would carry the armor of truth and a virtue that is undeniably its own reward.

"I'm a writer."

We decided to walk over to the Jaguar Inn for some lunch, the only eatery in the park functioning at the time. That's when we met Ray walking along the same road for the same reason. Middle-aged and affable, Ray would fit somewhere inside everyone's notion of average. Of medium height, he wasn't fat, but his chest had sunk into his paunch. He had short hair, thinning on top in the back, and an almost perfectly round head. He had found a trekker's hiking stick and poled himself along with it.

Like us, Ray had a tent in the park at the campground where most overnighters stayed. There weren't any showers anywhere, but there was a pump with a handle that, after a few quick pulls, would yield water.

A sign on the pump warned that the water was limited for drinking only and strictly forbade using it to wash clothes or bathe. The sign might just as well have had another sign appended to the bottom telling you to ignore the first sign, for all the good it did.

In late April, we were still a few weeks away from the start of the serious rainy season that would run well into October. The heat, humidity, and mosquitoes were not nearly the force they would shortly become. With a modest amount of repellant, it was possible to sleep unmolested at night in the string hammock I had haggled for in a market in Oaxaca, Mexico. Still, it was midday in the jungle and the heat was on.

The Jaguar Inn, a few bungalows and a café located in the park just a half-mile away from the ruins, was the area's sole provider of "indoors." Lunch at the Jaguar was the same as breakfast and dinner—black beans and rice, and eggs. And cold beer. The service was slow and the waitress still mixed up people's orders, even though there were only three items on the menu. On the other hand, it had a ceiling fan and was a place to sit where the sun and mosquitoes weren't. As soon as the cold beer arrived all three of us snatched up the bottles and touched the icy wetness to necks and faces. The chill stung exquisitely, like a love bite.

In the silence that settled in around us, Bev asked Ray about himself. The friendship was an hour old and she had already transformed from a Beverly to a Bev, and now the whole tapestry of our existences seemed to be fair game for discussion. That's how fast it can work with strangers who know they will never see one another again after a day or two. Inquiries that would be impertinent in any other context are acceptable in this one.

That's why we were surprised when her request, "So
Ray, tell us about your life," threw him into a brown
study. In the unnatural quiet we sensed an uncauter-
ized wound had been touched by the most routine of
inquiries. She hadn't asked him about his work, which
would have been easy for him to handle. A person can
hide behind his job all day, and besides we had already
covered that one. He told us on the walk over that he
was a contractor who built things on U.S. Army bases.
He traveled all the time doing this. He also played the
piano and after hours jammed with pick-up bands of
soldiers, other pretty good musicians who got together
when they could.

The waitress brought the food. Beans and rice with a
fried egg on top for all of us, along with a basket of fresh
hard rolls and a second round of beer. We ate a little to
fill the spaces in a conversation becalmed in doldrums.
We could see Ray's composure was fragile. Finally he
spoke. "I'm sorry."

"Want to tell us about it?" Bev asked, with a slight
grimace that begged a pardon if asking was making
another mistake.

And that's when Ray told us about the inconceivable
dual reality he had been living for twenty years. One
life was spent as a straight-arrow husband, the father
of two children, a self-made businessman and amateur
musician. Regular churchgoer. The works. In life number two Ray was addicted to all manner of homosexual
activity, mostly with enlisted men, in rec halls on the
bases. There had been officers, too, even a major. He described furtive gropings in bathrooms and public buildings. He held nothing back. As he unrolled his map of
two decades, we were riveted. He operated on one set of

standards at home and a completely different set on the road. As much as anything else, we were struck by the utter aloneness of his existence.

Lately, and increasingly, the separate colors of his two lives had started to run together. A lover from some- where on the road had called his home a few times. He counted it no less a miracle than the parting of the Red Sea that he got to the mailbox first on the two occasions when letters came from a one-night stand with requests that were particularly graphic. "How did he find out where I live?" Ray asked the middle distance in front of him.

"Army bases have computers," Bev offered. "You're a contractor, so you're in the database. I was madly in love with my biology professor a couple years ago. That's how I tracked him down. It was easy..." The last couple of words flattened out as she trailed off, expelled a be- traying sigh that wound down to a tiny puff. In nothing more than a parenthetical fragment, I thought we may have seen a door behind which she keeps an entire world sealed off for good.

"He drives past my house," Ray said. Public exposure loomed, and with it community revulsion, heartbreak, devastation. In addition, his business had been in a long rough patch and was in jeopardy of going down. The crows were gathering and Ray was feeling maybe it wasn't worth it. None of it worth anything.

Ray had come to Tikal to decide whether or not to kill himself.

When somebody tells you something like this, you're supposed to reach out, touch them meaningfully and urge, "No, wait, don't...all human beings are infinitely precious." And Bev did just that. In almost those exact words. She leaned in close, across the table and, I swear to God, touched his arm. I couldn't have gone there to save my life. I felt sorry for him but I've never been very good at this, and deep down in the nethermost dust bunnies of my soul, I wonder how long or happily everyone is supposed to live. Also, I don't impulsively touch gay men and even if I did, I don't say "precious" to anybody.

It would have been useless to remind Ray that, on the whole, double lives are good things to avoid, because there are enough deceptions and gray truth to keep track of in just one life. So I went for the more practical, "Were you thinking of taking a dive off the temple?" That was the start of Bev kicking me under the table.

"Oh my God, no," Ray replied. "I'm much too chicken." Not wanting to inconvenience others, Ray would do something less dramatic with drugs or gas when he got home. He had started to accumulate a lot of life insurance and would try to make it look like an accident. "But I did think about it when I was up there," he said.

"So you got all this stress and anguish. And the idea of killing yourself is to escape from that into oblivion?" KA-KICK!

"Something…anything…I just don't want my family to…"

"But what if peaceful nothingness isn't what happens?"

He was wary and irritated at what he thought I was getting at. I got an inkling we weren't the first people he'd had this conversation with. "Oh yeah, the burning fires of hell," he said. "Well, I don't buy into any of that."

"I don't either, but of course we never know. And that's the point. Nothingness is only one of a zillion possibilities. What if your suffering still exists and you're somehow trapped in it? I mean isn't that why ghosts hang around and haunt things and rattle chains?" Ray rolled his eyes. *Enormous kick.* But I had moved my legs and Bev caught the post under the table.

Bev, ever the good cop, jumped in. "This isn't something you've definitely made your mind up about is it?"

"No."

She added, "…because it sounds like you're thinking out loud. I feel like you're trying to desensitize yourself…like you're working up your courage." Direct enough, I guess, considering what she had been doing to my shins for saying what I thought was much the same thing. Neither of us had any way to know how far along he was in his plans, how definite, or if he was a serial crier for help or what. But I thought Bev was right. In front of us, two strangers he would never see again, he seemed to be seriously test-driving the idea.

"Maybe I am," he answered.

Bev and I didn't have a plan for where to take this, but we were connecting. Bev had ventured into euphemisms early on, referring to him as a borderline homosexual and bisexual, but I felt almost certain that wasn't true. I was sure Ray was gay as a box of birds and that whatever had been going on with him and his wife the past twenty years, he had been faking it all the way. That was my two cents and Ray didn't contest it when I brought it up. Bev sat beside me, and Ray across from us alternated looking at me, then her, then me, eyeball to eyeball with each of us. Every time my turn came around I was terribly aware I was looking deeply into

the eyes of a man who bats for the other team. Not good
for my homophobia, and it required a manual override
of my autonomic fight-or-flight.

"Ray, you need to get real," I finally said. "You've
obviously built a life you don't like and your business
is going into the toilet, but you're talking about killing
yourself, pulling the plug for all time. Forever. I think
you need to quit playing games and think this thing
all the way through because *death is pretty fucking ir-
reversible*." That last part may have been delivered just
a smidgen too loud. Every head in the place whipped in
the direction of our table.

We stayed in the restaurant for three hours, holding
down our corner as the rest of Tikal's gringo tourists,
"Banana Republicans" we christened them after their
sartorial sameness, drifted in, ate their beer and beans,
and left. I told them of my own decision-in-progress,
about whether to keep on working in an office or risk all
doing the writing I really wanted to do. If it didn't also
involve my wife and kids, no problem, but not being able
to provide for them, that was the scary part. The fantasy
itself was superb. Getting up in the morning, taking my
coffee cup and laptop up the ladder to the treehouse in
the woods out back. Banging out deathless prose to feed
a world of hungry hearts. Coming down only to put on a
tux and go to White House dinners. "Nice hallucination,
huh?" I concluded.

"The best." Ray winked.

Ray eventually began to lighten up. Nothing like a
few cockroach stories to put everyone in a festive mood.
Did you know some kinds will eat your eyebrows
while you're sleeping? Life stories of broken loves were
swapped and it was determined that nobody gets out

of this world with their heart in one piece. In the end, a conspiracy was hatched. Sunset on top of Temple IV. Maybe the Mundo Perdido temple because it would be less of a tourist magnet come sunrise if we decided to do an all-nighter.

The only problem was the guards posted after the ruins were closed to the public. "Leave them to me," I assured my companions. The universal language that unites all mankind isn't love. It isn't even money or the barrel of a gun. It's cigarettes. Marlboro, to be exact. They've gotten me through more closed doors and gates and into the good graces of tinpot dictators with rubber stamps in more places than I can remember. I don't smoke them but it seems like everyone else does. But when we arrived, the guards weren't around. They shooed the tourists out of the park before dusk, hung around to guard for awhile, and then left themselves.

The path into the restored part of Tikal was ours for the taking as the sun hovered through the treetops at a steep angle but still decently above the horizon. Provisioned with beef jerky, *mucho* bottles of piss-warm beer, three-quarters of a bag of sat-on Oreo cookie dust, and four useless packs of cigarettes, we scampered up the high temple giggling like kids who had snuck into a ballgame.

We arrived atop the temple in time to watch the sun fall into the seamless covering of treetops spread out below us. We listened to howler monkeys, which sound like jaguars, and jaguars (which also sound like jaguars), down below and around on all sides of us—staking out their territory for the night. We were in the middle of deadly earnest, non-Disneyland jungle. And now it was dark. In retrospect, smart people would not have been where we were.

"What do you suppose killed this civilization?" Bev asked. "War?"

Ray knew. "They ran out of sacrificial virgins. They had nothing left to appease the gods with and so naturally the gods destroyed them."

More thinking aloud than speaking, I added, "We're pretty much out of virgins back home, as far as I can tell."

"Not a good sign," Ray said.

While waiting to be eaten, we held a free-flowing and slightly inebriated all-night dissection of the souls of all three of us. Ray wondered if I had any personal objection to "gay." Feeling no need to pony up the usual preface "I have many friends who are gay," I simply told him that some time ago I arrived at the conclusion that "gay" is a stupid waste of time, and that Ray's pothering over his identity in the middle years of his life proved my point. It didn't, but somehow this made total sense in the moment.

I recited a couple of poems and was rewarded with their laughter and approval. They really liked the one about Attila the Hun and concurred that my life would be better spent pushing words around on paper than pushing papers through the colon of some great bureaucracy. We worked on our jaguar growls and taught Bev "Me and Bobbie McGee."

Bev found another giant ant, or rather it found her. She dispatched it with a swat and then started to demonstrate the fingernail bit with one of its friends. If it clamped her nail and didn't bite the finger, Bev would take it as a sign from God that she should pursue her dissertation. We

had been urging her to do that all afternoon and the ant
backed us up. The little bugger held on to beat the band.
Ray hailed her "Dances with ants."

We even discovered a use for the Marlboros: mosquito
repellant. We lit six at a time and set them all around
us. We would have been driven away by "blood-sucking
arthropoda" (a bugologist in the jungle can be endlessly
informative), but the breeze above the trees kept most
of them at bay, just as the stars and the companionship
anchored us there until night melded into daybreak.
The sunrise would have been outstanding if it hadn't
been for the fog. In the dark of pre-dawn, as the dew
was forming all over us like rain appearing out of thin
air, the night's coolness and the still-warm earth married
to produce a pea-soup shroud that rose from the jungle
floor. Before it surrounded us and blocked out the stars,
the fog climbed the temple stairs until it covered the
treetops at our feet, washing us in reflected moonlight.
We pretended to be the last three survivors of a castled
city built on a cloud.

Somewhere in the night I leveled with him. I said,
"Ray, you need to figure out whatever the hell it is you
are and then have a talk with your wife. Maybe the first
real talk of your whole marriage. Chances are she already
suspects you're gobbling army men since you've had sex
with her like what, twice?"

Bev agreed, "I'm sure she must know, but maybe
doesn't want to know." There on the top of the temple
of ancient Tikal, we made Ray raise his right hand and
swear before the orchid bedecked primordial gods of a
disappeared people, that he wouldn't do anything dumb
like the Mayans did. No human sacrifices. And that he
would tell his wife what he should have told her twenty

years and two children ago. At dawn we descended back into the present century. The tall wet grass soaked our boot tops as we headed along the path from the ruins, past surprised guards who had come on duty at sunrise. Back to the campsite to say goodbye, roll our gear, and depart on separate buses to our individual destinies, however enriching or pathetically tragic they would turn out to be. The fearsome threesome, unlikely to have met and even more unlikely to meet again. Dances with ants. Dances with words. Dances with soldiers.

❧ ❧ ❧

Senior Vice President of Editorial and International for United Press International (UPI), Larry R. Moffitt has visited eighty countries in the past two decades. From the Amazon River to North Korea, from Angola and Guatemala to Soviet and post-Soviet Russia, he has mispronounced his way around the world and eaten the unidentifiable. Mile markers along his life's path would be labeled husband and father, farmer and beekeeper, short-story writer, editor, amateur chef, stand-up comedian, and so-so poet. He lives in Bowie, Maryland.

꙳ ꙳ ꙳

Confessions of a
Travel Writer

It was all too good to be true ... for a while.

MY CAREER AS A TRAVEL WRITER BEGAN INNOCENTLY enough: I was looking for a way to deduct the $10,000 my five-month honeymoon in Asia had cost.

"Why not write an article?" my wife suggested. "You could write about honeymooning in Japan."

The piece I wrote about our nights in the love hotels of Japan slipped out of the computer with almost no effort on my part and was published in quick succession by the *San Jose Mercury News*, *Chicago Tribune*, *San Francisco Chronicle*, *Orange County Register*, *Sacramento Bee*, and Salon.com among others. Suddenly and unexpectedly I had become a writer.

Within weeks press releases began appearing in my

mailbox. A small flurry rapidly evolved into a blizzard of offers to visit destinations exotic and remote as well as domestic and mundane. Without ever knowing how, my name found its way onto the mailing lists maintained by the tourism authorities of Austria, Panama, South Dakota, Australia, Switzerland, Britain, Hawaii, Anaheim, Orlando, and the Quad Cities of Illinois and Iowa. All wanted me to visit. All offered free food, flights, accommodations, and the promise of a story that only a writer of my caliber could bring fully to life.

Like most free offers, it was all too good to be true. I didn't know it at the time, but I had effortlessly merged onto the literary road to ruin; the road known as travel writing. In reflection, I now see that I started on the trip to rock bottom, like so many others before me, in Las Vegas.

"Hi, this is Patrice," the preternaturally cheery voice on my answering machine stated before asking that I "please excuse the message, however, my attempts to notify you personally have been unsuccessful." Patrice buoyantly went on to inform me that I had been "selected to receive two, fully-paid round-trip airline tickets as well as two nights deluxe hotel accommodations in the heart of Las Vegas, Nevada. Congratulations." All I had to do was call an 800 number and confirm.

"This is so cheesy," I said to Nina, as we pulled into the parking lot of a nondescript office building halfway down the San Francisco peninsula. "I can't believe we're doing this."

"Come on," she insisted. "It could be fun. Plus, it's free."

Ninety minutes later we left the time-share presentation with a coupon redeemable for our free trip to Vegas.

"Don't you feel dirty?" I said to Nina as we drove home.

"Of course I do," she said. "But I'll wash off in our Las Vegas hotel room. It's freeeeee!"

When we got to Vegas, I had the taxi wait outside the Wild West Motel. Despite what Patrice had promised, "deluxe" is not the word I would have chosen to describe our room at the Wild West or the smokers' lounge that was filled with truckers or the small pool that was crowded with their wives and children and surrounded by a chain-link fence.

"Let's go someplace else," I said.

"Why?" Nina said. "It's just a room. And it's free. Plus I want to get to the Liberace Museum today."

"I have something else in mind," I said.

By the time of this trip I was already an "award-winning travel writer," thanks as much to any native talent as to the fact that the number of annual awards given out by the travel industry makes the people behind the Emmys look like pikers. We made our way back to the Strip and the looming, gold-mirrored complex where the local Four Seasons occupies the top floors of what is otherwise known as the Mandalay Bay, and where the publicist was more than happy to accommodate us...since we were in Las Vegas anyway.

"Better?" I asked Nina as we looked down on the neon from our room on the thirty-first floor. Our bathroom at the Four Seasons was significantly bigger than our room at the Wild West. No doubt the plush terrycloth robes had more thread in them than all the Wild West's linen, carpet, curtains, and towels combined. "It's O.K.," Nina said as she moved over to look at the rate card affixed to the back of the door. "But I'm not paying $425 a night."

If Las Vegas began my descent into travel writer's hell, then a call from *San Francisco* magazine completed the trip. Would I be interested, an editor wanted to know, in helping to inaugurate "He Drives/She Drives," a special advertising section in which a married couple drives a luxury car to a luxury destination every other month or so and then writes about it.

"You've called the right people," I said without hesitation.

For our first trip we were given a baby Benz and a lovely suite overlooking Monterey Bay. "You know," I said to the hotel manager, "if we were able to visit your new spa, I'm sure we would have that much more to write about."

"I'll see to it right away, Mr. Strauss," the man said, dispensing with the knowing wink that surely would accompany such a request in a Hollywood movie.

"What?" I said to Nina who was glaring at me, her jaw slightly cocked to the side in an expression I had come to know as one that combines disbelief with disgust.

"You *are* a whore," she said.

"So I guess then I'll be going for the salt-rub exfoliation by myself?" I asked.

"I didn't say that," she said.

"You've gone over to the dark side," my writer friends told me before explaining that as far as responsible journalism was concerned there was no place held in lower regard than special advertising sections such as "He Drives/She Drives," where any pretense of a separation between commercial and editorial interests disappears altogether. I wasn't troubled. "He Drives/She Drives" was a gig I hoped would go on forever. We were traveling around California in a style more typically associated with newly minted IPO babies than with lowly travel writers.

Despite the wit I attempted to infuse into each junket, our handler at *San Francisco* did not see us as heirs apparent to Tracey and Hepburn. When, for its gay pride issue, the magazine opted for an all-male "He Drives/ He Drives," we lost our pole position forever. For me, as a writer, it was already too late. I *had* gone over to the dark side.

In the beginning, I had been productive, reliable, conscientious. Then something happened. The concept of actually having to pay for a trip out of my own pocket, whether or not I would or could actually write a story about the experience, became distasteful. Why should I fork out for a trip when so many were begging me to visit? Trying to get something for nothing had become a game between two fixtures of the lower species of the modern literary world; the professional travel writer and the publicist. I had reached a point where paying for a meal, or a hotel room, or an airline ticket, or a round of golf, seemed like something only commoners did. Why bother with Motel 6 or a Holiday Inn when an e-mail could secure a luxurious suite where a complimentary fruit basket, bottle of wine, and a handwritten note from the manager were sure to be waiting? If invitations had started coming to me from Faustus Public Relations I would have been only too happy to accept. How, I wondered, could I have fallen so far? Not long before I had been enrolled at a Quaker college.

My wife and I maintain a "things to do in life" list, a list that includes watching a space shot, seeing the aurora borealis, building a house, and owning a small island. One of the items has long been riding the Blue Train, the famed South African railroad that runs between

Pretoria and Cape Town. I called an editor friend and was given a loose assignment that was just solid enough to extract a free luxury cabin.

We never should have gotten on the train. After all, I still "owed" stories on the cruise we took to Napa on a luxury yacht. And on the nights at the Hotel Mediterraneo in Rome. Then there was the personalized cooking class we took in Archidosso, in Tuscany, where the chef himself hosted us in his castle-like home. And what about the safari at Tiger Tops in Nepal? Or the days spent on the pure white sand of the Full Moon Beach Resort in the Maldives? And would I ever get around to writing something about the mountain biking and helicopter excursions I'd been given at Whistler in British Columbia? Or the free rounds of golf at Mauna Kea in Hawaii? I mean to write about all of them. I do. Honestly.

Even before boarding the Blue Train in Pretoria, I had a sense that this was a train too far. Despite the irresistible attraction of soaking in a full-size tub on a moving train, I should have turned down the assignment. I should have known better. The guilt I had accumulated over free trips and unwritten pieces had become disabling. But instead of saying no, I took the Blue Train's offer and built upon it, asking for free rooms at some of South Africa's top hotels. They all said yes.

I couldn't help myself. I had become a free travel junkie and each fix had me lusting for the next. Of course I had no one to blame but myself. Yet an addiction like this can't thrive without willing dealers.

Less than a year earlier a woman had called from Colorado to ask if I would be interested in four days of free skiing at Vail and Beaver Creek. Sure, I told her, before explaining that I was moving to Africa in a month and didn't think I'd ever have time to write about it. Plus, I told her, practically begging to be let off the hook, "I don't write 'skiing'."

"No problem," she said in the ever-upbeat tone that seems to belong exclusively to those in marketing and publicity. "You might some day. I'll send you a ticket." Like Al Pacino in *The Godfather III*, I knew very well that I needed to get out—but I kept letting them suck me back in.

The Blue Train was fabulous and lived up to every bit of its reputation. Twenty-seven hours on board was hardly enough. Had I the money to spend on such a trip, I might have even considered paying for it myself. And then there was the dinner in Paarl, in the heart of the wine country, at Bosman's, one of the country's best restaurants. On the veranda, under a full moon, it could not have been better. The cherry encrusted steenbok was gamy, delicate, and sweet all at once. And there was the free room at Johannesburg's elegant Westcliff and at its sister hotel in Cape Town, the Mount Nelson, where, quite by surprise, we were given two nights in the re-furbished Royal Suite, inaugurated not long before by Prince Edward himself.

"Not bad," Nina said as she took in the vast, two-room suite where everything was done in mirrors and shades of gray and where the television rose up out of a mirrored box at the foot of the four-poster bed on some kind of hydraulic lift system one would expect to find only in a love nest designed for Austin Powers.

In fact, although everything about our trip to South Africa was wonderful, I have been unable to craft a story worthy of the many thousands of dollars of transportation, food, and accommodation that we were "comped," as they say in the trade. There are, after all, only so many things one can say about sumptuous meals, luxury transportation, jade-green golf courses, and expansive rooms in five-star hotels.

In the months since our trip to South Africa I have written failed draft after failed draft. I have been up for hours, frozen at the keyboard, blocked for the first time since I began writing years ago. I suppose it's some type of cosmic torment for the promises I have made and failed to keep. I'm sick about the whole thing.

At long last, I think I have learned my lesson. I can no longer handle the angst of taking something for nothing and carrying the weight of a debt unpaid. The offers of free meals and hotel rooms keep coming. Despite my love of travel I cannot accept them and remain at peace with myself.

Not, of course, unless they throw in the airline tickets, too.

❧ ❧ ❧

Robert Strauss has had stories published in several Travelers' Tales editions.

MARK JENKINS

~≈ ~≈ ~≈

The Ghost Road

Hello heart of darkness.

D
OWN DARK PASSAGEWAYS, RIGHT AT ONE
corner, left at the next, no idea where I'm going.
On a main street in the town of Namsai, I spot three
armed Arunachal Pradesh border policemen up ahead.
It is the spring of 1996, and I'm traveling in this north-
eastern Indian state illegally. I slide into the flow of
tasseled trishaws, pedestrians, clicking bicycles.

A vintage white Ambassador—that lumpish fifties-
era sedan still found throughout India's hinterland—
creeps along within the bright human throng. Behind
it a young tribal girl carries two buckets of water on a
bamboo pole. I step up alongside her. She smiles, then
covers her face. I snap off my baseball cap and place it
on her head. She laughs and unwinds an orange cotton
wrap from around her shoulders and hands it to me. I

knew she would do this; it's not possible to give a gift in this part of the world without receiving one in return. I dive both hands into one of her buckets, slick back my shaggy hair, and whip the fabric into a turban around my head. Then I step to the rear passenger door of the Ambassador and jump in the backseat.

I find myself sitting beside a large Buddhist lama in maroon robes. I adjust my disguise and scan the crowd outside.

"You are being chased," says the lama.

"I am."

The lama speaks to the chauffeur. The chauffeur taps his horn, maneuvers around a Brahma bull seated in the road, speeds up. In the outskirts of Ledo, we roll onto a long grassy driveway, pass a freshly gilded stupa, and stop in front of a group of wooden buildings. The lama lifts his frock above polished black shoes and steps out.

"My name is Aggadhamma," he says, in British-accented English. "This is the Namsai Buddhist Vihara, a monastery for boys. You are safe here."

That evening I have dinner with the lama and a dozen shaved-headed acolytes. We are seated on the floor around circular tables. The walls are Easter-egg blue. A tin plate heaped with rice, *dal*, vegetables, and burning-hot, fuscous curry is set before me. I eat with my right hand.

After the meal, the boys slug back a last tin of water and scatter into the warm, lampless dark.

"Now," says Aggadhamma, "please tell me, what brought you to this distant corner of our earth?"

I don't have any reason not to be truthful. "I want to travel the old Stilwell Road and cross into Burma."

I outline my obsession. Six decades ago, during

World War II, American soldiers under the command of General Joseph "Vinegar Joe" Stilwell carved a 1,100-mile road, starting in Ledo, in the Indian state of Assam, through a wilderness of dripping mountains and leech-infested jungles in northern Burma, and across the border into southwestern China.

No one even knows if this old military road still exists. Perhaps it has vanished entirely, consumed by the jungle like a snake eaten by a tiger. It's a mystery I've been hoping to solve.

"This is your plan, despite the fact that Arunachal Pradesh is in the midst of civil unrest—car bombings, assassinations, and the like—and therefore closed to foreigners," responds Aggadhamma. "I take it you are here without government permission."

I admit that I do not have a Restricted Area Permit.

"It's not as serious as it sounds," I add. "Mostly just a game of cat and mouse with the border police."

Aggadhamma eyes me. "You can get away with this in India," he says. "India is the greatest democracy in the world. The government here is like an old elephant: vast, but slow and avoidable. Clever people can keep from being stepped on."

I don't tell him that I have already been arrested, and escaped, a half-dozen times, but he already seems to know.

"You are clever, then," he continues, "and yet you wish to sneak into Burma and play this same game?"

I just nod.

For the next three days I hide out in the Namsai Vihara. I help spade black soil in the vegetable garden and teach the eager pupils American slang in their English classes.

My last night in the monastery, Aggadhamma tells me he has someone for me to meet. After supper, he introduces me to a nine-year-old boy named Myin. The boy is as beautiful as a girl, with brilliant eyes and a perpetual grin. He is also an amputee, his left leg vanished at the hip.

"Myin is from Burma," says Aggadhamma, and tells the boy's story as Myin stares at me with a guileless smile.

Myin is a Jinghpaw, or Kachin. The Kachins are an ethnic group whose homeland includes most of northern Burma; they are one of seven major ethnic minorities—along with the Karen, Karenni, Mon, Chin, Shan, and Arakanese—that make up about 30 percent of the country's population (68 percent of the 50 million citizens are Burmese), each with its own state. All told, there are some 140 ethnic groups and 100 dialects in Burma.

Two years earlier, soldiers under the military regime burned Myin's village to the ground and took all the boys. They were tracking pro-democracy Kachin guerrillas through the jungle. The soldiers knew the trails were booby-trapped, and they used Myin as a human minesweeper, forcing him to walk alone in front of the soldiers. He was seven years old and couldn't have weighed forty pounds when his leg was blown off.

"We have several boys from Burma here," says Aggadhamma. "Each has been maimed in one way or other. This is what Burma does to humans."

After dark I leave Namsai Buddhist Vihara. Aggadhamma shakes my hand with both of his hands, holding on tightly even after I release my grip.

During the late eighties and early nineties, I went to the Himalayas on a mountaineering expedition every two years. When I was stormbound at high altitude, the best escape was always a good book, so I blame historian Barbara W. Tuchman for my original fascination with the Stilwell Road. Deep inside my sleeping bag at 23,000 feet, with waves of graupel slamming the tent, I read her 1971 Pulitzer Prize-winning book, *Stilwell and the American Experience in China, 1911-45*, and was transported to another world and another time.

By the time the United States entered the Second World War, Imperial Japan had been penetrating ever deeper into China for more than a decade, gaining control of nearly one-third of that weakened giant. In the first five months of 1942, Japanese forces rapidly subjugated much of Southeast Asia: the Philippines, Hong Kong, Singapore, Malaysia, Indonesia, and a large swath of Burma. If China fell, all of Asia was threatened, from the rice fields of India to the oil fields of Baghdad.

America had been attempting to bolster the Chinese Nationalist forces of Chiang Kai-shek by supplying his forces via the back door, through India. Pilots were flying ordnance and ammunition from India to China over "the Hump"—the dragon's tail of the Himalayas that hooks south into northern Burma. But China was still losing. General Stilwell, commanding general of the China-Burma-India Theater, believed these supply flights weren't enough. A tough, wiry West Point graduate who had spent years on clandestine missions in China, Stilwell was a military traditionalist. He was convinced that in order to adequately supply the Chinese, an all-weather military road had to be created from India through the unknown mountains and swamps of northern Burma. This 478-mile road, dubbed the Ledo Road, would connect with the old Burma Road, a convoluted 717-mile track built by the Chinese that ran northeast from Lashio, Burma, to Kunming, China—creating an 1,100-mile supply route called the Stilwell Road. (Today, it's popularly, if erroneously, known as the Burma Road.)

British prime minister Winston Churchill characterized Stilwell's endeavor as "an immense, laborious task, unlikely to be finished until the need for it has passed." Stilwell was undeterred.

Completing the road cost $150 million and required the labor of 28,000 American soldiers, almost all of them black, and 35,000 ethnic workers. It was a dangerous job; casualty rates were so high that it was dubbed the "Man-a-Mile Road." Japanese snipers, monsoon floods, malaria, and cholera took the lives of 1,100 American soldiers and untold numbers of Asian workers before the Stilwell Road was completed, in January 1945. Over the next seven months, 5,000 vehicles and 35,000 tons of supplies traveled it. Then the atomic bombs were dropped on Hiroshima and Nagasaki, and the Japanese surrendered.

In October 1945, the U.S. abandoned the road. Churchill had been right.

Over the following decades, the old Burma Road across southwestern China remained in use, but the stretch of Stilwell's highway that crossed the remote fastness of northern Burma reverted to a blank on the map, an enigma that became my obsession.

Detouring on the way home from various mountaineering trips, I managed to travel the entire Chinese section of the road by the early 1990s. I would sit on the roofs of listing, overloaded trucks grinding up and down hundreds of switchbacks across the gorge-scarred Yunnan province. It was my own private adventure. I didn't talk about it, didn't write about it.

But minor triumphs gradually set the foundation for great expectations. Over the years, my desire to get into Burma and traverse whatever was left of the Stilwell Road began to displace my passion for mountain climbing. Mountains were simple, predictable beasts, compared with nations. I knew the unknowns—the brutal cold, the avalanches. I knew how to suffer, how to summit, and how to fail. What I didn't know was Burma, a different kind of impossible challenge.

In late 1993, during an expedition into eastern Tibet, I tried to enter Burma from the north with a partner. We were caught by the Chinese border patrol, interrogated, and jailed for a couple of nights. We signed a confession and were released.

In the spring of 1996, I traveled to the Indian state of Assam to write a magazine article about wildlife poaching, then veered off to Ledo to try my luck again. Two weeks after leaving the Namsai monastery and traveling most of the twenty-mile stretch of the Stilwell Road through Arunachal Pradesh to the India-Burma border, I was nabbed. I was detained for three days in Tezu and politely interrogated (tea and scones were served) by Indian army officers, all of whom assumed I was a CIA agent. On the fourth day I was placed in a jeep with two armed guards, driven to the banks of the enormous, mud-brown Brahmaputra, put on a leaky tug dragging a mile-long raft of timber, and deported downstream to Assam.

Still, I felt that I'd successfully completed my appren-
ticeship in duplicity. I knew how to operate alone, how
to lie, how to stay calm while looking down the barrel of
a gun. I had completed the Chinese and Indian sections
of the Stilwell Road. All that remained was the 458-mile
ghost road in Burma.

Back home, I wrote to the Myanmar embassy in
Washington. (Since 1989, Myanmar has been the military government's name for the country.) In 1996, with
great fanfare, Myanmar launched a campaign to pro-
mote tourism, and visitors could obtain a visa to travel
in the southern part of the country, but northern Burma,
including the region the Stilwell Road passed through,
was off-limits to foreigners.

After pestering the embassy and its representatives
for several months, I managed to get an appointment
with U Tin Winn, Myanmar's ambassador to the United
States. I did my political homework before our meeting.

General Aung San, leader of Burma's Anti-Fascist
People's Freedom League, demanded independence
from Britain in 1947. While writing the constitution,
Aung San, along with six of his ministers, was assassinated, igniting a series of bloody coups and bringing
Prime Minister U Nu into power when independence
was granted, in 1948. In 1962, General Ne Win overthrew the civilian government and abolished the constitution. A gallows hood was dropped over the face of the
nation. Through coercion, repression, state-sponsored
murder, and Stalin-style domestic terror, Ne Win maintained control for nearly thirty years.

By 1988, conditions were so unbearable that pro-democracy demonstrations erupted throughout the coun-

try, led by returning exile Aung San Suu Kyi, daughter of Aung San and head of the National League for Democracy (NLD). These demonstrations were brutally crushed by the dictatorship—between 3,000 and 10,000 peaceful protesters were killed—and the State Law and Order Restoration Council (SLORC), a cabal of Burmese generals, was created to run the country.

In 1989, SLORC declared martial law and placed Aung San Suu Kyi under house arrest. Diplomatic pressure and agitation by the NLD forced SLORC to hold general elections the next year. When the NLD won a landslide victory, the generals declared the results invalid and subsequently imprisoned hundreds of NLD members. In 1991, Suu Kyi was awarded the Nobel Peace Prize—perhaps the main reason she is still alive. In short, Myanmar has the dark distinction of being one of the last totalitarian regimes on earth.

At my meeting with Ambassador Tin Winn, I outlined my plan for traveling the Stilwell Road across Burma, tracing the route on a WWII-era U.S. Army map. Ambassador Tin Winn was enthusiastic about my "daring historical journey" and introduced me to an embassy official named Thaung Tun, who was to arrange a special visa and assist me in navigating the Myanmar bureaucracy.

On the phone and in a series of letters, Thaung Tun was invariably gracious and upbeat. "Everything looks good—we're on course. Proper papers are assembling," he told me. "Things take time only." At first I believed him, but as the months passed, I came to recognize this behavior as classic puppeteering. After more than a year of strategic confoundment, Thaung Tun suggested I break the impasse by seeking permission in person.

He knew who I should talk to. I flew to the capital, Rangoon (renamed Yangon), in the fall of 1997.

For three days I sat in a hot, dank hallway waiting to meet Thaung Tun's government colleague. Making you wait is how bureaucrats exercise dominance. I took to bringing bread crumbs for the rats that scurried along the walls. When I finally met the man, a pinched homunculus with nervous eyes and no eyebrows, he pushed me right out of his office.

"Stilwell Road gone!" he screamed. "Disappeared! No possible!"

This only served to incite me. Stilwell and his men had faced countless obstacles, too—torrential rains that raised rivers twenty feet, titanic mudslides, jungle diseases—and Stilwell had been repeatedly told that it was impossible to build a road across Burma. I began to envision defying the Myanmar junta as not merely just, but obligatory. I was still young enough to believe—bewilderedly, arrogantly, passionately—that through sheer force of will, I could bend the world to my ambition.

In February 1998, I return to Assam and the town of Ledo, the beginning of the Stilwell Road. After several weeks of bureaucratic wrangling, I manage to sidestep obtaining a Restricted Area Permit and inveigle permission to travel the road up to the border of Burma. A platoon from the 28th Assam Rifles garrison, led by Commander Y. S. Rama, is enjoined to escort me on foot from Nampong, the last Indian outpost, up to Pangsau Pass, on the border, and then directly back. It is illegal to cross the border in either direction.

The night before our hike, I pull out several bottles of whiskey and start pouring drinks. The soldiers regale me with tales of the horrors unfolding nearby in Burma. There is a command post somewhere past Pangsau Pass, and the soldiers there are almost starving. Many have malaria. Rice is in short supply, and they never have salt. Salt is worth anything to the Burmese soldiers. They sneak over the border with something they have taken from the Naga or Kachin tribes—a bearskin shield, a wooden mask—and trade it for salt. Pangsau Pass, they say, is a punishment posting for Burmese soldiers who have run afoul of the military leadership.

Commander Rama, in his blue uniform and white ascot, sits ramrod stiff after polishing off most of a bottle of whiskey by himself. "Across the border is the end of the world," he declares. "You can go backward in history, Mr. Mark. Americans want to believe that everything goes forward. But if you went forward on this road, you would go backward."

When I leave at five the next morning, the platoon is fast asleep, as if the warm night air were an anesthetic. I know I have a head start of only a few hours at most. The road hooks uphill, disappearing into the black Patkai Range, taking me with it.

My intention is to cross over into Burma, alone and illegally. I don't think I'm delusional; I have a plan. I also know that my plan might fail. The difficulty itself is no small part of the appeal. If success is a certainty, where is the challenge? I am still entranced by the road, but now the seeds of something darker have taken root inside me.

The Stilwell Road was built to stop the spread of totalitarianism. For 2,000 years, from Caesar to Stilwell, building roads was how one nation conquered another. That ended with the rise of air power: Planes in the sky,

not trucks on a road, would thenceforth largely determine the course of warfare. Some generals could envision this not-so-brave new world, but Stilwell was not
one of them. It was an airplane that dropped the atomic
bomb and pushed us across a new rubicon of technological morality.

The Stilwell Road is a paradigm for failure, another
one of humankind's grandiose exercises in futility. As
I know in my heart, this means that my own attempt
at traveling the Stilwell Road is stained with the same
futility. But of course this doesn't stop me. On the
contrary, I charge forward, carrying through with my
complicated, contradictory convictions. Is this not what
all humans sometimes do? We deftly lay out snares and
then proceed to walk right into them.

I leap the giant tropical trees that have fallen across
the track and move between the moss-sheathed embank-
ments. The road narrows to a tunnel. I step through
spiderwebs larger than me, strands clinging to my face.

In two hours I reach Pangsau Pass, a road cut through
mud walls. There is a rotting concrete sign atop the pass.
I snap a photo and walk into Burma.

Just over the border the road begins to disappear.
Light and sky are closed off by vines thick as haw-
sers, leaves large as umbrellas, bamboo stalks rooted
as densely as prison bars. I begin to wonder if the trail
might be booby-trapped.

A queer uneasiness comes over me: I'm being watched.
It makes me want to stop, but I don't. I keep walking.
When I finally look over my shoulder, two soldiers, as
if on cue, part the jungle with the barrels of their rifles
and step onto the road. Two more soldiers appear in
front of me.

They are small men in dark-green fatigues and Chinese-issue camouflage sneakers. They have canteens on their belts and AK-47s and bandoliers of rounds across their shoulders. One wears a large knife on his hip, another a black handgun in a polished black holster.

I wave to the two soldiers ahead of me and move toward them eagerly, as if I am a lost backpacker. Their jaws tighten. I hold out my hand, talking and smiling. The soldiers train their weapons on me, their faces flat and strained.

The soldiers behind me begin to shout. One soldier starts prodding my stomach with the barrel of his rifle, as if he's trying to herd me back where I came from, but I won't move. A soldier behind me grabs my pack and starts to pull me backward. I spin around and he lets go.

This is the moment—they know it and I know it. The soldier in charge, the one with the black handgun, steps forward and holds my eyes in a cold, searching stare. I stare back. I know what he's looking for: fear. Fear is what he most wants to see, what he is accustomed to seeing.

But I have a secret weapon: I'm white. My whiteness protects me. My whiteness is a force field around my body. I know it is unjust, immoral even, but my whiteness means he can't act unilaterally. White people can cause trouble. He knows this.

The soldier shouts in my face but drops his eyes. His men begin to march me down the road, deeper into Burma, barrels at my back. Eventually we arrive at a burned-out building in a clearing. Laborers in rags are squatting in the mud in front of the building.

Using machetes, they're hacking long bamboo poles into three-foot spears and hardening the points over a campfire.

From the color of their sarongs and the way they wear their machetes in a shoulder scabbard, I know they are Naga tribesmen. The Nagas were headhunters until the early twentieth century (British colonial authorities outlawed the practice in the 1890s); although the Nagas have their own language, architecture, religion, and customs, the junta lumps them in with the Kachins.

As I come close, the squatting men do not look up. There are soldiers all around. The soldier with the handgun continues up steep stairs cut into the mud embankment, while the other three remain to guard me. I drop my pack and lean against the roofless building and watch the laborers. Their machetes make muted hacking sounds, the sounds you hear in a butcher shop. The men themselves are silent, as if their tongues have been cut out.

I realize that this is exactly what I was not supposed to see. This is why northern Burma is closed, why so many remote regions of Burma are closed. According to the Free Burma Coalition, an international alliance of activists dedicated to the democratization of Burma, most ethnic minorities across the nation have been viciously persecuted; more than 600,000 have been removed from their villages and forcibly relocated. By interviewing refugees, Amnesty International has documented forced-labor camps hidden throughout the country.

I wait for seven hours, tearing engorged brown leeches off my legs and watching the blood run down into my boots. Late in the afternoon, the soldier with the black sidearm comes down the embankment, grabs me by the hair, and jerks me to my feet. I knock his hand away. He wants to hit me so badly the muscles in his cheeks quiver.

I am pushed up the mud steps. Seated against the building, I could see only the laborers and the rolling jungle. When I reach the top of the mud steps, I truly confront the world I have entered. It is medieval, something from the Dark Ages.

Before me is a 400-foot-high hill, stripped naked. Cut into the base of the slope, circling the mountain, is a trench, 20 feet wide and 10 feet deep. Two-foot bamboo spears, sharpened *pungee* sticks, stab upward from the bottom of the trench. Just beyond the *pungee* pit is an eight-foot-high bamboo wall. The top and outer face of the wall are bristling with bamboo spikes.

Past this is a strip of barren dirt too smooth and manicured to be anything but a minefield. Beyond that is another lethal bamboo wall. There are five walls and four strips of mined no-man's-land ascending the hill in concentric circles. The only break in the stockade is a narrow passageway that zigzags up the middle.

I am dragged over the first *pungee* pit on a bamboo drawbridge and through the first wall via a small, heavy door with bamboo spikes. We enter a tunnel, the walls and stairs dug out of the wet mud, the ceiling roofed with logs. Passing through the tunnel, I try to imagine some purpose for this surreal jungle fortress. It lies on a forgotten, forbidden border and would be a ridiculous target for any combatant. It can only be protecting the Burmese soldiers from the local people they have enslaved.

After passing through four doors, the mud steps rise back up to daylight. We are on top of the hill. I am taken to a table set in the red dirt beneath a canopy of leaves, behind which is seated a fat man with a pockmarked face. Underneath his sweat-stained fatigues, which have no insignia, I can see red pajamas. He is wearing green flip-flops.

There are four armed soldiers standing behind the man. He says something to them and my pack is torn from my back and a bamboo chair forced against the back of my knees. I sit down. One of the soldiers dumps the contents of my pack onto the dirt and starts rummaging through my stuff. I stare at the fat man, wondering who will interpret, when he speaks for himself.

"Passport. Give."

I take my passport out of my money belt and hand it to him.

His eyes don't leave my face. Without ever looking down, he flips through the pages, then throws the passport back, hitting me in the face.

"Visa. Show visa."

I open the passport to the correct page and hand it back. He studies the stamp. I make every effort to appear bored. I have an official visa for Myanmar. It is a large stamp that fills one page of the passport. At the bottom of the page, in blue ink that matches the stamp, I've blotted out the words ALL LAND ENTRY PROHIBITED.

He shakes his head and shuts the passport.

"Not possible. No one come here. Border closed."

I expected this. I am already unfolding two other documents from my money belt. I hand them to him. One is a personal letter from Ambassador U Tin Winn, written and signed on embassy stationery, inviting me to Myanmar and urging all officials to help me travel along the Stilwell Road. The other is an official Myanmar Immigration Department Report of Arrival. My photo is affixed to this document, and it, too, has an official stamp from the Myanmar government. Along with my name, passport number, and visa number, there is a list spelling out my itinerary and the towns in Burma I have permission to travel through: Pangsau Pass, Shingbwiyang, Mogaung, Myitkyina, Bhamo.

These are all forgeries, but I have confidence in them. He has no way of checking their authenticity.

The documents make him angry. "Where you get?" he demands.

"From the embassy of Myanmar. I had lunch with Ambassador U Tin Winn. He invited me to your country." I surprise myself with the calmness of my voice. I tell him I have brought gifts. I gesture for one of the soldiers to bring over a sack from the pile of my belongings. Inside he finds a five-kilogram bag of salt, a package of twenty ballpoint pens, and three lined notebooks. Each notebook has a $100 bill paper-clipped to the cover.

He looks back down at the documents. All of his fingernails are short and dirty, except for the nail on his right pinkie, which is clean and long. I can only assume that he is the warlord of this lost jungle fiefdom—beyond civilization and beyond the fragile wing of morality—and that there is no law here, no God. He is God.

But I have these troublesome documents. I can see his mind working. Someone must know I am here. Why wasn't he informed? If these documents are real, he would've been notified of my arrival. I would've had a military escort.

He raises his small black eyes, stares at me, and says something in Burmese. Two soldiers leave. A few minutes later, a boy is dragged up to the commander. He is clearly a prisoner. Skeletal, wearing nothing but torn trousers, he has an angular head, protruding ribs, legs so thin his knees are larger than his thighs.

The commander barks at him and the boy cringes, then speaks to me.

"Why are you here?" His English is catechism-perfect.

"I told him already," I reply, feigning weariness. "I have been invited by the Myanmar government to travel the Stilwell Road."

The boy translates this.

The commander stands up and slowly walks toward me. He stops with his face in front of mine. Then he walks over and stands like a bear next to the emaciated boy and says something.

"He doesn't believe you," the boy tells me. "Why have you come here?"

When I give the same answer, the commander turns sideways and slams his heavy fist into the boy's rib cage. The boy screams and crumples to the ground.

The fat commander looks at me and laughs. The message seems to be: I may be someone it would not be prudent to harm. But this boy, this boy is perfectly expendable. This boy could easily disappear without a trace.

I am sickened by my naiveté. I've been willing to imperil my own life to travel this road, but not the life of someone else—that's why I chose to go alone. I should have known better. I've read shelves' worth of books about Burma.

When I refuse to answer any more questions, my audience with the warlord is abruptly terminated. I'm hustled back down through the mud tunnels and out of the compound. At dusk, my pack and my passport are returned to me, but my forged documents have disappeared. The film has been ripped from my camera, and all pages with writing have been torn from my journal.

I am marched back up to Pangsau Pass. Commander Rama and his platoon are waiting for me at the border. Rama stares at me with his old, oily eyes but doesn't say a word.

This should have been the end of it. But what began as a private passion, I now twist into a professional goal. I secure a contract with a publisher to write a book about the Stilwell Road. This, I think, will legitimize my bewitchment. Although my editor believes I already have enough material for the book, I insist I have to complete the route.

I return to India in the fall of 1999, hell-bent on finding a way around the Pangsau Pass military compound. The Naga tribesmen I manage to speak to refuse to guide me. No amount of bribery will change their minds, and I can't do it without them. I briefly consider bushwhacking my way into the jungle in a parallel traverse of the Stilwell Road, or whatever is left of it.

Instead, I decide to attack the problem from a southern approach. I'll take a train from Rangoon to Mandalay, then another train up toward Myitkyina, a city of 75,000 on the Stilwell Road. Recently opened to foreigners, Myitkyina is accessible only by plane or train, the region between it and Mandalay remaining closed. I intend to secretly hop off at the closed city of Mogaung, twenty-five miles southwest of Myitkyina, and light out from there, to the west and north, along the Stilwell Road.

I buy a black backpack and a dark-green bivy tent and dark Gore-Tex raingear. I conceal a knife and cash in the sole of one of my boots and obtain declassified Russian and American maps.

This all somehow seems appropriate to me. I have only one crisis of confidence.

While studying the maps on the flight to Bangkok, trying to guess where the military checkpoints along the road will be, I suddenly experience a visceral foreshadowing of my own death. It isn't a vision, just a profound blackness, a terrifying emptiness. My body goes cold, and my mind feels as if all the synapses are short-circuiting and exploding. Then I begin sweating profusely, soaking my seat. It is such a powerful presentiment of my own death that I begin to cry.

For several hours I convince myself that I will get on the next plane home. Instead, I write farewell letters to my wife, Sue, my eight-year-old daughter, Addi, my six-year-old daughter, Teal, and my parents. I mail the letters from Bangkok, but they never arrive.

Heading north from Mandalay, I climb onto the roof of a passenger car to avoid the conductor. The train lumbers along, stopping at every rice-pig-child village, then chugging slowly back into the country. Water buffalo chest-deep in black mud. Women bent in half in green rice paddies. Deep teak forests. Bicyclists on dirt paths. Asian pastoral—just like the brochures.

Twenty-four hours later, as the train slows outside Mogaung, I hop off, run down a dirt road, and leap into the first trishaw I see. The driver pedals me through

Mogaung, but there is a roadblock on the far side of town. He wants me to get out right there, in front of the soldiers. Wagging cash, I get him to pedal down a side street before I step out. Not five minutes later, the police pick me up off the street. They don't say a word. They are very young—adolescents with weapons, driving a souped-up Toyota Corolla. The driver flips on flashing lights, plugs in a bootleg tape of an Asian girl singing Cyndi Lauper songs, and flies north out of Mogaung.

We're on the Stilwell Road, heading toward Myitkyina. After half an hour, we pull into a compound across the street from the railroad tracks, on the edge of town. I peer out and shake my head in surprise and relief. They've taken me to the Myitkyina YMCA.

I register and am given a spare, clean room with a high ceiling. I shave, drop the key off with the clerk, and go back onto the street to explore. I hike muddy cobblestone streets between squat, nondescript buildings. I try to speak with people here and there, but no one will say a word to me. They ignore me, their eyes darting left and right. I end up in an outdoor market where wide-faced women sit under umbrellas amid a cornucopia of brilliant, alien fruits and vegetables.

Back at the Y, the desk clerk asks me how I enjoyed the market.

The next morning I hire a trishaw driver to take me out to the Irrawaddy River. When I come back, the clerk asks me how I enjoyed the river.

In the afternoon, it rains and I go for a walk alone, zigzagging randomly and speedily to the outskirts of town. At a wet intersection, I find one of the trishaw drivers who usually hang out in front of the YMCA waiting for me. I yank a handful of grass from the side of the road before accepting his offer to give me a lift back to the Y.

Early the next morning, I repack my bag, folding tiny blades of grass into my clothes and equipment. I leave and walk the streets of the town, returning to my room at noon. I find my pack right where I left it, everything folded precisely the way it was, but there are blades of grass scattered on the floor.

That night I slip through the window of my room and steal away, carefully climbing over a block wall with pieces of broken glass embedded along the top. I find an unlocked bicycle and take it, pedaling through the darkness to a corner where several old women, perhaps lost in opium dreams, sleep on the street. I lift a conical hat off the head of one of the women and slip a wad of bills into her shirt pocket. Now I'm disguised.

For the next five nights I leave my room and ride right past the roadblocks, with their sleepy sentries, and pedal out to the villages around Myitkyina. At dawn I return the bicycle and sneak back into my room at the Y.

In these neighboring villages, under cover of darkness, I finally find people who will talk to me. They are Kachins who are dying to speak to someone. A deluge of stories, always told behind closed doors, beside candles or oil lanterns that are frequently doused—and always in whispers. They are everywhere.

A shopkeeper who says that everyone is an informer here: "Trishaw drivers, businesspeople, teachers," he says. "Even good people are informers. This is the only way to protect their families: to give up someone else. It is poison."

This shopkeeper takes me to see a former government official who was tasked with beating tribals used for road gangs in the Karen state, in far eastern Burma.

"I was expected to hit them with a club," he says. "Not systematically, because then they could plan and train their minds to resist, but randomly. This works very well. It maintains the fear of the unknown. This is how to create terror in a human heart."

Sometimes I ask questions about the Stilwell Road, but they have stories of their own. What happened to me at Pangsau Pass is happening again: Traveling the Stilwell Road is becoming irrelevant, almost insignificant—a profoundly selfish misadventure, compared with chronicling these stories of suffering and struggle. On the third night, an interpreter is provided and people are brought to me at a secret location, an outbuilding on the edge of an old teacher's enormous vegetable garden.

A truck driver who uses the Stilwell Road delivering construction materials: "My wife washes clothes in the river for the bribe money," he says. "I must pay the soldiers every time I pass through a roadblock; otherwise they will take a part from my truck."

Two ancient soldiers who tell me about fighting for the Americans during the construction of the Stilwell Road, traveling ahead of the bulldozers and clearing the forest of snipers: "We knew the jungle," one says. "We could kill the Japanese. The Americans were brave but did not know the jungle, so we helped them. Then they left us. Now we are in another war against our own government, but America has forgotten what we did for them."

The son of a father who was imprisoned for friendship: "The bravest of all, Aung San Suu Kyi, came here in 1988," he says. "My father knew her; they were schoolmates. Just friends. When she left, my father was taken away. He managed to get letters out to us. How they tortured him with electricity. How they used an iron bar rolled on his shins. How they used snakes with the women. Put snakes inside the women's bodies. He was released after five years, and then he died."

A middle-aged woman who tries to speak but can only cry and wring her hands.

I write pages of notes, hiding them in a jar in the grass behind the YMCA.

On the fourth night, the woman who wept brings her daughter. The mother sits quietly in the shadows while her daughter speaks. She tells me she is 19 years old. She learned to speak English from Christian missionaries. She has dense black hair braided into a long ponytail.

"My mother came to tell you my story, but she could not do it," she says. "We have heard you are interested in the Stilwell Road." She tells me that, except in the far west, between Shingbwiyang and Pangsau Pass, the road still exists. She knows—she has been on it. Junta warlords have been logging in northern Burma and, in places, are rebuilding the road in order to transport the trees to China. Kachin households must provide one family member for the labor.

She was fourteen when she was taken away in a truck and put in a work camp with thirteen other girls. At night they were locked in a large bamboo cage in the compound. Nearly every night, she says, a different girl was dragged out and gang-raped by the soldiers. One of the girls in her crew bled to death. Another girl went mad. After a year, she was set free to find her way back home, walking barefoot back down the road.

She does not pause or weep as she tells me this, but her lower lip trembles.

"We have heard you want to travel the Stilwell Road. It could be done, but it would be very dangerous. I mean, not for you. For the people who would want to help you. But we would do it."

She tells me that since Myitkyina is now open to foreigners, tourists are coming. She believes someday there will be tourists on the Stilwell Road, and she wants them to know the truth. That it is not a road built by Americans. That was history. History is over. It's a road built by the Kachins.

"Do not believe it is a noble road. It is a road of blood. A road of death."

With both hands, she wipes away the tears now in her eyes, stands up, bows, and leaves with her mother.

My hands are trembling too much to write. I cannot listen to anyone else. I ride the bicycle around in the dark for the rest of the night, looking up at the cloudy Burma sky, asking myself, What am I doing here?

The next morning, the desk clerk asks me how my night was.

I look him in the eyes. He looks at me. He's on to me. I realize I've been endangering the people who shared their stories with me.

That night, to reduce suspicion, I decide to go drinking with the trishaw drivers. We end up in a bar, a dark, low-ceilinged place where women walk out on a little stage and sing pop songs under a ghoulish red light. When I'm ready to go back to the YMCA, my companions insist I have one more drink. A toast. It doesn't taste good. I drink some and spill the rest down my neck.

Something starts to happen with my eyes. Things begin to slide. My glass glides off the table and I reach out to catch it and knock it onto the floor. It shatters into little pieces that turn into cockroaches that scrabble away. I can't move my feet properly; they spill and flop like fish. Someone is slapping me, and I stand up swinging, screaming, spinning around.

I open my eyes. Nothing. Darkness everywhere. There's a bird over me in the dark, flapping.

I wake. My head is sideways. I try to focus. Lift my head. I'm naked, bloody, and filthy, covered with feces and dried urine. It's broad daylight. Two wide-eyed little boys are looking down at me. I sit up. I'm in the alley behind the YMCA.

I make it back to my room and fall asleep on the floor. The next time I wake up, I crawl into the shower, wash off the blood, and look at my bruises and cuts. Just beat up. Then I notice the words written in black ink on the palm of my right hand: LEAVE OR DIE.

Adventure is a path. Real adventure—self-determined, self-motivated, often risky—forces you to have firsthand encounters with the world. The world the way it is, not the way you imagine it. Your body will collide with the earth and you will bear witness. In this way you will be compelled to grapple with the limitless kindness and bottomless cruelty of humankind—and perhaps realize that you yourself are capable of both. This will change you. Nothing will ever again be black-and-white.

I spent a year of my life trying to complete the Stilwell Road, but I gave back the advance and didn't write the book. I wasn't ready. To this day, my arrogance, ignorance, and selfishness appall me. Adventure becomes hubris when ambition blinds you to the suffering of the human beings next to you. Only at the end of my odyssey did I fully accept that traveling the road didn't make a damn bit of difference. That wasn't the point. It wasn't about me. It was about Burma and the struggle of its people. And I plan to return the day the junta falls.

Since 1989, Aung San Suu Kyi has spent more than eight years under house arrest; according to Amnesty International, 1,850 peaceful demonstrators have been taken into custody, interrogated, and, in many cases, tortured as political prisoners.

In May 2002, after twenty months of house arrest, Suu Kyi was released by the junta. She immediately picked up where she'd left off, guiding the nonviolent democracy movement in Burma as much through her defiant, selfless bravery as through her words and speeches. "In physical stature she is petite and elegant, but in moral stature she is a giant," Archbishop Desmond Tutu said, in 2001, on the tenth anniversary of Suu Kyi's Nobel Peace Prize. "Big men are scared of her. Armed to the teeth and they still run scared."

On May 30, 2003, while Suu Kyi was on a lecture tour with members of the National League for Democracy near Mandalay, her small convoy was ambushed by members of a pro-government militia. Four of her bodyguards and some seventy supporters were reportedly killed, and hundreds injured, including Suu Kyi herself, who suffered face and shoulder wounds. Suu Kyi was arrested and held incommunicado at an undisclosed location. In late July, Red Cross officials met with her but were not permitted to give any details of her detention.

"Courage means that if you have to suffer for something worth suffering for," Suu Kyi told reporters prior to her recapture, "then you must suffer."

❧ ❧ ❧

Mark Jenkins is on the staff of Outside *magazine and writes a regular column entitled "The Hard Way."*

～～ ～～ ～～

Carbonaro and Primavera

In rural Cuba, faith in the old ways is rewarded.

ONE THING WILL NEVER CHANGE: CARBONARO MUST always be on the right. Five years from now, ten years, even twenty, if all goes well, Carbonaro will still be on the right and Primavera on the left, the two of them yoked together, pulling a spindly plough across the loamy fields in the hills outside Cienfuegos. Oxen are like that: absolutely rigid in their habits, intractable once they have learned their ways. Even when a working pair is out of harness and is being led to water or to a fresh spot to graze, the two animals must be aligned just as they are accustomed or they will bolt, or at the very least dig in and refuse to go any farther until order is restored, each ox in its place.

Carbonaro and Primavera were not always a pair. Twenty years ago Primavera was matched up and trained with an ox named Cimarrón. They worked side by side for two decades. But Cimarrón was a glutton, and he broke into the feed one day and ate himself sick, dying happy with incurable colic. It was an enormous loss. An ox costs thousands of pesos and must be babied along until the age of two and then requires at least a year of training before he can be put to work. It is especially difficult to lose half of a working pair: you have to find a new partner who fits the temperament and strength of your animal, and above all, you have to find an ox who can work on the now vacant side. Primavera would work only on the left. He could be matched only with a partner who was used to working on the right. It was a lucky thing to find Carbonaro, a right-sider and a pretty good match in terms of size, although to this day he is a little afraid of Primavera and hangs back just a bit.

Anyway, it was a lucky thing to find an ox at all. For a while oxen had seemed part of the Cuban landscape—huge, heavy-bodied creatures, with necks rising in a lump of muscle, their gigantic heads tapering into teacup-sized muzzles; homely animals with improbably slim legs and a light tread, their whip-thin tails flicking in a kind of staccato rhythm, the rest of their being unmoving, imperturbable, still. But then cheap Soviet oil came to Cuba, and chemical fertilizers, and, most important, tractors. In fact, during the 1960s and 1970s so many tractors were being sent to Cuba that there were more than the farmers could use. Sometimes when the Agriculture Ministry called the cooperatives to announce the arrival of more tractors, no one even bothered to go to the port to pick them up. During that time hardly anyone wanted oxen. With a heavy tractor a farmer could rip through a field at five or six times the speed he could with a team. It was, or it seemed, so much more modern, and so much simpler, than dealing with the complicated politics of a flesh-and-blood team. Hardly anyone was raising or training oxen. With such a windfall of tractors, no one imagined that oxen would ever again be anything other than a quaint anachronism.

Even during the time of abounding tractors Humberto Quesada preferred using Primavera and Cimarrón—and then, of course, Carbonaro—but Humberto is an independent sort of man. His grandfather was brought to Cuba as a slave and was put to work on a sugar plantation of 70,000 rich acres owned by a Massachusetts family. Humberto's father was a slave there too, and Humberto as a child worked beside him in the fields, so that he could learn how to do what he assumed he'd grow up to do. Although the Quesadas were slaves, they were mavericks. Humberto's sister Ramona, a tiny woman with tight curls and a dry laugh, married the son of white farmers down the road—a scandal at the time, but one that yielded a happy fifty-year marriage that became the warm center of the joined families. And of course Humberto went his own way. After the Castro revolution he became a truck driver, but he kept a hand in farming. It was different, because he was farming his own land, a piece of the old plantation. "The land is the foundation of everything," he told me not long ago. "If you have land, you always have something." He was encouraged to join a cooperative, but like many Cuban farmers, he chose to work alone. "There's always a lazy person in a group, so I don't like being part of groups," he explained. Moreover, he resisted each time the government tried to cut back a little bit of his land. Recently the government wanted to build a health clinic on a piece of his property, but once the official in charge of the appropriation realized that the magnificent sweet potatoes he regularly enjoyed were from Humberto's farm, he changed his mind and said Humberto should have *more* land, not less.

Once or twice Humberto rented a tractor, but he didn't like it. "It presses too hard," he explained. "The land ends up flattened, like a Cuban sandwich." Even when everyone else was using tractors, using chemicals, growing only sugar, Humberto ploughed with oxen; fertilized naturally, the way his father had taught him; cultivated tomatoes and corn and lettuce and beans—and sweet potatoes. Humberto never actually owned the oxen. He borrowed them from his neighbor, whose father had fought beside Humberto's father in the War of Independence.

When the Soviet money ran out, the battalions of tractors, now out of gas, rattled to a standstill, and oxen—quaint, anachronistic oxen—were once again worth their weight in gold. It was a lucky farmer who had never given them up, who still had a working team, who could still plough and plant even in the worst moments after the Soviet collapse. Luckier still was a farmer who had stuck with such crops as corn and tomatoes rather than being seduced by the money that had seemed as if it would flow forever from sugar. In such a moment a man like Humberto no longer seemed a throwback. Now in his eighties, slightly lame, wizened, Humberto is everything the new Cuban farmer needs to be: small-scale, efficient, diversified, organic—and, most important, invulnerable to the ups and downs of Cuba's gasoline economy, which once depended entirely on Soviet good will and has since come to rest precariously on Venezuelan. Most of the imported oil in Cuba these days comes from Venezuela, and because of the good relationship between Fidel Castro and Hugo Chávez, Venezuela's president, the price had, until recently, been especially favorable. But Chávez was nearly overthrown in April of 2002, and when he regained his footing, he suspended the shipments. Across Cuba gasoline prices rose by as much as 20 percent. It was a very good time to have an ox.

One recent morning Humberto stopped by to say hello to his sister, who lives with her extended family on another piece of the old plantation property. It was a brilliant, breezy day. Outside Ramona's little cottage a couple of chickens were worrying the dirt, and a litter of piglets were chasing around in a pile of hay. The cottage is tidy, old, and unadorned; there is something timeless about it, as if nothing here, or nearby, had changed in twenty or thirty or fifty years. And, of course, nothing much *has* changed in the countryside: the elemental facts, the worries over sun and water and whether the seeds have germinated and the eggs have hatched, don't ever change. In Cuba right now there is a sense of the moment, a sense that the country is on the brink of newness and change, a sense that the future is unfurling right now—but the countryside has a constancy, a permanence. And these days Humberto feels like a rich man. He said that everyone he knows is going crazy looking for oxen, and that you have to barter for them or apply to the government, and that anyone who still knows how to train a team—a skill that was of course considered obsolete when the tractors prevailed—is being offered a premium for his talents. He grinned as he said this, pantomiming the frantic gestures of a desperate man looking high and low for a trained ploughing team.

Someday, no doubt, the tractors will start up again, and the hills beyond Cienfuegos and the fields outside Havana and the meadows in Camagüey and Trinidad and Santiago de Cuba will be ploughed faster than the fastest team could dream of. Then, once again, oxen won't be golden anymore. They will be relics, curiosities. But this is their moment, just as it is Humberto's moment, when being slow and shrewd and tough is paying off.

After we'd talked awhile, Humberto got up and headed down the drive and over to his neighbor's, and a few minutes later he reappeared, leading the two oxen, who were walking side by side. He stopped in the yard near the cottage and brought the animals to a halt and stood beside them, one hand laid lightly on Primavera's neck. The oxen shuffled their feet a little and looked sidelong at the cottage, the chickens, a curtain ruffling in the breeze in Ramona's entryway. Humberto's straw hat was tipped back, and it cast a lacy shadow across his face; he leaned a little against the animal's warm gray shoulder and he smiled.

❧ ❧ ❧

Susan Orlean is a staff writer for The New Yorker *and the author of* The Orchid Thief, The Bullfighter Checks Her Makeup, *and* My Kind of Place: Travel Stories from a Woman Who's Been Everywhere.

PETER VALING

~ ~ ~

Where the Fighters
Are Hungry

It wasn't quite the "Rumble in the Jungle,"
but then again, they weren't Don King.

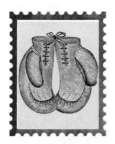

SUSPICION REIGNED AT THE ZIMBABWE-MOZAMBIQUE
border. It was a month or so following the controversial re-election of President Robert Mugabe, and the
border guards had their eyes peeled for trouble-making
foreigners, especially journalists. Having mingled with
members of the MDC (Movement for Democratic
Change), Mugabe's opposition, and several families
of white farmers, Mugabe's scapegoats, I now feared
complications exiting the country.

"Open." The word was spoken quietly but with an
air of command. Unclasping the top of my backpack, I
wondered what incriminating evidence I had forgotten

to destroy: an editor's business card, the address of one of the farms I had visited, an email contact? Again came the voice, this time softer, more inquisitive: "You are a boxer?" Two worn gloves protruded from my backpack. "Yes," I answered, looking up at the guard. "Mugabe was a boxer," I quickly added. To my surprise, his face soured. "Ah, Mugabe," he sighed. Next to me Neal was opening his luggage—one of his gloves also rested on top. "You are fine," said the guard, pointing at Neal. "You can go," he continued while shifting his attention to some of the crates arranged alongside our bus.

There is respect and passion for boxing in Africa. Mandela was a fighter, as were more unsavory characters like Uganda's Idi Amin, not to mention so many sons of Africa who made it big overseas: Louis, Leonard, Foreman, Ali… By instinct, I knew to bring gloves. One ambition I had as I prepared to travel to Africa was to somehow tap into this love of the "sweet science"—a latent love that lay beneath the surface like much of the continent's natural potential.

When I packed the gloves, visions of another "Rumble in the Jungle" danced through my head. Now, after having cleared Zimbabwe, I had two months and eight countries to shape this vision into a reality. But how? Where would one find the fighters, the venue, a welcoming audience, and receptive authorities? For the first "Rumble" in 1974, Don King had Ali and Foreman, the refurbished Kinshasa Stadium, the international press, and the helping hand of Joseph Mobutu, Zaire's flamboyant and attention-hungry dictator. For the budget sequel we had two sets of gloves, two mouthpieces, a cheap camera, and a dream.

We eventually made our way to Cape Maclear, a fishing village on the southern shores of Lake Malawi. It is a mecca for tourists, though the flow had tapered off in recent months due to the unrest in Zimbabwe. Darkness and silence were our only hosts when we arrived. With the minibus disappearing into the night, we walked across a sandy beach towards an illuminated sign announcing Steven's Resthouse. From the lake, which is one of the largest in Africa, shone dozens of tiny lights—sure indicators that the fishermen were busy at work.

Third-class travel had stiffened joints and atrophied muscles, so the next morning, following breakfast, Neal and I decided to pull out the gloves and go a few rounds. On a stretch of beach between the resthouse and the lake we loosened up, jabbing at each other, throwing in the odd right hand, circling back and forth over sand that grew warmer under our feet. Before we started traveling together, Neal had never boxed. But being naturally powerful, built of long lean muscles, he was learning the basics quickly.

And it wasn't long before we had ourselves a small audience. From the corner of my eye, I watched the young men and boys draw closer until around us they formed a loose ring. The resthouse staff came out on the patio, the curtains parted in one of the rooms, and the shipbuilders stopped hammering and gazed through the ribs of an unfinished hull.

The crowd didn't remain spectators for long. The young boys playfully began to push each other, the older ones mimicked our motions—the jab, the right hand, the footwork. Their conversations revolved around boxing. How did I know? Because "boxer," "box," and "boxing" were the only words I understood and they were repeated over and over amidst the laughs, squeals, and jeers.

In this Malawi village, we had stumbled upon a perfect venue for the "Rumble in the Jungle II."

Putting on a boxing card is no easy undertaking. I have witnessed cards take shape only to fall apart at the last minute due to absentee fighters, uncooperative commissions, and lack of interest. Anyone who has seen the documentary *When We Were Kings*—the account of the original "Rumble in the Jungle"—can appreciate the promoter's headaches and heartaches. Since neither Neal nor I had prior experience in the field, we could only expect worse, though lack of interest didn't seem to be a factor. One needn't be a pollster to recognize that here boxing, or at least the idea of boxing, was popular. Our gloves had disappeared into the center of the village, where they were being swapped among enthusiastic youths who swung at each other to the cheers of a steadily growing audience.

What we needed, above all else, was a liaison between us and the village—someone who could translate our desires, someone who knew the proper channels to go through, someone charismatic and bold.

He was young and handsome and he called himself "Snoop"—a name which he later put on his mailing address. His reputation preceded him. While in Blantyre, a city approximately two hundred kilometers away, I was advised to contact Snoop if I needed anything from snorkeling gear to Malawi Gold (marijuana). Snoop would surely sort it out. And among the beach boys—a group of young men who catered to the whims of tourists—Snoop was the "Main Man." He told me as much when we first met.

In the shade of a thatched-roofed bar, we plotted and schemed with the King-like character, whose hair jutted from his scalp—not in a graying afro like Don's, but in

tightly-wound dreadlocks. "First, we must see the chief,"
he advised us after we had laid out our plans. "The chief
will decide if the boxing can happen." Although I had
never met with a chief, I thought it easier to deal with one
man than an organized bureaucracy. We only had two
days for the card to materialize, and if we convinced the
chief we would be halfway there. "What about the fighters, a ring, and a place to hold the fight?" I asked. With an
entrepreneurial glint in his eye he replied, "Don't worry.
Snoop will sort it all out."

Cape Maclear was, in fact, much larger than I had
imagined. Nestled between the mountains and the lake,
the village was home to more than 10,000 Malawians.
Down the dusty road Snoop, Neal, and I trekked towards
the chief's house, past hundreds of tidy huts, a brick
church, an abandoned mosque, and a newly-built medical
clinic, through fields planted with corn, across irrigation
ditches bridged by boards. Dusk was settling on the village, the peasants were returning from the fields and
from behind the dry-grass fences came the sounds and
smells of dinner. My mind was filled with anticipation,
my belly growled for the meats and flatbreads that were
being prepared.

Suddenly, Snoop became very serious. We stopped a
hundred meters from the chief's house and could only
make out a dozen or so silhouettes sitting beneath an
acacia tree. "The chief is in a meeting," Snoop whispered.
"We must wait here."

So we waited, and the moon came up and the fishermen set out and the darkness was pierced by dozens of
celestial and water-born lights. Eventually the silhouettes dispersed, and Snoop returned with an invitation
from the chief.

On the porch of his modest home the man sat. I believed that we were finally face to face with the chief, but in fact, it was his translator—the chief sat somewhere in the shadows behind us. Snoop introduced us and after a pause, the translator asked: "What would you like from Chief Chumbe?"

I inhaled deeply and set forth our plan as clearly and decisively as I could muster. "…With all due respect… big boxing fans…Rumble in the Jungle, 1974…African fighters: Louis, Ali, Tyson…brought gloves…village affair…children enter free…admission divided between the fighters, charity, and the chief…would he agree?" After each point, I'd allow for a translation. From the shadows came a clearing of the throat, a few words and here and there, a chuckle. It was going well. I could feel it.

As it turned out, the chief, in his younger days, was a boxer in South Africa. His favorite fighter was the "Brown Bomber," Joe Louis (whom I had fortunately mentioned in the sales pitch). We were told that he'd think it over, discuss it with the elders, and we should return tomorrow for the decision. Thanking him for his time, we staggered home in the darkness. No electricity existed in the village proper.

Early the next morning, we began to make preparations. It was then that I realized how few resources we had at our disposal. Even the most basic boxing card requires certain staples: a ring, round cards, mouthguards, a bell. To survive in Africa, one must be innovative and resourceful at the most basic level. If we needed round cards, we would have to make them. If we lacked mouthguards, we could rely on the local craftsmen, who turned what would be considered refuse in the West into intricate toys and trinkets. No bell to start the round. Why not substitute a bongo drum?

Establishing a workshop on the resthouse patio, our preparations were soon noticed by a group of volunteer English teachers from England. They agreed to help. At one corner of the table, Neal and I converted an old calendar into round cards by folding it over and stencilling numbers on the back. At the other end, several teachers squabbled over designs and translations for the fight posters that would be posted throughout the village. By overlooking the larger obstacles—the chief's permission, absence of a ring and fighters—the project began to gain momentum.

Snoop arrived with good news. He had sorted out the material for a ring and found a potential venue. His association with the card had bolstered his status in the village and he was now committed to its success. "Let's go look at where we can have the boxing tonight," he said.

"Shouldn't we go see the chief first?" I replied.

He winked. "Today is the chief's drinking day. We will meet him in a bar later. It is better that way." Before we departed, Snoop picked up one of the posters. "What is mayhem?" he asked. I looked at the poster. "It's sort of like Malawi *craziness,*" responded one of the teachers, the coiner of the slogan.

The venue was perfect. In the enclosed courtyard of the Top Quiet Resthouse we would put on our tribute to the monumental Ali-Foreman showdown. There was enough room for a fair-sized ring, seating for several hundred spectators, and because it was enclosed, it would allow us to control the gate and collect the ten *kwatcha* admission. The only catch was that the owner wanted a piece of the action. Shrewd negotiations on Snoop's behalf resulted in the owner agreeing to 20 percent of the gate and profits from food and beverages sold.

The ring was our next challenge. Snoop had convinced several villagers to lend us some fence posts (which were little more than thick branches) and a length of rope. He had also organized volunteers: young boys who, enticed by the promise of ringside seats, were eager to help.

With whatever tools were not being used on the fields that day—three homemade hoes and several dull machetes—we set to work. We dug in the posts, secured them with rocks, and lashed them together with four lengths of rope. It was touching to see everyone working towards the same goal, happily, energetically, without pause, without a word of complaint. When it was completed it wasn't pretty, but it was sturdy and would contain the fighters, which we still didn't have.

From bar to bar we searched for the chief. The posters had been distributed and word was spreading fast. The children, especially, took to the idea and throughout the village they greeted us, yelling: "Boxer! Boxer!" Walking alongside, they grabbed at our hands and tried to impress us by throwing punches into the air. One boy even staged a convincing stagger as if the knockout punch had just been landed. The dormant passion had come to the surface.

It was the kind of passion that must have vitalized Ali's heart, giving him the will to defeat a stronger, meaner George Foreman back in '74. We experienced only a fraction of what "The Greatest" must have felt doing his roadwork in Kinshasa to the screams of "Ali, Boom-By-Ay!"

At Thomas's Bar sat the chief, his translator, and two others. Following Snoop's advice, we had made preparations for the card without the chief's final approval (a similar trick used by King to sign Ali and Foreman, knowing that at the moment he didn't have the money to pay either fighter). Now I was worried. Had the chief heard? Would he be offended? Would this former pugilist put an end to the card?

It was hard not to stare at the chief—this old man, this old fighter—no doubt a former heavyweight, judging by his still-solid frame and large fists. He was more than I had imagined in last night's shadows. A fan of the "Brown Bomber" he was, and no fan of Louis could resist a live display of boxing, I thought, as I ordered a round of beers.

Like Mobutu years ago, the chief could not attend the event, though for different reasons: Zaire's dictator feared assasination; the chief had pressing business in a nearby village. Nonetheless, he gave our fight his blessing. "The chief believes it will be good for the village," pronounced the translator. Looking into his eyes, one glazed by a cataract, the other still sharp, I thanked him. He enclosed my extended hand in his boxer's mitts.

The fights had to be over before the sun set. Otherwise, the audience would be paying to watch silhouettes trip over each other in the dark. On the posters, the bouts were scheduled to begin at 4:30 P.M. At 5:00 P.M. the courtyard was empty and the stick-and-rope ring began to look a little pathetic. Only Snoop remained optimistic. "Don't worry, Peter, they'll come," he said, staring down the dirt road that led up to the resthouse.

By 6:30 we had about 100 spectators, mostly children who were admitted for free. By 7:00 there was a crowd gathered at the gate and Snoop and I collected the tattered notes in a burlap sack. The men, especially, had all the reasons for why they couldn't pay the nominal admission: "No fish caught today." "My friend will pay later." Many reeked of booze but my sympathies for them waned each time a little boy or girl managed to offer up a folded bill. The only way for the men to enter free was to fight, and those who had read and accepted the offer on the poster were being organized in the back by Neal.

Intermittently, Neal would emerge from within his growing stable of fighters to confer with Snoop and me. "I've got four big guys, two short ones, and a skinny one back there. Is there a chance that we could get two more big guys?" Or, "That guy over there, Isaac's his name, I think—he doesn't want to fight anymore." Or, "Pete, the sun is starting to set. We've got to get this show on the road!"

With a little more than an hour of sunlight remaining, it was time to shut the gate and begin the bouts. Those who came late or refused to pay could still see the action from across the gate or from several vantage points along the mountain that bordered the resthouse.

The joy of the moment is hard to convey, and walking towards the ring I made a mental note of each detail, for I knew that no matter what life had in store for me later, it was difficult to imagine an occasion that would rival this in intensity, passion, and beauty. At the center of our small universe, enclosed by the mountains, the jungle, and the sea stood the stick-and-rope ring with its apron of freshly-raked sand. Around its perimeters sat the children, half-clothed, wide-eyed, and brimming with anticipation. The next tier consisted of the women, gathered in small groups, some cradling babies, others making eyes at the men who stood in line next to the gloving table. Finally, there were the men—those who weren't fighting—leaning against the chipped stucco walls, hanging around the gloving table and in the corners, where they inspected with an "expert" eye the stools, spit buckets, and drums. Dispersed thoughout the crowd sat the English teachers, their cameras at the ready, and Snoop stood in the center, beckoning me to enter.

I spoke, Snoop translated, and together we introduced our tribute to the original "Rumble" to the villagers of Cape Maclear. It was obvious that the names Ali and Foreman were not forgotten here, for at their mention the crowd responded with claps and cheers. When the intro was over, it was time for Neal and me to stage an exhibition bout. And there and then the card nearly came crashing down.

One pair of gloves lay on the gloving table, and the other was nowhere to be found!

Panic: searching under the table...Panic: searching around the ring...Panic: running in and out of the bar and restaurant...Restlessness in the crowd...Restlessness in the fighters...Restlessness in all those who dropped a creased bill into the burlap sack in anticipation of an event that they sensed was teetering on the brink. At one point Neal began to wrap towels around his fists.

We were desperate.

A card is not a card until both fighters stand gloved, face-to-face, in the center of the ring. King must have been swallowing his tongue when he was informed that Foreman had sustained a cut over his eye only days before the scheduled bout. Though postponed by several weeks, "The Rumble in the Jungle" eventually materialized, as did "Malawi Mayhem," due to Neal's quick thinking and his even quicker sprint back to my room where the gloves lay on my bed.

Kicking off our sandals, we laced up our fists and slipped between the ropes. We needed to recapture the crowd and so before the drum sounded the beginning of the bout I told Neal to hold nothing back. I would keep my hands low.

He tore into me with a viciousness that I didn't expect. The punches were undisciplined, but they came from all angles and thumped hard on my temples, off my chin, and off the exposed parts of my ribs. Some experienced fighters hate fighting "Green Guys" (inexperienced fighters) because they are unpredictable. Neal was certainly "Green"—and strong as a bull.

On the stool, "Softie," my corner man, rubbed my shoulders and poured water over my head. The sand burned under my feet and my brain was a bit clouded from the barrage that Neal had laid on me. But the crowd loved it and when the bout was over, it had set a standard, which each successive set of fighters either matched or surpassed.

The gloving table was in a state of pandemonium, crowded by men and boys who were trying to help in some way. My gloves were yanked off and laced on the next fighter in line. Mouthpieces were rinsed, dropped in the sand, rinsed again and placed upside down in open mouths. Neal, with the list of fighters in one hand and a glove on the other, was frantically searching for one of the fighters. Meanwhile, I stretched a pair of latex gloves (part of our first-aid kit) over my hands and jumped though the ropes to referee the next bout.

Boyson vs. Edwards, Issac vs. Jeff, Simon vs. Phoenix, Stephan vs. Justice, Chico vs. Billy—five fights, three 3-minute rounds, a half-hour of sunlight left.

It took me years in the gym to loosen up enough to

throw and take punches half-naturally. Here, it was different. Their movements were fluid, their bodies rhythmic, and the commonplace observation that white fighters are "stiff" and "starchy" was reinforced in my mind each time one of these novices threw a slick combination that would take many pros years to master. I'm not trying to make stereotypical divisions between black and white athletes—I am merely stating what I saw and measuring it against a decade of boxing experience. I was very impressed by the natural talents of the locals.

Halfway through the card, the sun dropped behind the mountains and darkness descended on Cape Maclear. The resthouse manager turned on the outside lamps, which barely illuminated the walkways beneath. The remainder of the card would unfold in an incandescent half-light.

When Chico entered the ring, the crowd went frantic with delight. He was a pocket-Tyson, with a compact turret of a torso and two muscle-clad barrels for arms. Word around the village was that Chico was the strongest of all the Cape men. Billy, his opponent, either didn't know or didn't care. His demeanor was calm and confident until the punches began to land.

Chico didn't waste a second and when the drums sounded to commence the round he ran at Billy, unleashing such a fury of blows that Billy's rear soon kissed the sand. Parting the fighters, I sent Chico to a corner while counting out the knockdown. At the count of three, Billy stood up and seconds later was again ass-in-the-sand. Chico was too much for Billy, whose backside graced the apron twice more before he finally gave up.

This was the only victory that was easy to call—the preceding fights were so close, and I was so occupied with refereeing, time keeping, and keeping the round-card bearers out of the ring during the action, that I scored most of them a draw. No sense in creating bad blood in the village, I thought. Especially among men who were putting on such a valiant display of boxing prowess.

This was to be the last fight of the night until Neal rushed over to inform me that he had two young boys who desperately wanted to knock each other about. One last time we rinsed the mouthpieces, laced the gloves, and sounded the battle drums.

They came at each other, conserving nothing, fearing nothing, the boldness of youth coursing through their veins. I was amazed, and at the same time concerned about what might happen to them if they continued. Several times I broke them apart, pleading with Snoop to warn them to take it easy or else I'd call the fight. To these instructions they nodded their heads, threw a light jab or two, and then, as though we had all disappeared, they ran each other around the ring to the drumming and screams of the fans.

In the middle of the second round, I put an end to it. They could return to fight another day when they were a bit older, a bit wiser.

Neal poured the Dettol across a gash in my back and I winced with the pain, wondering in which round it was that a fighter had run me up against one of the corner posts. Neal, Snoop, and the manager were gathered around a table in the office, counting the gate. Snoop emptied the sack and Neal sorted the money. When the count was complete, the card had earned 800 *kwatcha* (approximately $15)—laughable by Western standards, but in Malawi where the per capita earnings are $180, it could be stretched.

Outside, the fighters were eagerly awaiting their cut. Inside, the atmosphere was that of some dingy cubby hole in the back of a 1930s fight club where the promoters, managers, and sycophants parcelled up the blood money of some poor, punch-drunk journeyman. The resthouse manager wanted more for the use of his facilities, Snoop was eyeing up the coins, and Neal and I feared the consequences of not giving each fighter a fair shake.

One by one we gave the fighters their purse (approximately $1). "Just think of the possibilities if we had $100 dollars of our own to donate," said Neal. He, like myself, didn't appear comfortable dividing up such a pittance for so brave an effort. I felt like a miserly headmaster from *Oliver Twist*, doling out lumps of porridge.

With the fighters paid, we had enough left over to buy the chief a bottle of Tanzanian Brandy, as recommended by Snoop. As for charitable causes, we had nothing left and consoled ourselves with the thought that those who came to the card would remember it and those who fought in it might further pursue the "sweet science" in Africa. To this end, we left Snoop our gloves and mouthguards, as well as a promise to send more equipment when we returned to Canada. "Now, I can organize more fights," he said with a smile.

Two weeks later, in Tanzania, when all of this had already slipped into the recesses of my mind, I was reminded of what it was that I was trying to find in Africa when I had packed boxing gloves for the journey.

On a beach, amidst dilapidated hulls of fishing vessels, I saw him circling. Jab...jab...then left hook into a fishing buoy suspended from a tree. He wore old ski gloves and he hit the heavy bag hard. Watch out, all you would-be contenders. In Africa, the fighters are hungry.

※ ※ ※

Peter Valing is an award-winning writer currently living in Vancouver. He likes the ponies and the fights and a good bit of adventure now and then. His hope is to one day move to Mozambique to start an artists' colony.

꙾ ꙾ ꙾

Gringa Morisca

A building speaks to her of eternity and mortality.

W HEN I WAS FIFTEEN I COULD STILL SURRENDER
myself, in the way of a child, to pure magic.
I went to a place in Spain where I found the palace
of the Nasrid sultans riding on a hill like a great ship,
high above the plain and beneath the snow-laden Sierra
Nevada. Around it, across the low slopes and valleys,
lay the city of Granada. The whitewashed walls of the
ancient Arab quarter crowded the nearest hillside, and
behind that rose the hill called Sacramonte, pockmarked
with caves where Gypsies lived.

I wandered the palace for hours and hours that
seemed like days out of time. In trying to describe it
since, even to myself, I have had to fall back on poor
analogies—a fantastic wedding cake, a Disneyland—because there are no other analogies, no frame of reference.

This high flowering of Islamic art in Spain, the last glorious sigh of the Moors' eight-hundred-year reign—the
Alhambra—was an alien aesthetic for an American girl
like me. It was so completely alien that I was left, inevitably, with another sorry analogy but one that accurately
reflected the experience: I floated around in that place
like a visitor from another planet, amazed, uncompre-
hending, delighted to tears.

And so, twenty-five years later, I went back to see if it
would be the same.

In the center of a marble-floored room, a low fountain bubbles in a small round pool. Its overflow is taken
away in a narrow channel along the floor to mingle with
other waters in an adjoining courtyard. The fountain is
the only movement in the room. The walls breathe deep
silence, which is strange to contemplate since every inch
of surface on those walls, and up to the ceiling, and overhead, is filled with a chaos of decoration—up to about
chest height the walls are covered with geometric knots
worked in colorful tile, and above this there is an abrupt
transition to pale sculpted stucco, which lofts upward
in dense, delicate interweavings of Arabic script and
flowers and vines and pomegranates and stars. The eye
wanders over this, into this, led by curling lines to other
curling lines, bumping suddenly into hard geometric
shapes, because the whole system, it turns out, is based
on contrasts. It also becomes clear, on dizzy examina-
tion, that there is, everywhere, both infinite variety and
rhythmic repetition.

It is seductive to stare into it, and yet it is quite possible to look at it and simply feel soothed; as busy as it
is, it makes a gentle music. You can imagine a sultana

reclining on pillows on the floor: she is daydreaming and the walls are the soft background of her dreams, and then for no clear reason she notes a certain pattern in the lines, arches enclosing a stylized trefoil of leaves, and her memories sharpen (a remembered look, a word, and what she said in answer), and then she bites a fig and breaks the spell.

The "h" is silent in *Alhambra*; this place holds silence within itself. Luxurious quiet is its essence, in rooms like these, and in the small courtyard nearby with its ethereal, slender alabaster columns, and in the Court of the Myrtles with its long reflecting pool. And down all the shadowy walkways with their arched windows looking out over the city and the plain and the gorge of the River Darro at the foot of the walls, far below; and in the gardens, awash in the scents of orange blossom and jasmine and the lullaby-sounds of flowing water. The quiet is so carefully cultivated that it has made me wonder, what noise were they trying to forget? I think I understand, after two visits there, some of the answer to that question. Or, at least, I understand the question.

I haven't wanted to know too much. At fifteen I simply did not know, had some romantic notions that were the product of that particular adolescent moment—just past the age of surrendering my free-spinning childhood fantasy life, and trembling on the threshold of big ideas. I was pale and skinny and not very tall, wore tomboy shirts to hide my breastiness, and had straight brown hair that was longer than it will ever be again. Twenty-five years later I had mostly grown up, but I wanted to inhabit the same kind of wonder.

There are two ways you can visit a place. One way is to learn everything you can before you go, reading up

on the culture, the history, the geography, the food and
the people and the politics. Or you can go in cold, and if
you do, there's a lot of nuance you won't catch. Chances
are, unless you stay a long time, you'll never reach that
next level of understanding that would have been your
reward had you gone in educated. But if you do your
homework first, you lose your chance to be utterly, head-
scratchingly amazed. You'll have amazement, probably
plenty, but it won't be in the same class, can't be.

There are practical reasons for learning the lay of
the land before setting foot on it; depending on the
destination, it could be foolish, even dangerous, not to
know enough going in. But I'm not talking about going
somewhere completely uninformed, I guess I'm thinking about the possibility of isolating some aspect of a
place, say, the legacy of the Moors in the south of Spain,
and encountering it in my own way, without becoming
familiar, without learning the language that people use
to talk about it.

When I knew I was going back to the Alhambra, I
decided to resist too much study. I wouldn't completely
avoid what the scholars had to say—I am not so proud
as to think I can learn without learning—but I wanted to
be careful what I sought out, what I read, so I would not
expose myself to the point that I was talking their talk.

What I decided I was after was the best kind of naïveté. In my information-saturated world it would be a
treat to have one object of attention that I approached
this way.

An unmediated experience. Immersion in a language,
without an interpreter. The essence of childhood dis-
covery: encountering wonders without preconceptions,
without preparation, without a lot of ideas of self get-

ting in the way. Like an infant seeing colors and shapes, before there are words or even ideas for them.

I was the same and different person, back again, in the Alhambra.

Another small room, the walls too close for echoes. Close enough together that two people hand-in-hand with arms outstretched could reach across, fingertip to fingertip, and touch them. But the ceiling lofts high above, a grand feeling for such a sheltering, intimate space—a paradox, like that other paradox, the deep silence that contrasts with the intense visual music of every surface. And it *is* music—the Arabic script weaving through it like musical notation, the tiny leaves and loops and petals dancing, like grace notes, around the larger motifs. And every surface is, indeed, involved, with the exception of the floors, which are mostly plain tile or stone; not just walls and ceilings, but every archway between rooms, every filigreed lattice gracing a window, every door—of which there are few, all of them tall, ceremonial, inlaid with fine woods worked in complex geometric designs.

This room is different in one way: it has a window. Its shape is a simple, small arch, set in the middle of a wall of that gossamery stucco-relief the color of sand. I stand before the window, and what I see framed there are the pretty houses of the Albaicín, the old Arab quarter, gleaming white in the sun, and other hills in the distance, green and brown, with grids of dots that are olive groves. I am struck by the balance between the interior view, of wall and window, and the view outward. The idea is not simply about looking out, as it usually is with windows; I am held within the room, even as I am

invited to see outward. There is a point on the floor that
is perfect for this balanced view, and if I move too close
to the window I lose the equilibrium, step back too far
and the world outside recedes too much.

But there is something else, I realize. Something
wrong with what I'm looking at, how I'm looking. It
comes to me all at once, as I'm standing there contemplating the view while other visitors come and go—they
stay a minute, walk up to the window, look out and
move on, it's a small room, after all, and a lot like all the
other rooms. I see how they stand around, how they lean
on one leg, then the other. I think about the people who
lived here, how they sat on their pillows and carpets,
their portable furnishings, the legacy of their nomadic
culture. They sat on the floor. I wait for the room to
empty—it takes a few minutes, because these two are
leaving but now another is drifting in—he has that
blank tourist-stare from too much looking—but now he
is gone, and I sit down on the cool plaster floor and look
up to the window, and I see: blue sky.

It is hard, as a Westerner, to imagine people actually
living here, within these walls, beneath these ceilings—as
I sit there I look up and lose myself in the intricate, dense
stucco of the corners, which drips down from the ceiling like swarming bees clinging to branches. I close my
eyes and see lines and vines curling and leafing outward,
around delicate starbursts and flowing Arabic cursive, all
of this quivering against the background music of trickling water, always nearby, and I simply cannot picture
people living here. It is my favorite man-made place on
earth but I can't picture it as anyone's *home*.

For a moment I try to imagine a table or chairs in
this room, but there were none, there were divans in the

alcoves, carpets and pillows on the floor—the Spanish word for pillow, *almohada*, is, like many Spanish words, from Arabic. It is a stretch for me, I find, to conceive of domestic comfort without a lot of furniture. This is my problem, of course, not theirs. It occurs to me that the restraint of their furnishings, the lightness of their physical presence, explains how they got away with the overwhelming decoration of their walls and ceilings.

I wonder if their fascination with walls came from a cultural memory of not having them: they were nomads. As if they built this place convinced that, now that they had them, they would have the ultimate walls, no part undecorated, not even the tiniest pinpoint place. The essence of a wall is its static quality, and these walls are extraordinarily static, yet light. And the Alhambra, with all its fragile stucco relief, is the ultimate non-portable building—a statement about what constituted the aesthetic and concrete opposite of a nomadic life.

When I was fifteen years old I wasn't doing this sort of analysis. I'm not sure what I was doing. I wasn't seeing people in those rooms, I wasn't even thinking of people. I saw the Alhambra in its glorious emptiness and imagined that's what it had been made for.

I get up when I hear people coming in, and prepare to move on. I stay long enough to watch a Japanese family arrange themselves in front of the window for a picture. I don't know much about Japanese culture, but I am sure that this Moorish palace is as alien an aesthetic for them as it is for me, though in different ways perhaps. I see, in the walls around me, the contrast with everything that is my legacy as a Westerner—from Elizabethan gardens to chamber music to Frank Lloyd Wright to Gertrude Stein—but I have no way of knowing, can't get under that skin to know, how this all looks to someone whose cultural heritage includes tea ceremonies, haiku, samurai, Zen.

They are smiling for the camera. Except for one pale, quiet girl maybe fifteen years old, who, just as I'm slipping away, turns her head to look out the window. I think, again, of the Moors, and what they saw and how they lived. They did not see what we see out the window. They did not live as we live. They are not us. They saw the sky, because they were sitting on the floor.

Who were they?

The south of Spain was first inhabited by Iron Age and Bronze Age people, and then by a tribe called the Turduli, who were followed in turn by the Romans, who built bridges, roads, and fortifications in the place they called Illiberi, later Granada. When Rome fell, the Visigoths conquered Spain, and the city continued to grow, important for its strategic location between the mountains and the sea. In the year 711, the Muslim invaders came, mainly Berbers from North Africa, and the Visigoths were history.

In the eight centuries that followed, the Moors would conquer much of Spain, and lose it again to the Christians. Their control lasted the longest in the south, though much of that time was marked by violent strife and uneasy truces between different kingdoms. The Berber dynasty of Zawi ben Ziri established Granada as its capital in the eleventh century, and improved the fortifications on the hill called Sabika, the future site of the Alhambra, and built a complex there on top of the old Roman fort.

The story of the Alhambra as we know it dates to 1238 when Banu 'l-Ahmar led his army to the top of

Sabika, where he found the old fortress in ruins. He overthrew the Berber dynasty and established himself as the first of the Nasrids, a pure-blooded Arab family who would spend two hundred years, under twenty different kings, building their great palace.

Two of the later kings, Yusef I and Mohammed V, would be the most important builders—Yusef responsible for constructing many of the rooms and towers, while Mohammed saw the great project to its completion. But Banu 'l Ahmar had the original vision, which guided the work for two centuries. He was the one who ordered the construction of the watercourse called the *Acequia Real* which brought the water of the Darro into the Alhambra, and which still flows today, pool to pool, through the rooms and gardens. The Nasrids were infatuated with water, coming as they did from a hot desert land, and were fascinated with everything they could make the water do, using the technology bequeathed to them by the Romans and taking it to a breathtaking new level.

The historical moment that gave birth to the Alhambra, however, is about more than a visionary conqueror's rich dream. Before Banu 'l Ahmar even began construction, he was forced to a grim reckoning with the Christian monarchy who by then had retaken most of Spain. He rode secretly to a Nasrid town under siege by the Christians, and met with their king, proclaiming himself the monarch of Granada but also the vassal of his Christian rival. Thus began a couple of hundred years of tolerant truce, which allowed Granada to flower, growing wealthier from trade and culturally richer from contact with the Christian world, but touched always by uncertainty, by the knowledge that the dream was ending.

The Alhambra wouldn't have been the same place if Granada had been blossoming during the rise and consolidation of the Spanish Islamic empire; instead, it came into being in the wake of all that, in a time of decline, of slow territorial, religious, and political disintegration. The warlike Moors had lost their confidence, their conviction, but there were things they knew, about beauty, about the contemplative life, that they hadn't known before, hadn't had time for before. There had to have been melancholy there, bittersweetness. I think of them watching their own decline, seeing the inevitability of it, even as they were soothed by the bubbling of their fountains and the hypnotic rhythms of the exquisite *attawriq* stucco all around them.

The Arabic writing on the walls of the Alhambra repeats, everywhere, the phrase *"Wa al-Ghalib bi 'llah,"* (There is no conqueror but God.) It must have offered solace, and sadness. It would have reminded them at every turn of the transience of all this beauty they had created, of the faintness of their own imprint on the earth.

If you go up to the ramparts of the *Alcázar*, you can see, far away on the misty horizon, the mountain pass called the Moor's Sigh, where the last king of Granada, Boabdil, took his final look back at the Alhambra as he fled into exile in 1491, surrendering it to Ferdinand and Isabella who would take it once and for all for Christendom.

When I was fifteen years old and knew very little of all this, I felt something akin to the melancholy the Nasrids felt—felt it but didn't know it, only understood it later, on my second visit. Like them, I was witnessing the end of something, and the feeling of waking, really waking, from childhood was a revelation to me, nothing I would ever want to give up, but it came, I knew even then, at a cost. I had a longing for a time that was pre-intellectual, pre-analytic, for a time before I knew my limitations, just as they must have longed for a time before they *knew*. I dealt with this feeling by standing still before those walls, just trying to soak them up. Thinking to myself how I'd never comprehend this place, and being glad of it. Studying those cursive lines of Arabic prayers though unable to read them, following where they blended into placid abstraction.

There is one last place I must tell you about: the Patio of the Lions, perhaps the most perfect, the most beautiful human-made space on earth. The scale is intimate. The color of everything—more accurately, the color that results from the coming together of all the colors, paler and darker—is almond. The space is rectangular, with a central fountain featuring eight lions—small panthers, really—in a circle facing outward. Around the courtyard's perimeter, a shady walkway behind slender alabaster columns invites the visitor to make a circuit. The columns are not much bigger in diameter than a wine bottle; some of them stand alone but others are grouped in twos or threes as if to accentuate their individual slightness. They have delicate floral-motif capitals, and above these the filigree-stucco takes over, flowing up into arches between the columns. The construction, in actuality, is simple post-and-lintel, and the arches are just for looks, non-structural, a visual trick. These pseudo-arches should look impossibly heavy in contrast to the narrow columns, but they don't; they have the lightness of lace, which is what they most resemble—dense, delicate threads netted with air. The

illusion of lightness is an ingredient in the larger, struc-
tural illusion, the illusion that there is no lintel above the
post. Everywhere in the Alhambra, there is this passion
for surface and contempt for structure, perhaps, again,
related to the Moors' nomadic legacy—hungry for
beauty and ornament but not interested in buildings for
their own sake—though I didn't see it at fifteen. But I
saw the magic just as well, may have grasped that magic
more purely, with nothing in the way of it.

There was one thing about that small courtyard that
I did grasp when I was fifteen and still did at forty. I
learned that it was made for walking, not for sitting. I had
the fun of discovering, not once but twice, how to walk
around the perimeter, slowly, and watch the columns beside me cross in front of the columns across the way, making lovely, shifting, rhythmic geometries before my eyes.
A pair of two would pass before a group of three, and then
as I turned a corner, three groups might converge, cross,
separate, the near columns, of course, always moving at
a quicker speed past my eyes than the ones on the other
side. This walking, and watching, were hypnotic, and it
was easy for me, both times I did it, to imagine a contemplative Moor, taking his slow turns around and around.
My imaginary Moor was experiencing exactly what I
was—falling in love with the grace of those columns, with
their stillness even in motion.

My first visit came at a particular, extraordinary moment. Twenty-five years later I was able to dwell in a
rich nostalgia for that moment which was the same, in
its essence, as the nostalgia the Nasrid sultans felt—indeed, were drenched in—in their Alhambra. I was there
in search of the fifteen-year-old I had once been, but I
didn't find her, not exactly; what I found was my mem-

ory of her. It's a fine distinction, and indeed the distance between us was, at times, so slight, so slippery, that as I passed a certain reflecting pool, I thought, for an instant, I saw her mirrored there.

She is as ethereal as the tint of almond in the Patio of the Lions. And maybe my present self is, too, so that I may need to go back one more time, in another twenty-five years, see how the place feels, how I feel, inside a new skin unimaginable to me now. I will pass the happy hours, walking in the Alhambra, conjuring communion with the past. I will make my way to a certain room, and sit down on the floor, and find the blue sky out the window.

❧ ❧ ❧

Sally Shivnan's travel essays have appeared in The Washington Post, *and other publications and her fiction has been published in journals including* Glimmer Train *and* Rosebud. *Prizes for her work include a Silver Rose Award from the ART Foundation for her short fiction. Sally lives in Annapolis, and teaches creative writing at University of Maryland, Baltimore County.*

~≈ ~≈ ~≈

Life, Interrupted

A chance meeting with her literary hero,
Spalding Gray, inspired her to write.

T HE ABSOLUTE LAST THING YOU EXPECT TO SEE AT A
nude beach is any sort of public figure. But by the
third time I passed the alarmingly familiar man squatting at the water's edge—his skinny butt looking like
a flesh-tone "W" hovering just above the sand—I realized who it was. Christ in a sidecar, I'd happened upon
memoirist and actor Spalding Gray.

This was 1994, at the now-closed Black's Beach just
north of San Diego. It was the first time I'd ever been nude
in public. That summer I was rereading Gray's first memoir, *Sex and Death to the Age 14*, a book I'd initially gobbled
up in college, becoming consumed by his rollicking style
and searing candor. I'd never read anything like it. I swore
that, goddamn it, one day I would write like that.

I was lying on the blanket, the sun beating on my breasts, while I reabsorbed revealing passages from *Sex and Death* and bemoaned my inertia. I was twenty-six and still I wasn't writing, like my beloved Spalding (whose every book I'd read and held aloft like a plate of communion wafers), or anyone else. I got up to walk the beach. And then—suddenly, magically, unbelievably—he appeared: Spalding Gray, the closest thing I'd ever had to a role model, a god figure, a chieftain. And he was naked as the day he was born.

My fight-or-flight response surged as celebrity anxiety kicked in. I wanted to run, but I knew I'd never forgive myself if I did. Then I had to wonder if he was really there at all, or if I had snapped and he was a figment of my unconscious mind gearing up to scold me for my literary reticence. Because, really, what were the chances of this?

I tried not to gawk. Instead, I surreptitiously crept by two more times, growing dizzier with each pass. Spalding stayed right where he was, his skin an even oak color with nary a tan line, his frizzy gray hair bouncing in the breezes as he searched for guppies at the edge of a tide pool with a cherubic toddler, also naked. He wasn't an apparition; the man was real.

I had to talk to this hilarious, sincere, confessional storyteller who, in regularly laying bare his soul, had inspired me like no other. Never mind that he would see parts of me only gazed upon by paramours and my physician. The time was now. What was I going to say?

I approached softly, but with purpose, hoping not to shatter any sort of reverie he had going with the boy. "Are you Spalding Gray?" I asked.

"I am," he said, rising from the guppy search and

slapping his hands together to get the sand off before offering up a shake.

The short monologue I delivered then fell from my mouth in an ungraceful tumble. In a rush, I told him that reading *Sex and Death* in college was pivotal for me. The book made me feel like my neurotic spew—if I could ever get off my ass to put it onto the page—might actually be entertaining. Marketable, even. I was sure he'd heard the same stuff from fans the world over, but I was relatively certain he'd never heard it from someone who was naked.

"Oh, *Sex and Death* is not my best," he said humbly, almost shyly. "Have you read my first novel, *Impossible Vacation*?"

We talked naturally then, like new neighbors over the fence. I ceased with the gushing and he wasn't pompous. And it didn't matter one iota that we were nude. Speaking with slow California contemplation braided with a Rhode Island accent, Spalding asked me what I did for a living and why I was at the beach at that moment.

I was unable to ramble much about myself; I was, rather simply, a journalist on vacation. I'd also set up a job interview in the area, and we talked about my bad timing: Just months before, two local dailies had merged, creating a giant glut of journalists. It didn't look like I'd be making a career in San Diego.

I tried like hell not to look at Spalding's crotch, but I couldn't help it. He was uncircumcised, and there were tiny globs of sunscreen lodged in his penis's various folds. But he was a better man than I; not once did I catch him sneaking a glance at my parts.

In a languid tone that seemed at odds with the frenetic pace in his work, Spalding told me he was in town performing his most recent monologue, "Gray's Anatomy," and was headed to London after the following night's show. We talked about his thoughts on nude beaches as compared to nudist colonies (beaches are better). We spoke of the scary cliff we'd had to scale to get down to the beach (much fear and sweating); the hang gliders above; the child, his first son, playing at our feet.

Spalding offered me comp tickets to his performance that night, just a few miles away. I was touched, but self-conscious about accepting. I'll buy my own, I said. No, he insisted. He told me where he was staying in La Jolla, gave me the room number and his intended whereabouts for the rest of the day so I could figure out when to come by and pick up the tickets. We said warm goodbyes, he wishing me luck on the job interview, and I wishing him luck with the performances.

Later, I was relieved he wasn't in his room when I called up from the lobby. I didn't want the day's exchange on the beach to be marred. I wanted it to stay etched in my memory as it already was: sunny, naked, self-contained, celestial and intriguingly awkward— what with the sunscreen globs and all.

I bought a ticket and went to Spalding's performance the next night.

And when I got home, I started to write.

Over the years, when I wasn't on deadline with a personal essay, I continued to read and reread everything Spalding Gray created. My mom would send me newspaper clippings when he delivered a performance down in South Florida. Friends would call if they heard a mention of him on TV or saw him interviewed. When his work turned more sweet than neurotic in *Morning, Noon and Night*, I rejoiced for him. I wanted him happy.

I wrote about meeting him on Black's Beach, but then sat on the piece for a spell before I considered sending it to him. Would he remember me, five years later? Would he like my work? Or would he find it silly and derivative, and just toss it on a pile to join all the other packages from simpering, sycophantic would-be memoirists? Finally I kicked all that aside and sent it, getting his address from directory assistance in Sag Harbor, New York, where he mentioned relocating in *Morning, Noon and Night*.

And then I waited, dreaming up all sorts of fantasies. Spalding would be so floored by my stuff, he'd call his agent on my behalf and we'd all meet for lunch in New York. Or he'd feel so connected to me through my writing, he'd invite me up to Long Island to hang with his new wife and kids. All of that was ludicrous, I knew, but I couldn't help myself.

I kept waiting. Months went by. I figured he might be traveling, or on a hairy book deadline, so I remained patient. But then, rereading one of his books, I came across a passage about how he was often inundated with other people's writing and found it annoying and overwhelming. Blood rushed to my face. There was my answer right there. My hopes of hearing from him drained through the floorboards.

I stopped waiting, which was a good thing, because Spalding never wrote.

I gathered all his books and put them back on the shelf, sneering when I passed them. Pretty soon I found another neurotic, self-deprecating memoirist to fuss over: David Sedaris. Spalding now seemed to me like a first boyfriend, one you think back on and grimace. What was I thinking?

I got over the scorched feeling, though, and soon I could look at Spalding objectively. Serendipitously bumping into him broke through something in me, and thrust me into writing: I had since landed a personal column in the *Baltimore City Paper* that soon had a sizable following. I was writing for magazines and I was working on a book project, a memoir. I was deeply grateful to him for that.

One recent autumn day, I was flipping through a copy of *GQ* in my doctor's office and came across a piece on Spalding. The news wasn't good. He'd been in a terrible head-on car crash in Ireland in 2001. The crash resulted in debilitating injuries and crippling, disorienting bouts of depression. The following year, he'd even tried to kill himself, which his mother had done, too—only she'd succeeded.

Haunted, I went home and re-immersed myself in the waters of Spalding. I pulled all his books off the shelf. I rented *The Killing Fields* so I could introduce my husband to Spalding and have another look myself.

I was rereading *Swimming to Cambodia* on the morning an e-mail came in from a friend, telling me I needed to go to the CNN website right away. There, I found the report: Spalding was missing, thought to have committed suicide. On January 10th, he had taken his kids to the movies, brought them home and then vanished, leaving his wallet behind. People reported seeing him around the Staten Island ferry.

I read every report I could in the days and weeks that followed, hoping poor Spalding had maybe slipped into a fugue and wandered off into the woods, and that some nice person would take care of him, get him to a hospital. But I knew better. He was likely dead, replicating the legacy of his troubled mother. Or was he? I chose denial. Yeah, someone would find him all gnarly and speaking in tongues in the woods and bring him home. There, rest and meds would cure him and he'd return to the Spalding I saw on the beach—tan, happy, serene, vital. Yes, that's what would happen. I picked up *Sex and Death* for the fourth or fifth time, hoping my reading it again might send some good vibes into the universe that would radiate back down to him, wherever he was.

Almost two months later, I was in my car turning out of my neighborhood when I heard the news on NPR, that the body of Spalding Gray had been found in the East River. It was likely a suicide.

I went heavy and slack-jawed, no longer paying much attention to traffic lights or road signs. He was gone. Really gone. My original, powerful inspiration, taken by madness. He left a wife, two sons, a stepdaughter, and countless indelible images in people's heads and hearts, that raving guy in the plaid shirt. He'd changed everything for me, and I had never been able to thank him.

✌ ✌ ✌

Suz Redfearn is a freelance reporter and essayist based in the Washington, D.C. area. Her work has appeared in many publications, including Salon, Slate, The Washington Post, *and* Men's Health.

LENNY KARPMAN

≈ ≈ ≈

Working Men of Tokyo

The warmth of urban Japan rises before the sun.

J ET LAG HAD SENT ME TO BED EARLY. I AWAKENED AT 4:30
A.M., about the time my tour companions staggered
in from the bar. As they fell into bed, I tiptoed out, heading into the dark with Tsukiji Fish Market written in
Japanese on the back of a card and the name and address
of the hotel on the front. Confident that the little Japanese
I had learned would carry me through, I greeted the taxi
driver with a polite honorific salutation and he grunted
and rasped a totally unintelligible guttural response.
I asked where we were, and he grunted *"Niu Otani
Hoteru"*—the name of the hotel. I asked the direction we
were heading, and he grunted *"Tsukiji Sakana-ya,"* the
name of the fish market—no more conversation—no
more information.

There was little traffic on the black streets of Tokyo

until the taxi neared the Tsukiji Fish Market, the world's largest, selling 5 million pounds of seafood a day. As we drew closer, we passed battalions of small trucks and divisions of motorized carts. He grunted one last time and deposited me in front of a maze of buildings that looked like airport hangers. There were fires in metal trash cans marking the route and warming the hands of an indistinct army. I joined the processional and marched in. I was out of uniform without pants legs tucked into knee-high rubber boots and with a camera hung from the neck of my bright pumpkin-colored flannel shirt.

The shadowy figures became illuminated as they entered the vast halls, but the colors of the fishmongers hardly changed in the soft light. They wore only shades of gray, dark blue, or black jackets, pants, sweatshirts or sweaters. They sloshed in boots that were all black. It was colder inside than out from tons of block ice. Narrow wet aisles separated small stalls, each selling one or two items. Wooden boxes and stainless steel trays full of glistening, slippery harvest from the sea sat edge-to-edge on tables illuminated by blue-white neon that made it all even more surreal.

Some of the fish were smaller than a thumbnail, some had razor-sharp predator's teeth, and some wore faces befitting a *Star Wars* bar scene. There were at least three different kinds of eel, all squirming in glistening tangles and more colors and sizes of shrimp than I had ever imagined. There were sea cucumbers, cockles, jellyfish, yellow and green groupers, red snappers, yellowtail and barracuda, small squid and huge squid, flanked by cuttlefish and octopus, raw and cooked. Those that were cooked were white-fleshed inside and dark red outside if they had been pickled, or golden if they had been cooked in soy.

The variety of fish roe, too, was beyond belief: silver gray, pale yellow, iridescent orange, golden, and crimson. These delicacies were displayed in unadorned mounds, clinging like barnacles to strips of seaweed or encased like sausages in semi-transparent tubes. Seaweed came in all shades of green, from lime to dark forest, and in black, brown, and dark purple. The clams, oysters, scallops, and crabs went from teaspoon-tiny to platter-large. There were miniature periwinkles and giant conchs.

The vendors were generally friendly and much more communicative than the taxi driver had been. A few did produce a deep-throated growl on occasion, as if to accentuate a word or phrase. They seemed amused by my exuberance and curiosity and answered my questions as slowly and simply as they would if they were responding to an inquisitive toddler. Closer to dockside I saw dozens of large tables with electric band saws. Workers in surgical gloves and rubber aprons operated on 200-pound headless and tailless frozen tuna bodies. They would cut the tuna lengthwise along their backbones, then load them onto carts for delivery to the buyers' mini-trucks waiting outside. The place sounded like a sawmill.

One vendor, who had been patient with me and had struggled to welcome me in English two hours before, smiled at me and bowed slightly as I tried to find my way out. He had exhausted his English with his greeting, but was adept at charades. I returned his smile and his bow, carefully bending my head a little more than he had, as a sign of respect.

"*Sumimasen*"—excuse me—"New Otani Hotel, *doko desu ka*"—where is it? "*Yukuri, kudasai*"—Slowly, please. I handed him the card with the hotel's name, and we both tried our best. The hotel was not nearby, however.

He tried to draw me a little map but seemed unwilling to give it to me because it was rough and not to scale. He was a stern self-critic and kept apologizing. He frowned and tucked his chin under the neck of his black windbreaker. I apologized for disturbing him and thanked him as profusely as my limited language skills allowed. I was going to take my leave when we both said, *"Gomen nasai"*—I am sorry—in unison, as if we had been rehearsing.

Both of our faces erupted into ear-to-ear smiles. I extended my hand. He took it in his and accepted the bond of a handshake. He became resolute; he raised his chin high, puffed out his chest, and chuckled deep in his throat. He obviously had hatched a plan. He asked me if I knew Japanese numbers. I nodded yes. He asked me to count and I counted to 20, then by tens to 100. He smiled and bowed. He then opened his cash box, gave me a large bill and directed me to change places with him. He pointed to the golden, soy-cooked octopus pieces in the metal tray, and slowly articulated an order: *"Tako, ichi kiro han, kudasai."* I got the message. I lifted a plastic bag onto the scale, pretended to fill it and pressed my index finger down to move the needle on the dial to 1.5 kilograms. I calculated the cost, took the bill, gave him change and presented him the empty bag with a bow and a thank you very much.

Mr. Yamamoto introduced himself and so did I, repeating each other's names aloud and exchanging salutations. He then rather abruptly hurried away and left me behind the counter to tend his money and tentacled wares. I surmised that he had gone off to find an English speaker to give me directions.

A small gray-haired woman in a long dark raincoat walked by three times. The first time she stole a glance out of the corner of her eye as she stepped by in her plastic rain shoes. The second time, she paused ever so slightly, then quickened her pace and turned away after a closer look.

Finally, she stopped and whispered in a high falsetto that she wanted half a kilo of the octopus. Her eyes darted back and forth from the octopus to her purse to the scale, but she avoided my eyes. She extracted exact change and handed it to me from the greatest distance possible. She watched the scale as I put successive pieces into the plastic bag with metal pincers. When I reached the half-kilo mark, she inhaled barely audibly, and bowed her head almost imperceptibly. I handed her the package with a bow, a thank you, and a smile. Her eyes were trapped and she smiled back. She placed her package into a crocheted shopping bag. She seemed very pleased with herself for her courageous purchase from the bearded *gaijin* in the loud shirt. Me, too! I noted the sale on a small pad next to the plastic bags. I would have affixed a gold star had there been one.

Mr. Yamamoto returned with a little boy who was barely visible in a down jacket and a knitted ski cap and gloves. The boy could have been six or seven. He hopped up on the wooden stool and took my place. Before I could figure out how to brag about my sale without destroying my veneer of humility, Yamamoto-san was steering me down the aisle. We walked briskly through two cavernous buildings and out a door into an alley.

We negotiated the maze to and over the bridge and onto a commercial street with open-fronted shops selling shaved bonita flakes, sushi, noodles, pottery, and kitchen utensils. He walked quickly and silently. I had to press to keep abreast. At each turn he smiled at me and angled his head a few degrees in our new direction. We descended into the subway. He bought two tickets from a vending machine and we were off.

He seemed less willing to play charades with me in this public place than he had in the partial privacy of his fish-stand. He used hand signals to beckon me in and out of the spanking clean subway cars. With his hand opened, palm facing downward, he flexed his four fingers toward his palm two or three times rapidly, signaling me to follow. I tracked very closely behind him and marveled at his agile figure, walking rapidly but never touching another human, even with the brush of a sleeve or elbow.

We exited onto a busy street in an upscale neighborhood. I resumed my position at his side, a quarter of a pace behind, like an obedient dog who had been instructed to heel. A few blocks later, we arrived at the door of the hotel.

He refused payment for even the subway tickets. I offered him a drink inside but he politely declined. We repeated our bows and handshakes. He gave me his business card, which I could not read, and I gave him my business card, which he could not read. "*Sayonara, dewa mata*"—goodbye, until next time, he said. Then he hurried away down the drive toward the street without a backward glance. Inside the lobby, the clock read 10:45. My tour mates were heading into a breakfast buffet.

"Where did you go?"

"To the fish market."

"Why would anyone want to go to a fish market? Didn't it stink?"

I donned the requisite smile and nodded my head, not to affirm, but to leave them, politely. "*Sayonara,*" I said softly, but from a deeper, raspier part of my throat. That is how we, the working men of Tokyo, speak.

Lenny Karpman lives in Costa Rica and writes a food column and restaurant review for AM Costa Rica.

❧ ❧ ❧

Balkans? No Problem

As the Iron Curtain was coming down, getting to Bucharest was not so easy.

I STRETCHED OUT ON THE HARD BACK SEAT OF THE AGING diesel Mercedes and saw…the Balkans. It is not so easy to know where the Balkans are. Ask anybody in the region if they are Balkan and the answer is, definitely not; the Balkans start in the next country. But I knew I was there. Two hours after setting out from Belgrade, the car was winding up a curving road. I could see fir trees passing by above me. Night was falling. Wolves, I felt, could not be far away. I knew from the map that this was definitely the Balkans—the mountain range carrying that name. I was in Serbia and the next stop was the Bulgarian border.

"Maybe we have small problem at frontier," remarked my Serb taxi driver. "Bulgarians difficult people. Animals, really." This was a different story from three hours ago, when I agreed to part with $600 to be driven through the night from Belgrade to Bucharest.

"Don't worry. I take Associated Press correspondent this way during war. No problem," he reassured me. Yes. No problem. That was what he told me back then, too.

That afternoon, I had watched an airliner heading for Bucharest crawl out to the runway of Zurich airport without me on board. I was on a late connecting flight. It was June 1990 and the Iron Curtain was shredding. Hungary had opened its borders, the Berlin Wall had fallen, and Czechoslovakia was ruled by an anti-Communist playwright. Six months before, Romania's Communist dictator Nicolae Ceausescu had been murdered in a violent coup. The Reuters news agency no longer needed to distribute its news through state monopolies. It was time to bring uncensored news to the liberated peoples, and go out and sell to whomever would buy. I was off prospecting for business for Reuters.

The trip to the Balkans seemed over almost before it began. My first appointment was at 10 A.M. the next morning in Bucharest, the Romanian capital, and there were another five lined up. "But," said the obliging Swissair woman, "you're lucky. Tonight is the weekly China Airlines flight from Peking to Bucharest, and it stops over in Belgrade. You can take our flight to Belgrade and catch that." And so I did.

At the transit desk in Belgrade, they confirmed the Chinese had a weekly flight to Bucharest stopping over at Belgrade. Only it was tomorrow, not tonight.

"Marcus," said an inner voice of cussed stubbornness, "you have got this far and you are not going to give up. You've worked behind the Iron Curtain. You know how to deal with situations like this."

I was not so sure. But I blurted out, "How about a taxi to Bucharest?"

The dark young Serb in front of me raised an appreciative eyebrow. I was showing the right spirit of Balkan improvisation. At the same time, he drew in his breath. "Yes, taxi. Why not? But be careful. They all sharks out there."

I looked out beyond the passport control. The concourse swirled with loitering males, every one of them a shark.

"But I have friend. No problem."

Friend turned out to be one of the most prominent sharks among the waiting taxi drivers. After a brief financial skirmish, we were on our way to Bucharest.

First, via a dilapidated tenement block testifying to Yugoslavia's impending economic collapse. Belgrade was then still the capital of federal Yugoslavia, soon to be torn apart by civil war. His wife, warm-hearted and slightly frayed, brought him his pullover and plied us with juicy strawberries and bars of chocolate. She correctly calculated that her husband was relieving me of the average monthly wage for a single night's work. Take another bar. Enjoy the trip.

Everybody's minds were working. While she did her sums, I was calculating my chances of recovering the $600 from Swissair. Also, how likely it was that I would get to Bucharest by the next morning. My taxi driver was thinking how much to tell me, and when. He did not want me to give up too soon.

"We not cross Romania at night. Too dangerous. Too many people with guns. We go via Bulgaria," he announced. This is when instant recall of geography helps. On the map, Bucharest is more or less straight east from Belgrade. His assessment of the gun situation was convincing, but Bulgaria seemed way down south. I told him of my 10 A.M. appointment the next day.

"No problem. I get you there in time."

At the border, my driver began shouting at the Bulgarian officials. I murmured in a conciliatory way, foreseeing a nasty incident, but nobody took any notice. It was just a softening-up exercise. My driver, who had sworn in Belgrade I did not need a visa for Bulgaria, knew that I did, and it would be available for a price. He was doing his best to ensure I would not pay too much. He seemed reasonably satisfied that I parted with $35, and we were off again into the night.

Inside Bulgaria, the only signposts not in Cyrillic letters said "Istanbul." That did not seem right, but the driver churned on through the darkness, albeit with some muttering about where the turn-off was. "Ah!" he exclaimed and plunged off towards a Cyrillic expression.

After an hour or two of fitful sleep, he woke me. "I not take you as far as Bucharest. I hand you over to Bulgarian taxi driver in Ruse. He take you to Bucharest." Somehow, he had omitted to tell me the previous evening that he needed a special permit to enter Romania, and did not have it.

"Don't worry. I take Associated Press correspondent this way during war. He get there O.K."

Confronting Ruse with a befuddled 5 A.M. mind is daunting. First of all: Where on earth is it? I wished I had paid more attention to geography at school. In fact, it is situated strategically on the Bulgarian shore of the Danube, overlooking one of the last crossings on that most majestic of rivers.

It nevertheless has a certain ramshackle anonymity. I wondered how many taxis would be plying for hire at 5 A.M. My driver knew better. Sure enough, outside the monumental gray railway station looking like a Hapsburg palace buzzed a swarm of tin-pot Russian-built pseudo-Fiats, ready to bear me on to my destination.

The Serb radiated ethnic superiority. He pushed a fistful of Yugoslav dinars of doubtful value towards the candidate he had chosen for the run to Bucharest, and transacted with a disdainful flourish. A rip-off? Well, I still felt the $600 was a fair go if I was going to get to Bucharest. The Bulgarian looked pleased to have a fare for a sixty-kilometer journey. We were both eager. I asked for a receipt, and Swissair later refunded it.

The comfort of the tin-pot pseudo-Fiat left something to be desired compared with the twenty-five-year-old Mercedes I had just left. We bounced and clattered along the road at a fair lick until we came to the queue. Half the downtrodden races of the world seemed to have gathered there, with their belongings piled high, preparing to make what must be a truly epic crossing. They stretched as far as could be seen, patiently awaiting their turn to move from one rundown country to another. What motivated these huge crowds to travel through this part of Europe was a mystery. Suffice it to say that they felt the urge to assemble in the thousands, numbly undergoing yet another obstacle to their meager hopes for a better life.

My Bulgarian driver slowed. What now? I was in a typically Balkan dilemma. I had three courses of action and they were all wrong. I could join the queue or turn back home, but in both cases my trip would be useless and I would be letting my employers down. Or I could jump the queue, which gave me an unfair advantage over the others. Whatever I chose, I was going to be morally compromised. If you are going to get on in the Balkans, it is best to get used to this. I took a deep breath, and said, "Drive to the front of the queue." He knew what the answer was going to be; everybody else in the queue knew, too. Nobody batted an eyelid. It was as if they had known me for a long time. They knew I was a creature from another world, one who went ahead.

At the frontier, the driver busied himself with the passports. In the fresh morning air, a young man in a black leather jacket was standing beside me. "Do you have any magazines?" he asked. I abruptly denied that I had any Western news material with me. Let's not get caught smuggling propaganda. "If I were you," he said, "I would look a bit more carefully." He sauntered off.

Wake up, Marcus. You've given the wrong answer. The secret police have their people here. You've been spotted, and they are glad to see you. Black leather jacket will decide how soon you continue your journey, and he wants something to read. I leaned back into the car and pulled out *Newsweek* and *The Economist*. He personally retrieved our passports, and three minutes later, we were heading for the Danube. It was becoming a nice morning.

A vast bridge rose in an arch ahead. We drove and drove, with the endless stretch of water spreading beneath us, until, just over the hump of bridge, we ran into a mighty gush of water spurting into the air. Pipes ran across the bridge, and that morning one of them was badly in need of a plumber.

"Romania. Terrible country. Look at all this. Everything falling part. They're like animals," confided my Bulgarian driver.

Back on terra firma, we came upon the other half of the world's downtrodden races waiting to be processed by the Romanians. This was the queue the first half eventually wished to join after their few days with the Bulgarians. The Bulgarian driver, cocky with his new-found sense of ethnic supremacy, scarcely slowed before accelerating onwards at the wave of my hand.

Two kilometers further on, a row of khaki-dressed army officers sat at a wooden trestle table by the side of the road. This was the frontier post. Time was marching on. I remembered the name of the Romanian State news agency.

"Good morning. I'm from Reuters. I have a meeting with Rompres in Bucharest at 10 A.M. May I go through please?" My thumb pressed a burgundy-colored British passport meaningfully on to the wooden table.

"Rompres…Reuters! Welcome to Romania," exclaimed the commanding officer with rhetorical gusto. Stamps banged across the passport. "Enjoy your stay in our country, Mr. Ferrar!"

"And my Bulgarian driver?" With a barely perceptible gesture of dumb insolence, the chauffeur pushed over a passport of a different color. "Bulgarian driver?" The Romanians' faces darkened. I was close to going too far, to abusing the hospitality so generously offered. But since I could not move without the cheeky Bulgarian, stamps clattered once more over the table, and we hit Highway E85.

Twenty kilometers on, we swerved erratically round a bend and found three-quarters of the road blocked by a jackknifed lorry with a collapsed axle. There was a small space through which we could squeeze. A truck coming the other way had the same idea. The Bulgarian spurted ahead, and so did the truck, but my driver drew the last resources of speed out of the tin-pot pseudo-Fiat to beat the oncoming juggernaut to the gap.

No problem. As we approached the outskirts of Bucharest, the road deteriorated into a mess of broken cobbles. Sixteen years earlier, I had visited a relaxed and relatively well-off Bucharest with the encouragement of a Romanian regime courting Western journalists. But the Ceausescu swagger had turned into a nightmare of Byzantine oppression, condemning his people to poverty and humiliation. Tractors with trailers gathered listless, ill-shod groups of villagers waiting at the roadside to go to work. Packed trams swayed and bumped their way gingerly over crooked and broken rails, rusty doors scarcely hanging to their hinges.

The Bulgarian's knowledge of Bucharest was vague. Neither he nor I had a clue where the Intercontinental Hotel was. With a flash of inspiration, I urged him to drive to the tallest building.

As we approached, a young man poked his head into the car window, and politely said: "Good morning. Welcome to hooligan land. I'm afraid you can't go any further."

Hooligan land? Protesting students were occupying the street outside the hotel, and the president had accused them of being hooligans. There was a stand-off, with miners said to be moving on Bucharest to beat up the students.

I grabbed my bag and walked around rubble over the remaining 150 yards to the hotel. The door was stuck. I pushed and it gave way. It was 9:15 A.M. I was exactly on time. Thirty minutes later, I had checked in, showered with cold water, and was waiting in the lobby to meet my first contact.

The hotel was packed with journalists. My colleagues of Reuters, hale and hearty young lads, were working vigorously to inform the world, aided by a bevy of beautiful young female interpreters. They seemed to find it a good assignment.

Business took me to the state television building on the outskirts, where some of the fiercest fighting had taken place six months earlier. Decades of neglect had seriously weakened the lift's resolve. It wobbled slowly higher, and every now and then went back down a few floors, before finally delivering me on the eleventh floor. The director greeted me courteously in his wood-paneled office riddled with bullet holes. We agreed on a contract and I moved on, to a weed-infested Stalinist palace of culture. Another promise of a contract. After two days, I had done what I could to bring free news to the people of Romania.

I had also learned a little respect for the Balkan way of doing things. To a Westerner, this may seem in equal part reckless adventure, chaos, and deceit. But when a Swiss airline made a wrong booking, a Serb "shark" proposed a last-minute alternative. His plan to travel south through Bulgaria and hand me over to a Bulgarian driver turned out to be perfectly viable. When he said, "You will be there on time," his word proved to be his bond. Both the Bulgarian secret service and the Romanian military had done their bit to speed me on my way. Extraordinary and improvised though it all was, this is how Balkans get through life every day. Without them, I would have gotten nowhere.

Balkan improvisation had outperformed the sophisticated technology of Europe's strongest economy. How embarrassing.

But no problem.

❦ ❦ ❦

Marcus Ferrar is a former Cold War Reuters correspondent and co-author of Slovenia 1945: Death and Survival after World War II. *He lives in Geneva.*

MURAD KALAM

❧ ❧ ❧

If It Doesn't Kill You First

Making the hajj tries a pilgrim's soul.
But then something else happens.

I WANDER BAREFOOT OUT OF THE GRAND MOSQUE
through a cruel blanket of Saudi heat, floating in a
sea of strangers from almost every country on earth. It's
my third day in the city of Mecca, where I've come to
take part in the hajj, the annual five-day pilgrimage to
some of Islam's holiest places. This trek is required once
in the lifetime of every able-bodied Muslim, and I'm one
of 2 million people, part of the largest mass movement of
humans on the planet.

The birthplace of Muhammad, the prophet of Islam,
born in the sixth century, Mecca sits at the base of the
Hejaz Mountains in western Saudi Arabia, forty-six miles
east of the Red Sea port of Jidda. To someone watching
from atop the thousand-foot peaks that surround the city,

we must look like countless insects as we spill out of the high, arching gates of the 3.8 million-square-foot Grand Mosque, the most important religious site in the Islamic world.

Mecca is home to 800,000 gracious people, any of whom will tell you not to worry about your well-being when you're here. "This is Mecca," they say. "No one will harm you." Maybe not, but the less devout might steal from you—I'm barefoot because somebody ran off with my sandals this morning when I removed them, as required, before entering the Grand Mosque to pray.

Meanwhile, it's a fact of hajj life that people die all around. Earlier, I watched the Saudi religious police— the *mutawaeen*, stoic, hard-faced men with henna-dyed beards—carry green-shrouded gurneys holding the bodies of five pilgrims who died today, setting them on the marble floor of the Grand Mosque for funeral prayers. In one twenty-four-hour period during my pilgrimage, eighty-two hajjis will die. People perish in many ways, from natural causes like heart attacks to unnatural ones like dehydration and trampling.

Trampling is what I'm concerned about at the moment, and with each frantic step I become more worried about my safety. The problem is the hajj's sheer numbers. Despite many improvements, the hajj facilities and infrastructure—which are managed by the House of Saud, the iron-fisted royal family that has ruled Saudi Arabia since 1932—haven't expanded to meet the fourfold increase in attendance that has occurred over the past thirty-five years. The result is that people too often wind up in death traps.

In 1990, a stampede in the pedestrian tunnel leading from Mecca to Arafat, a rocky, arid plain twelve miles southeast of Mecca and one of the final way stations of the hajj, killed 1,426 pilgrims. Another 270 were trampled to death four years later at Jamarat, a site just east of Mecca where a ritual called the Stoning of the Devil takes place, and the most crowded of all hajj settings. In 1997, 343 pilgrims burned to death and another 1,500 were injured in a giant fire started by a gas cooker in the tent city of Mina, an encampment a few miles east of Mecca where all pilgrims gather near the end of the hajj.

It's a bizarre sensation, but I keep imagining my own demise, visualizing my shrouded body being carried into the Grand Mosque above the wheeling masses. Every Muslim knows that a believer who dies on this journey is guaranteed a place in paradise. Personally, though, I'd much rather live to tell about it.

Why take this risk? The answer starts with my spiritual beliefs. I've been a Sunni Muslim for nine years. (The Sunnis make up 90 percent of all Muslims but are the minority in Shiite-dominated nations like Iran and Iraq. Sunnis and Shiites differ on major theological matters—like who should have succeeded Muhammad after his death, in A.D. 632.) I was born in Seattle in 1973 to a Jamaican father and an American mother, grew up a lapsed Baptist-turned-agnostic in Phoenix, and started college in Boston, at Harvard, in 1994.

As an undergrad, I happened upon an English translation of the Koran, the written version of Muhammad's revelations from Allah. I was so floored by its persuasive power that I converted to Islam, stopped drinking, and adopted an Islamic name, Murad Kalam. Like many new converts, I was zealous and naive at first. I bought the fundamentalist line that the cause of all the Muslim world's problems—poverty, corruption, and repression—boiled down to a simple failure to apply the tenets of the religion, and nothing more.

Like every American Muslim, I've had a lot to think about in the past few years. When Al Qaeda launched its attack on September 11, 2001, I was a third-year law student at Harvard and an aspiring novelist. I had not yet traveled to Muslim countries, but I had made friends from Egypt, Saudi Arabia, and Jordan, and they'd schooled me in the complex realities of Muslim life. While Islam is dear to the majority of Muslims, they said, Koranic law should not be taken as the cure-all for everything. In many Muslim societies, religion was a smoke screen for old-fashioned greed, tyranny, and hypocrisy, as well as numerous distortions of Muhammad's ideas for twisted political goals.

Among the worst examples of that last problem, obviously, is Al Qaeda, which has been a scourge in the United States, Afghanistan, Kenya, Yemen, and, more recently, Turkey and Saudi Arabia itself. Though Saudi Arabia, birthplace of the exiled Osama bin Laden, has been relatively safe from terror in the past, that changed after my pilgrimage, which took place in February 2003. On May 12, 2003, Al Qaeda truck bombers hit a housing complex in the Saudi capital, Riyadh, killing twenty-six Saudis and foreigners working in the country, eight Americans among them. On November 8, terrorists, probably linked to Al Qaeda, killed seventeen Arabs in a similar strike.

The hajj itself has never been the target of a terror strike, but according to published reports, in a raid carried out not long after the November bombings in Riyadh, the Saudis uncovered a plot by Islamic militants to booby-trap copies of the Koran, allegedly in order to maim and kill pilgrims during the hajj.

The Saudi government has to be worried about terror oc-
curring under its watch, since its role as keeper of the holy
places is a major pillar of its legitimacy. The closest thing
to such an attack occurred back in November 1979, when
a radical cleric named Juhayman ibn Muhammad and
hundreds of followers barricaded themselves in the Grand
Mosque for two weeks to protest what they saw as political
and religious corruption in the House of Saud. Before it
was over, dozens of soldiers and more than a hundred of ibn
Muhammad's partisans had died in gunfights.

Even though the hajj was not in progress, attacking the Grand Mosque was an incredible blasphemy,
and the punishment was swift. After their capture, ibn
Muhammad and his band were executed in cities and
towns throughout Saudi Arabia—dispatched by means
of public beheading.

Throughout the international turmoil following 9/11,
I remained a devout Muslim, and I found myself torn
between my beliefs and my country. I've worried that
President George W. Bush was too heavy-handed in his
war against terror, both overseas and in the U.S. At the
same time, I've felt oddly insulated from any anti-Muslim
backlash. Too pedigreed to lose a job, too American-
looking to be assaulted, I felt alienated from my fellow
Muslims in Boston, some of whom were attacked on the
street by angry locals. I was drifting, missing prayers. I
worried that I was failing Islam. So, in late 2001, I started
thinking about trying the hajj.

To prepare for my trip, I read narratives of pilgrimages to Mecca, beginning with the hajj chapters in *The
Autobiography of Malcolm X*, the 1964 book about the
political and spiritual quest of the famous black Muslim

activist. In older books I found tales of desert caravans, raids by Bedouin clans, near starvation, and hard-won spiritual enlightenment. For 1,500 years the hajj has been the ultimate Muslim adventure. It remains a soul-rousing journey that, I decided, could snap me into shape.

The hajj itself predates the prophet Muhammad. According to Muslim belief, Abraham established it and built the sacred Kaaba—a fifty-foot-tall window-less sanctuary made of black granite—but over time the rites in Mecca degenerated. Pagan Meccans set up 360 idols outside the Kaaba, and Mecca became a center for worshipping cult, tribal, and polytheistic gods.

Muhammad, born in A.D. 570, received his call at age forty and risked his life to establish Islamic monotheism in Mecca. Persecuted and facing imminent assassination for teaching that there is no god but Allah, he fled with his followers to Medina in A.D. 622. Later, after several battles between Muslims and nonbelievers, the Meccans converted to Islam, and the prophet returned to rule. During his final hajj, Muhammad stressed the equality of man, respect for property, and the importance of prayer, fasting, and charity.

The pilgrimage itself is a twenty-five-mile trip, made by bus and on foot, that starts and ends in Mecca, with shifting dates determined from year to year by the Islamic lunar calendar. Pilgrims begin arriving two or three weeks ahead of time in Mecca, where they spend several days performing rituals and prayers inside the Grand Mosque. At this point, many hajjis take a multi-day side trip to Medina, the oasis city where Muhammad estab-lished his first community of followers.

In a transition that marks the official beginning of the hajj, all pilgrims start to converge on Mina, where they camp for the night. The next day they proceed five miles farther east to Arafat, to face the Mount of Mercy, a hill where they meditate on the day of judgment. The hajjis leave Arafat at sunset and walk three miles to the valley of Muzdalifa, to camp under the stars. There they pray and collect pebbles, which they'll take to Jamarat the next morning. At Jamarat, two miles northwest of Muzdalifa, hajjis throw stones at three fifty-eight-foot-tall granite pillars, symbolically warding off Satan. After completing this, pilgrims shave their heads or cut off a lock of hair, to mark the end of the hajj. Then they return to Mecca to complete their final rituals inside the Grand Mosque.

Initially, I'd wanted to do all this in the most rigorous way possible. My hope was to take a boat across the Red Sea from Cairo—where I was living for four months while researching my second novel—and then ride horseback from Jidda to Mecca, camping out in the vastness of the Arabian Peninsula.

But after checking in with the Saudi embassy in Washington, D.C., I discovered that the days of romantic pilgrimages were over. The hajj is too dangerous to allow everyone to chart his own course, and under Saudi law, to get a visa, every pilgrim who has the financial resources must make airline and hotel reservations. The embassy passed me on to the well-oiled D.C.-based hajj machine, Grand Travel, where I was informed that not only was a package tour required, but tours were segregated by nationality. I would be lumped in with ninety-eight other American Muslims.

Making one last stab, I asked the agent if he would book my flight and let me wing the rest. He laughed. "You want suffering, brother? You'll be suffering enough."

I set off for Saudi Arabia on January 28, 2003. Pilgrims prepare for the hajj by taking a ritual bath and putting on the symbolic robes of *ihram*, thereby entering a spiritual state in which differences of race, wealth, and nationality are erased. My robing took place in a hurry at the Cairo airport, where I followed a pimply-faced Egyptian skycap into a dimly lit industrial closet.

"Get naked," he said. For ten Egyptian pounds (two bucks), the young man expertly dressed me in two white sheets, one placed horizontally around my waist, the other over my left shoulder.

Afterward, I jumped on an EgyptAir flight to Jidda. From there I traveled by bus forty-six miles to the Al Shohada Hotel, in Mecca, where I met my tour group. Once in Mecca, hajjis immediately proceed to the Grand Mosque, a massive coliseum that contains the Kaaba, the cube-shaped granite shrine toward which Muslims all over the world direct their daily prayers. Pilgrims are required to circle the Kaaba seven times, counter-clockwise, praying as they go. This ritual is called *tawaf*. At the end of the hajj, when they return to Mecca, they must complete the *tawaf* again.

Two nights after I completed my initial *tawaf*, inside the airy, luxurious lobby of the Al Shohada, I got a first look at the American hajjis as we assembled to meet our tour leaders. Studying them, I felt a painful rush of our collective inadequacy. They were a collection of well-meaning people from all walks of life: taxi drivers, salesmen, mailmen, lawyers, doctors, and hotel workers. But they also seemed like a reflection of myself—slightly out of shape, self-conscious in pilgrim garb, clearly a little panicked.

We gathered in a hotel conference room, where Sheik Hussein Chowat, our spiritual adviser, paced before us, fielding questions. He's a squat, bearded, soft-spoken Arab in his forties who teaches Islam in northern Virginia. Here, it was his job to put the fear of Allah into us, stressing the need to do everything right. "You have to do the hajj carefully," he warned. "If you don't, Allah might not accept it."

Our group leader, Nabil Hamid, a grinning, Egypt-born chain-smoker from the Washington, D.C. area, also in his forties, sat by himself at a nearby table. He was the fixer, solver of the inevitable crises: lost hajjis, broken-down buses, sickness, emotional burnout. He fiddled with his prayer beads while Hussein responded to a question posed by a middle-aged woman, also from Washington, who had completed a hajj in 2002. (Like many pilgrims, this woman had returned to the hajj on behalf of another Muslim who couldn't make the journey.) She mentioned in passing that, at the end of her first hajj, she had not completed a final *tawaf* around the Kaaba.

"Sister," Hussein interrupted, "your hajj was invalid."

The woman was stunned. The sheik, with iron certainty, seemed to be telling her she had gone through great expense and weeks of pain for nothing. I wanted to find out the woman's name, but it wouldn't have done any good. I couldn't approach her or talk to her: Personal contact between unrelated women and men is forbidden here.

Now, it's my third day. With a pair of new sandals, I wander down the rolling streets to enter the Grand Mosque and pray. After ten blocks of wading through crowds, I come to the mosque's towering granite minarets, entering alongside stone-faced Turks dressed in olive-green, African women in flowery headdresses, and a gaggle of tiny Indonesians dressed in white cloaks. The whispered prayer of millions sounds like rustling water along a riverbank. The Kaaba rises above the marble floor, and I move closer, meeting the stride of the floating multitudes and chanting along with them.

I exit onto Al Masjid Al Haram, Mecca's main street, which is thick with lame and disfigured beggars. Crying children from Africa kneel on the grimy road; when they don't cry loud enough, their mothers appear from street corners and beat them. One girl has wrapped a gauze bandage around her little brother's head and smudged it with lipstick to mimic a bloody wound.

Tired, and starved for a glimpse of the world beyond Mecca, I retire to a cafe in the back of my hotel to watch CNN, hoping to get the latest on the still-pending war between the U.S. and Iraq. Inside, I run into somebody from my tour group, Aaron Craig, a handsome African-American engineering student from San Diego. Aaron is a recent convert in his late twenties, and he's dressed like a Saudi in a full *jallabeyah*—a flowing ankle-length gown worn by men. The robe isn't required for the hajj, but Aaron is signaling his burning desire to look 100 percent Muslim.

"You know," he tells me, sipping tea, "I've already seen lots of mistakes made by pilgrims. And the bumping and pushing and nationalism! And you wonder why we don't have Muslim unity."

This is Aaron's first visit to the Middle East. Like me when I converted, he seems convinced that pure application of Islam is the answer to everything.

"People are trying to change the religion, brother," he continues.

"What do you mean?"

"The sellout Muslims in America."

He's talking about moderates, people who live suburban lives, have non-Muslim friends, watch TV.

"Allah's religion is perfect. The sellouts want to say that jihad does not mean jihad. Meanwhile, Muslims are being attacked in Afghanistan, Chechnya, Palestine. You have to believe in it or you are a disbeliever."

This talk startles me. *Jihad* is a loaded word, referring to both armed resistance in defense of Islam and a private struggle to bolster one's faith. I wonder if he would think I'm a sellout. My jihad has always been intensely personal, concerning prayers, family, success, and finding the peace that lately has eluded me—peace that, so far, continues to elude me during this hajj.

In the evening, when the streets are empty, I call my wife, who's in the U.S., from a nearby cabin with pay phones. It's staffed by smart-alecky young Saudis dressed in Western t-shirts and blue jeans. They look like they'd rather be listening to Tupac or dancing in a club—anything but herding us pilgrims around.

"Why didn't you tell me the streets are filled with crooks?" I jokingly ask them in Arabic. "My sandals were stolen from the Grand Mosque."

"All Meccans are good, all Muslims are good," one replies robotically. He offers me a Marlboro, one of the few naughty pleasures tolerated in Mecca.

"No," the other declares. "Some Meccans are good. Some are bad."

It's three days later, February 3, and I'm standing in the hallway of the Dallah Hotel with Aaron. We have left Mecca, boarded a bus for Medina, and arrived at sundown, just in time to make the last prayers of the day. The ride here was soothing, with African pilgrims dressed in white walking the road beside us, chanting loudly, *"Labaik, Allah, labaik"* ("Here I am, Allah, here I am"). Medina is an oasis 210 miles north of Mecca. It's a smaller, more comfortable city, its streets cleaner and less congested.

The hotel is swarming with African-American converts and Kuwaitis. As we prepare to leave for the Prophet's Mosque, Aaron shares a big piece of news: His wife has been offered a position teaching English in Riyadh, and they're thinking of making the move.

"Murad," he says, "the Saudis—what are they like?"

There's a lot I could say about that. I spent a week in Saudi Arabia in 2002, and I was shocked by the restrictiveness of everyday life, where most pleasures, even innocent ones like G-rated movies, are banned. I've known too many American Muslims who studied in Saudi Arabia and found, alongside the unbearable dreariness, the same hypocrisies, vices, and bigotry that they thought they'd left behind.

In the end I say little to Aaron; I'm leery about interfering with his destiny. "The Saudis make loyal friends," I tell him. "But there is no social life here. I think you will miss the States."

Aaron sighs, then laughs. "I don't care," he says. "They've got Kentucky Fried Chicken and Burger King. That's all the culture I need. I just want to hear the call to prayer in the morning."

At twilight, Aaron and I wander down the windy street to the Prophet's Mosque. Set on flat land in the city center, its white granite walls are cast in beautiful greenish light. Six thirty-story minarets ascend from its corners, poking into the night sky. Inside, the shrine is huge, spanning 1.7 million square feet. At prayer time, each row of prostrate men extends nearly a mile.

Inspiring though it is, Medina does little to lift my sagging spirits during the six days we stay here. Aside from the physical discomfort—I'm suffering through my second case of flu, and my body aches from walking—something spiritual is missing. I cannot yet say that I'm feeling any different than before I arrived in Mecca, and I'm disappointed in the way the Saudis manage the whole thing, giving too little attention to safety and security. Not for the first time, I'm wondering if I'm crazy to be here.

After a week of Medina's prayer and quiet, our buses show up again on February 8th, a Saturday, to take us about 210 miles to Mina, where all 2 million hajjis are heading to enact one of mankind's grandest mass rituals, starting tomorrow. Bounded by mountains on two sides, Mina is home to a permanent tent city that sits between the plain of Arafat and Mecca's eastern boundary. It's a small metropolis of 44,000 identical fifteen-foot-high, aluminum-framed tents, placed on a square-mile quadrant. The Jamarat overpass—a huge two-level walkway that leads pilgrims to the three granite pillars representing Satan—sits roughly a mile to the northwest, in the direction of Mecca. A string of mosques borders the tent city in every direction.

We float into Mina, across the dirt roads between the tents, which are sectioned off by region and country. The bus stops before the entrance to what's called the Egyptian section. Nabil Hamid, our group leader, has placed us in an area called 42/2.

"Remember that number," he says sternly, pointing to a sign. "It's the only way to get back. If you are lost here, you are lost." We find our tent space, a 10,000-square-foot enclosure for fifty men.

After nightfall, Nabil leads us out to the site of Jamarat to show us the mile-long path from the tent and back. Just before we leave, Sheik Ahmed Shirbini, a forty-something Egyptian-born Muslim from Denver who's on his third hajj, issues a warning about the dangers awaiting us at the Jamarat walkway.

"If you lose your sandals, if you drop your money, your sunglasses, do not go back!" he says. "I was here four years ago, and I saw with my own eyes a man who'd dropped his wallet on the overpass trampled to death by the crowds."

Nabil carries a twelve-foot sign that reads U.S.A. We wander across the dark dirt lanes, past patches of paved road where pilgrims sleep on the ground. We turn a corner, walking down a longer road, until we come to the infamous overpass, a mile-long, 300-foot-wide structure. You can get to the three granite pillars from this bridge or an underpass below it. The structure is built to hold 100,000 people, but three times that number will crowd it in the thick of Jamarat. This overload caused a collapse in 1998 that killed 118 pilgrims.

One of our group, a young doctor from Pennsylvania named Shakeel Shareef, points to the street under the bridge. "That's where all the people were killed," he says.

Hearing this, Aaron swallows and his voice goes big. "Allah is all-knowing and all-powerful," he says. "If we are supposed to die at Jamarat, it is part of his will. What better place to die?"

But I can see the fear on his face. It's oddly comforting to know that he's as scared as I am.

It's eight o'clock on the morning of February 11, the day I'll perform the Stoning of the Devil ritual, and I'm lost. At the moment, I'm in Mina, walking on a street beneath the mountain valleys, surrounded by exultant pilgrims hustling toward Jamarat. On each side of me, the numberless tents sweep out beneath the mountains.

A lot has happened since this time yesterday. In the morning we left early as our bus raced toward the Mount of Mercy for the nighttime vigil. Hajjis in surgical masks streamed beside us in a fog of exhaust; young boys surfed the hoods of antiquated American school buses, their white robes flapping in the wind.

But this glorious motion didn't last long: We spent much of the day either stuck in traffic or walking around lost, and I got separated twice from my group. At sundown it looked like we might not make Muzdalifa by midnight. Sheik Hussein, our spiritual adviser, informed us that if we didn't get there by then, we would have to lay out cash for the sacrifice of a sheep in Mecca, to atone for this failure in the hajj.

When a pilgrim objected to this—shouldn't our group leader, Nabil, have to pay, since he is responsible for getting us around?—Sheik Hussein wagged his finger and said, "You do not understand worship! I don't care about the money! This is between you and Nabil! I am here to help you worship Allah!"

In the end we got there, but in these crowds, it's always easy to get lost again. Right now, pushing my way forward in the Mina morning, I have no idea where I am. I have a vague sense that my tent at the Egyptian camp is straight ahead, but Mina is so rambling, its hills so full of identical tents, that I can't be sure. I walk forward, pacing ahead of the crowds of half-sleeping pilgrims.

Two hours pass. When I finally get my bearings, around 10 A.M., I realize that I'm just one street removed from 42/2, but it's hard to get all the way there. Pushing through the crowds is like wading through waist-high water. I am caught on a street congested with pilgrims and tour buses, vans, and trucks on their way to Jamarat. Blocks away, pilgrims are flooding the street from both directions, coming back from Muzdalifa and racing toward Jamarat. Trapped in a hot, heaving crowd, I suffer the most terrifying claustrophobia of my life.

I force my way through the street until it is impossible to take a step forward. Suddenly there's an explosion of human pressure from all sides, and I find myself standing face to face with a small, neatly dressed Iranian hajj leader in wire-rim glasses. The Iranian's eyes go wide as pilgrims on each side of the road begin to rush toward us. Africans are shoving through. Saudi policemen stand on trucks and rooftops, doing nothing as they watch the street below them devolve into madness. Women shout "Stop!" in Farsi and wave their hands, but no one can stop the crowd from crushing in. I cannot move. I can only pray. The crowd erupts in frenzied screaming. A row of middle-aged Iranian women fall over like dominoes.

Nigerian pilgrims start pushing through violently. Feeble, veiled women shout the only Arabic words understood by every pilgrim: "*Haram! Haram!*" ("Shame on you!"). Women and small old men are getting trampled in the mud. I find an opening through the maelstrom and hurry to a parked truck. I climb into the truck, my sandals left behind in the street mud, my bare feet burning on the truck bed's hot, rusty metal floor.

Nigerians crawl onto the truck from all sides. I can do little more than watch as screaming Iranian and Nigerian women are crushed on the street beneath us, a sea of white *burqas*, angled shoulders, crying, pleading faces, the flashing of outstretched arms. I reach down and pull a young Nigerian woman into the truck. Like me, she is crying, her face racked with fear. An old Iranian woman in white clings to the Nigerian's waist as I pull her up, her body floating on a wave of white-cloaked women. In another language, she thanks me for saving her life.

And then, in what seems like just a moment, the street is somehow cleared behind us. Women lie moaning in the mud. The truck's engine chugs; it zips forward six or seven blocks down the now-empty street. I watch pilgrims in the distance climbing from the piled bodies to their feet on the muddy, empty road.

I jump off the truck and walk barefoot back to my camp through a cloud of diesel exhaust. The scene of the stampede is six blocks away, shockingly clear. When I return to it, the road has been swept of thirty or forty people who—I can only assume from what I saw—have been badly injured or killed. (I never find out, but the next day I read in the *Saudi Times* that fourteen people died a half-mile away in a different stampede at Jamarat.)

I am angry—angry at the Saudis for permitting such chaos. But beneath my anger, there is also exultation, something electric, happiness to have survived, the clarity that comes from facing death. Around noon, I finally reach 42/2, entering through an iron gate. Sheik Hussein is speaking with a veiled woman from the American group.

"I must talk to you," I tell him, sobbing.

He takes me by the wrist down a concrete path, and we stand in the shade of a fluttering tent. "I was almost killed, Sheik Hussein! There was a stampede in the street. I jumped into a truck. I pulled a woman up. I saved her life. I think people died there."

"It is O.K.," the sheik says. "It is O.K. if you touched the woman."

"No, no. I was not asking that. I wanted to tell you that I almost died today."

"Well, it is over now," he says, without emotion. Then he leaves me at the tent.

However deadly and frantic Jamarat is, it can't be worse than what I've just seen. Though I haven't slept in thirty-six hours, nothing matters now but completing this hajj. I step inside my tent and stare at my fellow pilgrims lying on a rug. Half of them have already gone to Jamarat and returned. They eat oranges or sleep blissfully on mats in the hot, cramped tent. The rest are waiting until evening, when Jamarat is safer.

I decide to go right now. I have lost all my fear. Along with Shakeel Shareef, the Pennsylvania doctor, and a few other pilgrims, I march to Jamarat in the midday heat, collecting pebbles along the way. The streets are congested, but we weave through the crowds. We watch a pilgrim coming back from Jamarat. He is bandaged and bleeding from the head, his *ihram* robes covered in blood.

We wander into a crowd of more than a million people. A couple hundred thousand pilgrims are striding on the overpass above. "Everyone is taking the overpass," says Shakeel, pointing. "The bottom level is safer."

We follow him, making our way through the rushing crowds to the smallest pillar to throw our seven stones, but we are too far away. Shakeel is not like so many other careless pilgrims. He will not throw at the first opportunity; he waits until he is certain he will not hit another person. I watch him, banged upon by rushing hajjis, measuring his throw, stopping, moving closer. I stand behind him, my hand on his shoulder, so that we stay together.

"We have to get closer," Shakeel shouts. "If we throw from here, we'll only be hitting pilgrims. Hurry."

We link arms and march into a wall of pilgrims. Hundreds of tiny pebbles pound against the sides of a granite pillar in little bursts of dust.

Right after Shakeel throws his last pebble, he is almost pushed down by a throng of Pakistanis. I grab him and pull him away from the scene. We run through the riotous crowd until we are outside again, safe, in the sun.

As we approach our camp, I turn and watch the arcing, sun-washed, overcrowded Jamarat overpass receding behind the tents. As I wander back, I realize I've made peace with the hajj, and with this rough, beautiful, holy place. Everything I have suffered seems almost necessary, because I am overcome with an unutterable serenity. How is it that, by some miracle, so many people can exist in the same small place at once?

We reach our camp, shave our heads, shower, change out of our *ihram* robes into *jallabeyah* robes, roll out our mats, and sleep hard on the Mina dirt.

❧ ❧ ❧

Murad Kalam's first novel, Night Journey, *was published by Simon & Schuster. He lives in Washington, D.C. and is working on a second novel set in Cairo.*

MICHAEL SHAPIRO

❧ ❧ ❧

The Longest Day

The grip of love reaches through time.

AS A PLANELOAD OF PEOPLE STARED AT THEIR TINY
seat-back screens, I raised the cover of the oval
window and witnessed my second dawn of the day. The
orange-pink light illuminated the crystalline snow that
blanketed Baffin Island below with a purity that made
me gasp. This second dawn, which kindled my waver-
ing hopes, brightened the horizon just a couple of hours
after my first sunset of the day, when our 747 nosed
above the Arctic Circle and into December's round-the-
clock darkness over central Greenland.

The brilliance of the second sunrise contrasted sharply
with the day's first dawn. My cell phone rang before seven
A.M. with a message from my wife that my father, who
was fighting cancer, had taken a sudden turn for the worse
and was slipping away. The iron skies over London barely

lightened as I packed; a friend drove me to the airport through thick, sepulchral fog. It was a typical December day in London, one in which the sun climbs meekly into the southern sky for a few hours before beating a hasty retreat from the bone-chilling cold and bluster.

Because my wife told me every minute could count, I intended to carry on my small backpack, my only bag. But it exceeded the airline's six-kilo limit, and despite the urgency of my situation, the gate agent refused to let me carry it on. After getting seated my frustrations mounted: we'd be delayed forty minutes due to the fog, the captain said. Forty minutes later he said the delay could be two hours because so many planes were stacked up waiting for takeoff.

That's when I began to sweat—I knew that if the delay became too long our pilots would be disqualified because they can only work so many hours. With an eleven-hour flight to San Francisco, we had to go soon or we could lose this crew. If the flight canceled, I probably wouldn't be able to leave London on any airline until the following day.

The captain said we'd been scheduled to take off at one P.M., exactly two hours late. We inched up the runway, and with every inch of progress I breathed a bit more easily. Two minutes before one P.M., I heard the engines rev. After rolling over the length of several football fields we left the ground.

As the anxiety of the delay ebbed, I recalled a trip my family—parents, grandparents, brother, and I—took to Venezuela when I was ten. When my mother attended summer camp in the late 1940s, she'd befriended a girl named Chata from Caracas, and they had stayed in touch over the years.

A generation later, seeking an escape from the New York winter, my family accepted Chata's invitation to visit Venezuela. After a few days in Caracas, Chata and her clan took us to their vacation house in the jungle. They'd warned us it was remote, which I thought might mean no television. Yet it was more exotic than I could imagine: never had I seen pigs sauntering down a dusty main street, never had I slept in a hammock draped by a mosquito net, and never had I observed an emerald snake slither silently into the shrubbery.

Chata told us we'd be going to one of the country's most beautiful beaches. But to get there we had to navigate through a horseshoe of sea caves. When we arrived at the caves' mouth, about two feet high and ten feet wide, the adults huddled and seemed agitated. Usually the water is about knee-high inside the caves, Chata told us, but the tides were high and the water would be above everyone's waist. We had enough young men in our group of twenty-some people to form a human chain and pass the kids through the deepest water, Chata said. My grandmother and mother stayed behind.

I boasted that I could swim through the caves, but when we got inside I realized the severity of the challenge: It wasn't just that the water was deep; it was that the tides could yank out to sea anyone who lost his grip. The concussive collisions of water against stone created a thunderous roar that reverberated inside the caves. As my father held my hand, we walked into deepening waters.

We gripped the caves' walls and stepped tenuously towards the chain of young men. My father reluctantly released his grip. In seconds I was passed from body to body, then steadied myself. Through the knee-high horizontal exit, a sliver of shimmering beach opened into a broad crescent of fine fawn-colored sand as the sea stretched into shades of turquoise, azure, and lapis. No one else was there. It was like a postcard made real.

Soon my father emerged and we lounged in the sand, talking about whether Walt Frazier and the Knicks would win another championship—they would three months hence—and whether the Yankees would ever get good again. The sun warmed us. Despite the moderate surf, the ocean beckoned. As we plunged into the tropical waters, my father told me to stay close to him. I floated on my back, stared at the cottony clouds, and let the waves ride me up and down, up and down.

"Michael!" my father shouted, shattering my reverie. Behind me, I saw him and the biggest wave I'd ever seen, both zooming towards me. My father grabbed my hand—we were too far out to beat the wave to the shore. After a few terrifying seconds, the wave began to curl over us in slow motion and envelop us with unrelenting force. The surf spun us around like driftwood; my father's grip tightened. As the wave slammed us into the scabrous ocean floor, he held on. And when the undertow began to suck us out to sea, his grip remained strong as he swam us—with his one free arm—towards the shore.

As I reflected on that thirty-year-old memory, I knew I'd make it home in time. I could feel my father holding on, across the dwindling miles. And I felt assured that despite the pain the cancer was inflicting on his body, his spirit wouldn't let go until we embraced one last time.

❧ ❧ ❧

Michael Shapiro is the author of A Sense of Place: Great Travel Writers Talk About Their Craft, Lives, and Inspiration. *Shapiro has biked through Cuba for* The Washington Post, *celebrated Holy Week in Guatemala for the* Dallas Morning News, *and floated down the Mekong River on a Laotian cargo barge for an online travel magazine. His work also appears in the* Los Angeles Times, San Francisco Chronicle, *and several national magazines. Some of his stories are archived on his web site, www. nettravel.com.*

PICO IYER

~ ~ ~

Prayer Flags and Refugees

The author pays homage to a most unusual
government in exile.

IDROVE BETWEEN AVENUES OF TREES, VILLAGERS
working in the lush fields around me, camels,
lipsticked girls with large bowls on their heads, signs along
the road saying, in India's inimitable fashion, "Thanks
for inconvenience." Up above, suddenly, in the radiant
spring sunshine, a few hours out of Jammu Airport, I
could see snowcaps, shockingly clear against the high
blue skies, and speaking for the even higher peaks of the
Himalayas just behind them. My rickety Indian-made
Ambassador lurched over mountain streams, on single-
lane bridges that looked ready to collapse, and then, as
we began to climb the pine-covered slopes, flashes of
rhododendron through the trees, I began to see more and
more people dressed in claret robes. We passed through

Dharamsala proper, the nondescript Indian town that sits at the bottom of the Kangra Valley, and then began to ascend a winding mountain road, past monuments to soldiers, army cantonments and an old Anglican church where Lord Elgin lies buried amidst the overgrown crosses. Finally, we bumped into the scrappy line of stalls, run-down guest-houses and spinning prayer-wheels that the world thinks of as Dharamsala.

"It's O.K.," said the Dalai Lama, breaking into a high chirrup of infectious laughter when I asked him recently about his adopted home (seconds before, he had been speaking about the gravity of the situation inside Tibet itself). "Now we have been in India forty-four years, in Dharamsala forty-three years, maybe thirty years from now everything will be fine." When first the Tibetan leader arrived here, with his devoted community, sight unseen, in 1960, he remembers the excitement of waking up to snowcaps and seeing wild flowers everywhere; his new home allowed him to tinker with his garden and to take long hikes into the hills, leaving his bodyguards breathless behind him. Every summer, though, he notes, with characteristic honesty, the withering monsoons for which Dharamsala is notorious would destroy all the flowers he had so carefully tended, making him home-sick, for a moment, for the high dry air of the Tibetan plateau.

As with much that he says, the friendly anecdote is a parable of sorts, and a kind of metaphor: Dharamsala is the place from which "by far the most serious" govern-ment-in-exile in the world (in *The Economist*'s words) has organized its more than 80 schools across India, the 190 nunneries and monasteries it has built since 1960, and the 50 settlements and communities that shelter hundreds of thousands of exiled Tibetans. In one corner of the hills is a Tibetan Children's Village where 2,000 kids learn their culture's language and history as they could never do at home (many of them are in fact sent out from Tibet over the Himalayas in order to get a Tibetan education here); in another, the Tibetan Institute of Performing Arts preserves Tibet's dance and opera traditions. Down one winding road sits a library containing Tibet's archives, and down in the valley a sumptuous cultural institute, the Norbulingka, where apprentices make scrolls and statues and wood carvings in a garden of walkways and flowers alarmingly reminiscent of Shangri-La. And yet, for all that, after almost half a century in exile, the Tibetans are no closer to a vanishing home that is on the brink of extinction now.

I go to Dharamsala—and have been going for almost thirty years—in order to savor its silent spaces, but also to witness the paradoxes of exile, and the mingled heroism and frustration of trying to build a new home that, at some level, its makers hope will one day make itself redundant, as a mandala does. If you want mountain views, I tell my friends, you're better off in Darjeeling, and if you wish to see Tibetan culture live as it might have done centuries ago, fly up to Ladakh; if you want to savor the wistfulness of a former British hill station, you may be better served in Simla, and as a center of the East-meets-West dance, nowhere is more colorful and comfortable than Kathmandu. Yet Dharamsala is the place where all the themes converge, in a sort of dizzying mandala in which a myriad cultures circle around one another, not sure of whether they're in search of enlightenment or something else. When I called up the

Dalai Lama's younger brother this spring, I was put on hold to the tune of "It's a Small, Small World."

When first you arrive in McLeod Ganj—the un-paved little heart of Upper Dharamsala (the Tibetan area that sits six miles by road above the Indian town of Dharamsala)—you may feel as if you've fallen into a bad trip, in every sense of the word, and a place as unmelodious and mongrel as its name. Languid blonde girls in harem pants and shaven-headed boys who haven't washed in days saunter past the Peace restaurant, en route to the Faith gift-shop, talking of dharma bummers and showing off a style that might best be called "McLeod Grunge." Ads for "Dream Yoga" and "Zen Shiatsu" and every kind of mishmashed transformation flutter from outside "Esoteric Boutiques" and "Buddhist Book Stores." Tibetan blades with silky hair down to their waists and slow smiles move around the dread-locks and the incense, seeing how they can turn their exoticism to advantage.

Yet Dharamsala is, if nothing else, a lesson in im-permanence and illusion, the Buddhist truths. Nearly everyone here is in flight—the Tibetans from China, the foreigners from home—and yet many a story you hear is one of suffering and surprise. That high-cheeked Tibetan stud in the black leather jacket, standing outside the "only Internet cafe where all profits go directly to the Tibetan cause," traveled fifty-nine days through the snow to get here, he will tell you, and if you ask him whether he has any contact with his family back home in Tibet, his eyes mist over and a silence falls. And that flamboyant character in ponytail and sandals turns out to be a volunteer who's left a job at an ad agency to teach English to the nuns who've escaped imprisonment and

torture to come here. Both parties are looking for salvation of a kind—a new life—but both seem to sense that
it will very likely go unfound.

The first time I came to McLeod Ganj, in 1974, I drove
straight up to the Dalai Lama's house (there was none of
the elaborate security then that makes even a public audience with him now a five-hour exercise), and as we sat in
his airy living-room, summer clouds floating through, it
was easy to feel as if we were truly apart from the world,
in the clouds, out of time. Even in 1988, when I came to
celebrate the Tibetan New Year here—long-horns sound-
ing from the roof of Thekchen Choeling Temple in the
pre-dawn chill—there was only one semi-comfortable
hotel in which to stay, and its dining-room was empty
save for me and a lonely French Buddhist nun. But after
the Dalai Lama won the Nobel Prize in 1989, and as
more and more people started going to Tibet, or finding
Tibet in their neighborhoods, suddenly Dharamsala—the
living heart of Tibetan color and wisdom and hope, and
home to its open-hearted embodiment--became dispro-
portionately well-known. Multi-story Indian hotels began
appearing on once virgin ridges and now a little directory
lists eighty-one guest-houses alone charging less than $7
a night.

"The thing that separates Dharamsala from Manali,
Dheradun and Simla," says Tenzin Geyche, the private
secretary to the Dalai Lama who's been working with the
Tibetan leader since 1964, "is that it's so international"; in
some seasons, the Dalai Lama's other private secretary,
Tenzin Takhla adds, the population here is 50 percent
Israeli (there is even a rabbi among the German bakeries
and wood-fire pizza joints of Dharamkot nearby). And
since Kashmir became something of a war zone, more

and more Indians look in on Dharamsala when they want a holiday in the hills. Nothing remains unchanged. "Some people say that when we came to Dharamsala, many of the Indians here were vegetarians," the Dalai Lama told me on my recent visit, exuding his characteristic delight in challenging himself and his assumptions. "But now, more and more are eating meat. So, that means"—his eyes crease up at the irony of it all—"that we Tibetans are teaching them bad habits!"

More seriously, there is always a potential for unrest as the 11,000 or so Indians of Upper Dharamsala watch the 11,000 or so Tibetans receiving all the attention and support of the world at large: even a tiny guest-house here sells itself as an "Exile Government Undertaking." A few years ago, a Tibetan boy stabbed an Indian, and small riots broke out in the area, the windows of Tibetan stores were shattered and even the government-in-exile's secretariat, a long walk away, was attacked. "A lot of the people who come out now, they don't even remember the old Tibet," says one of the men who was in the Dalai Lama's party when he fled Tibet. "All they think about is the Almighty Dollar."

For most foreigners, though, Dharamsala remains an often idyllic place of secluded temples and sunlit valleys, where a state oracle offers government advice in a trance and the heir apparent to Tibetan hopes, the 17th Karmapa, still a teenager, stays after his flight from China (the very word "Dharamsala," appropriately enough, refers to the shelter for pilgrims attached to a temple). One bright spring morning I scrambled down a mud path, just across from my cozy guest-house (itself across from the Dalai Lama's house and his private monastery), and found myself alone

on a rough shepherd's path through the trees, white butterflies twirling around me, and black-and-white crested
birds singing from the trees. In the distance I could just
make out the shining rooftop of a Buddhist temple, and as I
pulled open a creaky gate, I found myself, as in a fairy-tale,
at a small stone bridge leading to a sleepy monastery. Small
monks were sitting on a patch of grass, playing a board
game in the light. Prayer flags fluttered against the high
cloudless blue. A few steps down, some foreigners who were
staying (for $3 a night) inside the Tse Chok Ling temple, sat
above commanding views across the valley.

Those views are one reason why the British settled
upon the area in 1849, first setting up an army canton-
ment here, and then a whole community for escape from
the heat of the plains. A Forest Officer and a Deputy
Commissioner were soon ensconced in British cottages
here, and an army church built amidst the Himalayan
cedars, or deodars; if Lord Elgin had not died in 1863,
it is said, Dharamsala would have become the summer
capital of British India. The community was reduced
to rubble by an earthquake in 1905, and then again by
Partition in 1947, but in both cases it soon rose again.

"It was so remote," the Dalai Lama's younger brother,
Tenzin Choegyal, recalls of Dharamsala when he arrived here in 1960. "You couldn't get many things from
the market." The Dalai Lama moved into a small house
that is now, aptly, a Mountaineering Institute, and his
junior tutor into a place that is now a Meditation Center,
both of them enjoying the fact, no doubt, that centuries
ago the Kangra Valley was famous for its Buddhist
temples. Soon the calendar became as full of Tibetan
customs as the countryside all round. When I arrived in
Dharamsala this spring I saw explosions of red in every

corner of the town—in Internet cafes, in little video dens, in Japanese restaurants—as up to three thousand nuns and monks from around the Tibetan world gathered for the annual spring teachings, or "Great Prayer Festival," that customarily follows the Tibetan New Year (in late February or early March). As soon as the Dalai Lama concluded his two weeks of public lectures, the Shotun, or Yoghurt, Festival took over the Tibetan Institute of Performing Arts, and for ten days, every day, black-masked dancers and comical singers entertained crowds of delighted locals. Both prayer-halls of the central temple were filled from dawn to nightfall with monks praying (at the Dalai Lama's request) for world peace, and when the imprisoned 11th Panchen Lama's fourteenth birthday arrived, Tibetans carrying candles appeared all around the temple and banners were strung across the main street.

Something was always happening at the main temple, which now contains its own stylish museum, Italian cafe and shop selling "Quality Curative Incense." And as if in honor of the Buddhist teaching, the place was never the same from day to day. Sometimes groups of uniformed schoolchildren were crouched over drawings in a public competition held outside the main hall, sometimes the monks led a special prayer around a bonfire. Occasionally special auspicious food was handed out to anyone who wanted it, and sometimes there were esoteric dances and ceremonial mandalas. And almost every day, in the quiet afternoons, or after dark, I watched young monks perform classic Tibetan debating, one of them sitting on the ground, aspiring to look unmoved while the other fired questions at him and lunged towards him with a lightning clap of hands.

One day a whisper ran through town that the Dalai Lama was offering a public audience, and an unending line of Western nomads formed around the security office where passports were checked and passes handed out. Then, as the sun came out, the Tibetan leader stood outside his audience-room and a circle of silent votaries, first foreign and then Tibetan, lined up around his driveway for a quick blessing or a shake of his hand. After even the briefest of encounters, boys in swelling pantaloons and hoop-earringed girls issued forth with huge smiles, or tears in their eyes.

And around this constant flux the whole zany carnival of Indian daily life was always in full swing. One little restaurant inscrutably serenaded diners with a Muzak version of "Here Comes the Bride," while the buses outside said, "I love my India" on their sides, or "Oh! God save me." In many a dark, bare-walled opening, some resourceful kid had set up a DVD player and a flat-screen Sony, and projected five brand-new Hollywood releases a day ("THIS IS THE PROPERTY OF MIRAMAX STUDIOS. IT IS TO BE USED FOR SCREENING PURPOSES ONLY," flashing across the screen every five minutes). One over-eager Indian hotel, anxious to offer best wishes for the Tibetan New Year, Losar, had even strung a banner above Temple Road, leading to the Dalai Lama's house, announcing, in huge letters, "HAPPY LOSER."

The other component adding the final coup de grace to the whole cross-cultural swirl is the arrival of luminaries from everywhere—Martin Scorsese, J.F.K., Jr., Harrison Ford—to learn what they can from the Dalai Lama. Goldie Hawn is often seen on the debris-stricken streets and Steven Seagal clomps around town in full Tibetan gear. The McLlo restaurant, a loud place next to the central bus stand, features a picture of Pierce Brosnan tucking into its fare, a hand held to his heart (or is it his stomach?). And when you use a public toilet, you see that it was donated by Richard Gere, who has selflessly devoted time and money to the Tibetan cause for more than twenty years now, and actually set up a waste-management program to try to clean up the area's congenital mess.

And yet for all the brightness and sunshine of the Tibetan flowers and prayer flags and smiles—for all the magnolia against the snowcaps, next to golden wind-chimes, in the ravishing Norbulingka—there remains a strain of poignancy to the borrowed Elysium that reminds one of the archetypal traveler's truth that what is liberation for the visitor is often a painful imprisonment for the local. From my guest house I could hear a solemn gong through the trees and see monks playing tag on the whitewashed terraces of their monastery; yet on the road leading to it there were always Indian beggars and women waving receipts from hospitals to show the money they needed. One bright afternoon I drove up to Naddi, an Alpine village where green fields run up to a stunning line of snowcaps, the only sound a rushing stream far below; just two miles away, though, at the Children's Village, the bright creche was full of orphans, and the little girls who sang me a delightful version of "Jack and Jill" were very likely children who would never see their parents again.

I fell into conversation one day with a Tibetan woman and heard how she was an orphan herself, discovered by chance along the streets of Kathmandu by the Dalai Lama's sister. Now she had two children of her own, at the Children's Village, but the $2 cab fare and a leg ailment meant that she almost never got to see them.

Another bright Sunday morning, I stepped into a bookshop—McLeod Ganj shops are generally open on Sundays and closed on Mondays because, some say, the soldiers in British times wanted to shop on their one day off—and came upon a version of "This Land is Your Land," sung with Tibetan lyrics, by the bookstore owner, who had stolen into his homeland in 1980 and been moved to write about what he had seen and felt. Even the tire-covers on the jeeps in the Namgyal Monastery say, "Time is running out," followed by a line of gravestones. "Now we are finished," said a resistance fighter, mournfully. "Though I hope I am wrong. The Chinese are playing for time and we are playing into their hands." The Dalai Lama's decision that the most the world could hope for was a "saved" and not a "freed" Tibet still disappoints this onetime guerrilla. "Without freedom," he says, eyes penetrating and clear, "there is no hope."

The same day I walked into the sepulchral gloom of Nowrojee General Merchants, the Indian shop that has been supplying the area with its necessities since 1860, and found the last of the Nowrojees, as he sees himself, seventy-five years old, sitting in the dark, amidst dusty British ads for "Lux Toilet Soap" and "Andrews Liver Salt." His father, he said, had taken over the shop in 1904, and his elder brother, now deceased, had looked after it for sixty-two years. But he did not expect a sixth generation to take over because "Now nobody wants to live here."

"Dharamsala was so beautiful then, so peaceful," he said, recalling how all the family's sixteen employees had slept in the shop and went out each morning to pay calls on every bungalow. "I used to walk down to college, from 6,000 feet to 3,000 feet, four miles down, four miles up, every day. Everything was open: the Nature, the fields. Now sanitation is not there, administration is not there. You cannot believe that this was once the biggest enterprise in northern India." The old man can still remember when "we offered the land to His Holiness and the Tibetans. Then, an economic revival was there. But now"—a smile, with very few teeth in evidence—"now there has been too much revival. A flower blossoms and then it fades. Overcrowding, so much noise. I used to dream of growing old here, of dying here."

Not far away, in the Church of St. John in the Wilderness, founded by the British in 1852, a scratchy cassette is playing a version of "Onward Christian Soldiers" while birds sing in the rafters and the cheerful South Indian priest puts on a cassock above sneakers and jeans to deliver an Easter Sunday service. A ragtag group of worshipers has gathered in the draughty space to sing "Morning Has Broken" from a folder containing two photocopied pages (and concluding with "Have A Nice Day"). The plaques all around, put up by "Brother Officers of the Gurkha Rifles," recall men killed in Mesopotamia, Palestine, Baluchistan, and even one Thomas William Knowles killed by a bear on 25th October 1883, aged fifty ("In the midst of life we are in death").

The point of travel for me is to journey into complication, even contradiction; to confront the questions that I never have to think about at home, and am not sure can ever be easily answered. Dharamsala, alive with the sound of monks practicing dialectical reasoning, takes one as deeply into the dialogue of realism and hope as anywhere I know. The foreigners who stay here are often strikingly serious and compassionate, and spend months learning Tibetan or helping those in need; the place is bright with mystical paintings and prayer-flags and glorious mountain sunshine; the long walk around the Dalai Lama's house is always vivid with old Tibetans praying for the health of their leader and their home. And yet all of it remembers a culture that seems very far away. "As a human being, I am hopeful," says a Tibetan very close to the Dalai Lama. "But as a Tibetan...I don't know."

The Dalai Lama has worked as hard as anyone alive to make optimism and realism seem compatible. "If you look at things locally in Tibet," he told me this spring, "of course there is not much hope. But"—the famous gift for pragmatism takes over—"if some day there are 6 million Tibetans in Tibet and 10 million Chinese and they are Buddhist, maybe, something O.K." We don't know the future, he might be saying, but we have to act as if it will end tomorrow. He, his vibrant temples, the stirring institutions kept alive by the Tibetans around him, speak for hope; the stories that come out of Tibet, and the broken offices of McLeod Ganj, sometimes speak for something else. The visitor to Dharamsala tries to make sense of his competing feelings, and to make out the sound of the prayers above the klaxons on the road.

❧ ❧ ❧

Pico Iyer is one of the most popular travel writers of our time. He's journeyed the world covering distant places for publications like Time, Harper's, The New York Times, *and* The New Yorker. *His books include* The Global Soul, Sun After Dark, Cuba and the Night, Falling Off the Map, The Lady and the Monk, *and* Video Night in Kathmandu..

꘏ ꘏ ꘏

Circuit Broken

Zen saying: "Before enlightenment,
mountains are mountains; after enlightenment,
mountains are mountains."

M Y LAST AND PERHAPS MOST REDEMPTIVE ACT AS
a tourist in the Vietnamese central highlands
was to visit the Montagnard church in Kontum. There,
perched innocuously on the back wall of the parish office,
was a large painted-ceramic crucifix unlike any I had
seen before.

Whereas most images of the crucifixion depict a Jesus
agonized and exhausted by the pain of the world's sins,
the Montagnard Jesus looked downright chipper—his
hair feathered back in the manner of a 1970s rock star,
his mouth spread into a huge, toothy grin, his hands
(which had somehow pulled loose from the crossbars)
stretched out in a gesture of neighborly goodwill.

"Never mind the stigmata," the Montagnard Jesus seemed to be saying. "Let's have a barbecue!"

For devout believers, the notion of a Jesus so distracted and nonchalant in the face of his own crucifixion would seem a tad blasphemous. But for me—after a rather bewildering experience in the area—the sight of Barbecue Jesus came as a kind of relief.

"Forget about your expectations," Barbecue Jesus seemed to tell me. "Forget about what you think you're supposed to do. Look at me. Run your hands over my ceramic finish and you'll see: I am just as real as your expectations."

My trip to the central highlands of Vietnam had started on a note of euphoric optimism on Route 13, the main road through the region, around the same time half the people on my bus started vomiting.

Granted, watching a bunch of motion-sick Vietnamese farmers puke into plastic bags wasn't all that pleasant, but I enjoyed the quirky feeling of otherness, as I was the only foreigner there. I was intrigued by the details of the experience: how the women dabbed a green salve under their nostrils to ward off the stench of gastric acid; how the men squatted on small plastic stools in the aisles to compensate for overcrowding; how everyone shared water from a grimy Mickey Mouse cup that floated in a jug at the driver's feet; how the rounded corners and metal vent windows made our small bus look like an ice cream truck.

Route 13 gained distinction as being the home of some of the heaviest fighting in the waning days of the Vietnam War. Portions of the road, which to this day are virtually impassable to anything bigger than a motorcycle, were once part of the Ho Chi Minh Trail supply route from the Laotian frontier.

In retrospect, the sole reason I had for traveling Vietnam Route 13 was because it wasn't Vietnam Highway 1. The sole reason I was headed to the highland town of Kontum was because it wasn't the highland town of Dalat. And the sole reason I wanted to travel a potentially dangerous stretch of the Ho Chi Minh Trail was because it wasn't part of the Circuit.

In Southeast Asia, every country has a standard Budget Travel Circuit. In Thailand, the Circuit involves any combination of southern islands and northern hill-tribe treks, with a few intermediary days in Bangkok. In Laos, the overland Circuit almost always includes stops in Luang Prabang, Vang Vieng, and Vientiane. In Cambodia, no Circuit is complete without stops in Angkor Wat, Phnom Penh, and Sihanoukville.

Vietnam's Circuit roughly follows Highway 1 between Ho Chi Minh City and Hanoi. This largely coastal route features comfortable and convenient transportation, plentiful tourist facilities (from cheap motels to moped rentals) and sightseeing stop-offs from Haiphong to Hue to Hoi An. The problem with this, of course, is that so many travelers frequent this route that a person can go for weeks on the Circuit without having much interaction with the locals.

Perhaps no place illustrates this better than Nha Trang—a southern coastal city whose most famous citizen in backpacker circles is a small, visor-wearing woman named Mama Hahn. For about $7, Mama Hahn takes foreigners on all-day boat cruises that feature sightseeing, snorkeling, a nearly limitless supply of cheap beer and a floating lunch that features a man in a rowboat handing out marijuana cigarettes. Mama Hahn's cruise has proven so popular with backpack travelers that she has already spawned a couple of imitators (one of whom, confusingly, also calls herself Mama Hahn).

I joined Mama Hahn's boat trip one day after arriving in Nha Trang on the Circuit from Ho Chi Minh City. My seven Canadian boatmates (all of them friends, traveling together) were gregarious and funny—and the cruise through the bay was enjoyable enough—but I lost all sense of being in Asia within minutes of leaving the shore. It didn't help that Mama Hanh carried a loudspeaker, and continually used it to squawk such non-traditional Vietnamese aphorisms as "Let's party!" and "Who's ready to get fucked up?"

As usually happens when travelers get together, the Canadians and I shared our road tales. Various members of the Canadian crew had been to places like Tibet, Goa, Samarkand, and Tanzania. I hadn't been to any of those places, but my southeast Asian experiences seemed to meet with their approval. "I could tell when I met you that you were a seasoned traveler," one of the Canucks confided at one point.

The thing is, sitting on Mama Hahn's boat, I didn't feel like a traveler at all—let alone a seasoned one. And—considering that my companions' travel experiences seemed to center around sampling drugs in various far-flung corners of the earth—I began to wonder just what defined a "seasoned traveler."

I came ashore from my Nha Trang boat excursion with a sunburn, a mid-afternoon hangover, and the vague feeling that I could have experienced the exact same thing in Ontario.

Suddenly filled with the urge to do something different, I visited my guesthouse travel office and scanned the map, looking for a southern region that was as far from the Circuit as possible. I put my finger on an area near the Laotian border. "I want to go here," I said to the Vietnamese woman who ran the office.

"That's the central highlands," she told me. "A very wonderful place. We can get you a ticket to Dalat for tomorrow."

I knew plenty about Dalat. Dalat was a Niagra Falls-style highland resort town that boasted waterfalls, swan-shaped paddleboats on the local lake, and a "minority village" that featured a giant concrete chicken. Dalat—on kitsch value alone—was already a part of the Circuit. "I don't want to go to Dalat," I told the tour woman. I tapped my finger on the northern stretch of Route 13. "What's on this road?"

She thought for a moment. "Buon Ma Thot, Pleiku—but those places aren't so interesting. Kontum is good. It's like Dalat—lots of nature and hill tribes. But the road after Kontum is very bad. It's only for motorcycles, or maybe army trucks. Nobody ever goes that way. Kontum is kind of a headache. I think Dalat is better."

The next morning I went to the Nha Trang inter-city bus station and headed for Kontum.

It took me two days to get there—one day on a crowded, lumbering DeSoto bus bound for Buon Ma Thot, and one day on the ice cream truck vomitorium to Kontum. By the time I reached my destination, fresh air and leg-room seemed like glorious, decadent luxuries.

After checking into a cheap hotel near the bus depot, I set off down the sidestreets of Kontum, hoping to find some place—such as a market—where I could mix in with the local folks. Not far from my hotel, I stopped to hold a store-front door open for a young man overloaded with boxes. A minute later, he came jogging up to me on the sidewalk and handed me a plastic sack filled with coffee beans. He was dressed in a white t-shirt that read, enigmatically: AS BIG AND AS CLOSE AS IT GETS.

"Is this for me?" I asked. At the time, I had temporarily forgotten that asking a yes-no question to someone who doesn't understand English is possibly the most pinheaded mistake a traveler can make in Asia. Still smiling, the Vietnamese guy nodded.

I had no use for a big bag of coffee beans, but I was nonetheless touched by this seemingly generous gesture. Wanting to express my appreciation, I took out my Vietnamese phrase book and tried to make conversation. This proved to be a slow process, since spoken Vietnamese is a tonal language, and difficult for beginners. I mostly just communicated by pointing to words. It took me fifteen minutes to establish that my friend's name was Tran, he wasn't married, and his hobby was singing. I threw in a few personal bits about myself and showed him some pictures of my family.

As I made to end the conversation and leave, Tran seized the phrase book and flipped through the pages for a few moments. He stopped at the numbers page, pointed to "20" and looked at me quizzically.

"Twenty," I told him. "That's twenty."

"Twenty," Tran repeated in English.

"Is that how old you are?" I asked, still oblivious to the yes-no rule.

Tran nodded. "Twenty," he said. "O.K.!"

"Great," I said. "I'm twenty-eight."

"Twenty!"

I pointed to myself. "Twenty-eight."

Tran pointed to the coffee beans. "Twenty!" he said.

I suddenly realized, after all this time spent endearing myself to Tran, that he'd never intended to give me the coffee. He'd merely been attempting to sell it to me. Figuring it a cheap enough way to save face, I took 20,000 dong (about $1.50) from my pocket and held it out to him. Tran scowled and pushed away the Vietnamese money. He dug into his pocket and pulled out a dollar bill. "Twenty!" he said.

I shook my head and handed the coffee back, but it was too late: Tran was convinced I wanted the coffee. By the time I gave up trying to say no and started to walk away, the price was down to $12. Tran pursued me, dropping the price to $10, then $8, where it hovered for a good ten minutes as Tran backpedaled in front of me, waving the coffee in front of my face.

On paper, ten minutes doesn't seem like much, but when it's spent trying to wave off an absurdly aggressive coffee salesman, ten minutes is a maddening eternity. Finally, I broke. "No, Tran!" I yelled, coming to a halt on the sidewalk. "How many times do you want me to say it? No! No! No!"

Tran sneered and shoved the bag of coffee beans right up under my nose. Without thinking, I smacked it out of his hands. This sent Tran into a fury, screaming what I can only assume were the choicest of Vietnamese curses. I took it as my cue to leave when he spun around and kicked over a parked bicycle.

I never did find the market that night. I ended up weaving through the streets for upwards of an hour, trying to remember my way home.

It was after dark by the time I'd found my hotel. As I walked through the lobby, I noticed two little Vietnamese girls sitting on the couch, watching television. The older one looked to be about six years old, and the younger one couldn't have been older than three. They were both clutching orange sodas.

"Hello!" the older one cried as I walked past.

"Hello," I said. "How are you?"

"What is your name?" she replied.

"My name is Rolf. What is your name?"

"What is your name?" she said.

"I said my name is Rolf. But what's your name?"

The girl gave me a confused look. "What is your name?" she said, a bit uncertain this time.

I squatted down by the couch and gave her a friendly smile. "We know my name. What's your name?" I playfully wiggled my finger at her. Her face went blank. I pointed again. "Not my name," I said brightly. "Your name!" The girl looked at me as if I'd just said I was going to hit her on the head with a hammer.

Worried about the direction our conversation was heading, I stood up and tried to look as cheery and non-threatening as possible. "Time for me to say goodnight!" I said. "Can you say goodnight?"

At this, the younger girl suddenly burst into tears.

I went to bed that night feeling like some kind of tragically misunderstood cartoon monster.

The following day I rented a clunky one-speed bi-cycle, and rode out of the city in search of Montagnard ethnic minority villages. Following random roads out of town, I bicycled into a stunning landscape of river valleys, coffee plantations, huge white clouds, and far-off purple mountains. The roads were lined with broad fields of maroon soil, smoking brick kilns, cement graves painted mustard yellow, and mud-walled long-houses. In packed-dirt yards along the roadside, little girls coasted precariously on adult-sized bicycles while little boys ran around trying to urinate on each other. Tiny babies buzzed past on 100cc motorcycles, stoically perched on their fathers' laps.

After about three hours of pedaling, I arrived at a rural minority village that looked suitably remote and authentic. I decided to stop and check things out.

In a way, I've always been a bit confused about the purpose of hill-tribe tourism, which has become a travel fad in places like Thailand and Vietnam. I guess the rural treks are meant to expose travelers to an exotic way of life and provide contrast to the modernized ways of places like Bangkok and Ho Chi Minh City—but I suspect that such treks largely serve to validate the sentimental standard of foreign exoticism set by *National Geographic*.

My most immediate challenge upon arriving in the village was simply trying to figure out what to do. In my mind's eye, I envisioned a grand entry into the minority village, replete with tribal dancing, pigs butchered in my honor, and a hearty round of toasts with some ill-tasting fermented beverage. In reality, I found the town largely deserted at midday. The few dark-skinned locals I did see were wearing Western clothes with occasional ethnic flourishes, such as a woven sash or a porkpie hat, and didn't take much interest in me, even when I pulled out the phrase book and tried to make conversation.

After twenty or so awkward minutes of skulking around the village, I managed to insinuate myself into a group of teenaged boys, who were standing in a circle and kicking a chicken-feather birdie into the air. My rusty soccer skills were good enough to keep up with the boys, and we'd just managed to get a good volley going when a boozy, toothless old man wheeled my bike up and indicated that he wanted me to get on it and leave. The boys shouted angrily at the old man; the old man pointed at me and shouted back.

Then, without warning, the tallest boy cuffed the old drunk on the side of the head. As the old man reeled backwards, a second boy pushed him to the ground. When he tried to stand up, the tall boy kicked him in the rump. The others jeered and laughed. When the old man had scampered away, the tall boy looked over at me, smiled, and gave a thumbs-up.

Not comfortable with the notion that my new companions had just shown their hospitality by beating the bejesus out of the town drunk, I excused myself at the first opportunity and—after a few more halfhearted attempts at interaction with the locals—pedaled back to Kontum.

Independent travel is often an act of hope—an optimistic attempt to blur the line between cultures through somewhat random interactions. By my second night in Kontum, however, I felt more like an outsider than ever. I decided to make a play at salvaging my trip by moving on.

The next morning I managed to hire a battered green '70s-era Dodge van to take me to Phuoc Son along the Ho Chi Minh Trail portion of Route 13. The driver was a high-strung wheeler-dealer type, and by the time we left the blacktop at Dac Glei, he had managed to fill the remaining seats in the van with a motley assortment of Vietnamese farmers. Despite my protests, I ended up having to share the shotgun seat with a parcel-laden old woman. I noticed, with a bit of dread, that she was carrying a bottle of green salve.

Thirty minutes into our creep down a rutted stretch of road, the driver brought us to a rough and sudden halt.

An overloaded white transport truck had rolled over in the middle of the road and burst like a sausage, jettisoning torn bags of rice and smashed boxes of clothes in its wake. Our driver cursed and stubbornly honked his horn, but there was no way around it. Angrily, he threw the van into reverse and managed to get us mired in the gravelly mud on the side of the road. After several minutes of flooring the accelerator, he yelled at everyone to get out. The farmers made for the side of the road and began to take out their food, looking like they expected to be there for a while. The driver remained in the van, cursing and stomping on the accelerator.

At that moment, with the back wheels of the Dodge sending chunks of gravel thumping off into the trees, I suddenly realized that I had no good reason for being there. I had gone to a remote corner of Vietnam with no sense of the language or culture—with no host or guide or guidebook, and no specific ideas about what to find there. The decision that brought me there was not a savvy act of independent travel, but an insipid act of negation—a ritual of avoiding other travelers, as if this in itself was somehow significant.

Wearily resolved, I shouldered my pack and started walking back up the road. After an hour or so, I hitched a ride on a flatbed lorry and made it back to Kontum by late afternoon. Since no buses back down to the coast were available until the next day, I checked back into my hotel and went for an aimless walk that eventually landed me in the Montagnard church.

There I offered up my confusion to Barbecue Jesus.

There is no such thing as a seasoned traveler, because travel is an ongoing experience of the unfamiliar. Regardless of how many stamps you have in your passport, you eventually find yourself in a place like Kontum, Vietnam, inadvertently making small children cry, hopelessly trying to deal with people who see you as nothing more than a consumer, and haplessly walking in concentric circles until you can find something that resembles your hotel.

Sometimes, the Circuit is not a physical route, but a largely unavoidable state of mind that regulates your expectations. I had gone to the highlands looking for Vietnamese authenticity, but perhaps I was just looking for a generic affirmation experience—something superficial and positive to make me think I wasn't just passing through like a ghost.

Ironically, the utter lack of affirmation and positive interaction I found was—in its own, frustrating way—bluntly authentic. All too often, the random workings of reality simply don't match up with your reverent, idealized hopes.

Hanging there before me—strange, grinning, half-crucified—Barbecue Jesus seemed to understand.

❧   ❧   ❧

Rolf Potts is the author of Vagabonding: An Uncommon Guide to the Art of Long-Term World Travel, *and his travel stories have appeared in Salon.com,* Condé Nast Traveler, National Geographic Traveler, National Geographic Adventure, *and several Travelers' Tales anthologies. He keeps no permanent address, but his virtual home can be found at www.rolfpotts.com.*

DUSTIN W. LEAVITT

✢ ✢ ✢

Balinese Canoes

Observing the rituals of a dying craft,
the author tries to assess the legacy and the loss.

OUR SECOND ORDER OF BUSINESS, HAVING ALREADY
negotiated a daily fee for services rendered,
was to decide what we ought to call each other. "Your
people (meaning my people, Americans) use the family
name, is this not correct? And what is that name?" asked
the headman of Tanjung Benoa village. I told him my
family name, but suggested he call me by my given name
instead, as was customary in my country.

He hesitated and the corners of his mouth contracted
in consternation. "This would be difficult for me."
Silence, and then: "Please excuse me, what is your social
position?"

Consternation, this time mine.

"What is your...job?" he prompted, in an attempt to

clarify his line of inquiry. I considered for a moment and replied, "I'm a writer."

"Ah," he said, now wary. "Then you write for the government newspaper?" In Southeast Asia, where governments commonly harness the written word to their often unpopular political agendas, people view writers with suspicion.

"No, no, I'm independent...a scholar."

The headman's face brightened. "Independent! A scholar! And your father? Is he a scholar, as well?"

I bobbled my head in the affirmative.

"Then you are certainly a Brahmin. I am Sudra, a common man. And... forgive me for asking these questions...you are married?"

"No," I replied.

"Not married?" he said, incredulous. Our driver, a young man who spoke less English than he understood, appraised me anew with a sidelong glance. "Never mind, then. I will call you Mister Dustin Leavitt...this is correct? And you should call me Ktut Kami." I nodded, glad to have this apparently minor formality settled. "...Although it is not what the people call me, as I am married and I have children."

Consternation, mine again. I turned around in the front seat of the Toyota jeep as it negotiated the swarming streets of Denpasar, capital city of the island of Bali. "What do the people call you?"

"Ah," he replied. "That depends."

Boats had long captivated me—or more correctly, what boats represented loomed large in my imagination. To me, boats were small worlds unto themselves, roving islands of purposefulness in which the discipline of self-reliance passed for the law of the land. They projected order and utility. Yet, they remained compliant, ego-less, if such a thing may be said of an inanimate object, for they had existed among men for a very long time.

I had spent significant periods of my life working them as fisherman and sailor, and felt a nagging moral anxiety over their gradual disappearance from the face of the earth, although I was not certain whether my concern was for the boats themselves, for the lives of the watermen who built and sailed them, or for the abstractions they had engendered in me. I could not even say whether these were three issues or one.

When I speak of the disappearance of boats, I do not mean pleasure yachts, nor do I mean the monoliths of modern merchant fleets such as supertankers, container ships, or luxury liners. Rather, I am talking about the canoes and planked craft of indigenous watermen the world over, which represent not just one element of a complex corporate structure, but which underpin entire local economies.

And I am not talking exclusively about boats as implements of material culture, but also as vessels of cultural principles, principles I believed were worth preserving in spite of their apparent incompatibility with the grasping way of life sweeping the globe. Such a way of life was, I felt, unsustainable, if not devastating, and might benefit from the lessons in self-reliance and moral integrity that indigenous watermen could provide.

Thus, I had come to Bali seeking that which somehow defined me even as I sensed the decline in its relevance—and perhaps my own—in a changing world. We are loath to yield to the inevitable. And yet, where lies the virtue of human life if not in the struggle between our rooted moral will and our unrelenting destiny? We may not willfully attempt to determine our fate, but by understanding that it abounds with options, however inconspicuous, we may alter its course in unforeseen ways.

Our driver, whom I had chanced to meet a few days previously, had recommended Ktut Kami to me as a man who knew about Balinese boat building and who could introduce me to carvers of *jukung*, the traditional double-outrigger canoe.

"Kami is my given name," Ktut Kami explained, "and Ktut means 'fourth born.' We are all named Wayan, Njoman, Made, or Ktut: first born, second born, third born, fourth born." He laughed. "It's confusing, yes?"

I allowed that it was.

"He…" indicating our driver, "…is Made, third born. You should call him Made because he is just a boy."

I looked at Made, Made Suardika. I would not have thought him boyish at all, but a grown man of twenty-something. His dark face divided in a brilliant smile. "Yes, I am a boy," he affirmed shyly. "I am not married."

Personal names, "little" names, Ktut Kami told me, are bestowed on Balinese children 105 days after they are born. However, birth-order names (Wayan, Njoman, Made, or Ktut) are more commonly used to address them—or young women or men, like Made Suardika, who are as yet childless—even though the system is further complicated by the fact that the fifth-born child will be called Wayan (first born), the sixth-born Njoman, and so on. To avoid confusion among the dozens of Wayans and Mades who inhabit any given village or hamlet, birth-order names may be supplemented by the personal name.

When a Balinese has sired or borne children, however,

he or she ceases to be called by birth order name and is referred to instead by a new one based on the personal name of the (now) adult's last born child: Father-of-so-and-so, Mother-of-such-and-such, and when grandchildren are born, the people of the village begin to refer to him or her as Grandfather-of or Grandmother-of.

"Why aren't you married, Made?" I asked in what I hoped was a spirit of mutual interest, not to be mistaken for impudence.

He licked his lips, searching for words, and gave me a rueful look. "I want," he said. "I want, but not have money."

"Yes," Ktut Kami confirmed from the back seat of the jeep. "He is not yet a man."

Double-outrigger canoes had once lined the shores of Bali's coastal villages. In the south, on the beaches of Kuta and Legian, where Western tourists surfed and drank and sunned their breasts to the amazement of the native Moslem minority, few examples remained. The sun-grayed hulks of unfinished and abandoned canoes, on which the people had once depended to provide fish, Bali's cheapest and most obtainable source of protein, lay upturned along the margins of narrow lanes. No one in the southern villages now pursued canoe carving or its traditions. Most canoe carvers now worked menial jobs in construction or the tourist industry, casualties of the capital-driven juggernaut that was invading Southeast Asia and replacing self-sufficient village-based economies. Invariably, when I introduced myself to the inhabitants of the walled compounds nearby, searching for the owners of the discarded canoes, I was told they were not at home, but working as wage earners in the city, and I assuaged my disappointment with the thought that at least they had jobs.

Arriving in the village of Banyar Kubur, Ktut Kami introduced me to a canoemaker he'd heard of who had turned to shrine building. Having listened intently to Ktut Kami's explanation for my unexpected appearance in his quiet neighborhood, the shrinemaker smiled broadly and ushered us into his compound through a gateway of carved stone. It was midday, and he was dressed for work in a pair of canvas trousers and a thin plaid shirt whose lemony yellows and cerulean blues had faded to a uniform gray.

The shrinemaker had chosen his new trade wisely, for every Balinese house possesses a family shrine, a small, open sided pavilion with a thatched roof that perches atop a short wooden tower. Household shrines are typically hung with vivid decorations of beads and worked cloth—valances and banners and shrouds in Chinese red, saffron, green, and white—and contain offerings, but are otherwise empty. Balinese worship the Hindu trinity of Brahma, Shiva, and Vishnu, but venerate a supreme god, Sanghyang Widi, as well, who may be approached only by the priestly caste and remains obscure.

"He is a fat man," Ktut Kami whispered to me, referring to the shrinemaker, as we rounded the *aling aling*, a small wall that shielded the courtyard from the street and prevented evil spirits, who cannot easily turn corners, from entering. His tone, far from deprecating, was infused with awe. "I think he is a religious man, too," he added, sealing his endorsement with a solemn nod.

When we had removed our shoes and sandals and seated ourselves on the raised floor of the shrinemaker's open, tile-roofed communal *bale*, a sort of Balinese living

room, he leaned back against a polished wooden pillar
and spread his blunt workman's hands across his belly.
A breeze, laced with birdsong, quelled the torrid heat of
midday. As we waited for the shrinemaker's wife to prepare tea, I took note of his neat garden, the kitchen, the
household shrine, the private sleeping rooms—and in the
dark shadows of their doorways, the spellbound faces of
the old man's daughters peering out at me.

Since he was a "religious man," I asked the shrinemaker questions about the rituals associated with the
building of Balinese canoes. The old man listened atten-
tively while Ktut Kami translated, enthusiasm spreading
across his face as my line of inquiry became apparent.

"Balinese life," Ktut Kami began, translating for the
shrinemaker, "is ruled by *desa-kala-patra*. This is true.
We are a religious people."

I nodded encouragingly, and the shrinemaker, un-
comprehending, nodded as well.

"*Desa* is place; *kala* means time; *patra* is the law."

"Like *adat*?" I interrupted. *Adat*, a word I was familiar with, refers to traditional law.

"Yes…" Ktut Kami replied, shaking his head in the
negative. "…no. No, not *adat*. *Patra*…*patra* is the village
law. It is like agreement, you see. All things must be in
agreement…time and place and people…"

I nodded again, a little uncertain whether or not I did
in fact see.

"*Desa* means place," Ktut Kami continued. "To us,
place is very important. Where we are and where we
come from. Where you come from. Where we are in
relationship to each other. This is *desa*."

"*Kala* means time. This is very important, Mister
Dustin Leavitt. We Balinese never do anything until we

know when it is a good time. For us, the time must be propitious...this is the word?"

"Yes," I assured him. "Propitious means the right time according to the Hindu calendar, yes?"

Ktut Kami pressed his palms together and bowed his head in a single, deep nod. The shrinemaker mirrored his gesture. "Yes," Ktut Kami sighed. "Mister Dustin Leavitt, you understand our religion."

"No. No, not at all." I was quick to disabuse him of this generous but serious miscalculation. "I have heard about the Hindu calendar. You use it to calculate what days are good for doing certain things, and what days are not so good. That's all I know. Please go on."

"Thank you." Ktut Kami then explained to me how *desa-kala-patra* governs traditional canoe building, as it does every other Balinese occupation. It determines the confluence of where, when, and who, without which a canoe would remain not-a-canoe, and prompts the ceremonies without which the making of a canoe would lead inevitably to its own unmaking.

"The first ceremony," Ktut Kami explained, "is called *ngebah*."

"*Ngebah*," the shrinemaker echoed.

"He," Ktut Kami continued, inclining his head toward the shrinemaker, "celebrates *ngebah* when he cuts the tree. The second is a wedding ceremony. He calls it *makuh* or *ngakit*..."

"*Makuh*," said the shrinemaker.

Ktut Kami spelled the words for me. "He performs this ceremony when he begins to carve the canoe so the different parts will stay together, like man and woman who are married. Do you understand, Mister Dustin Leavitt? This is very important."

I tapped the notebook in which I had been writing. "Yes, I understand."

"Number three is called *nguag sendeng*." Ktut Kami slowly spelled the words, then consulted briefly with the shrinemaker, who shook his head and shrugged his shoulders. "This ceremony is performed when he puts in the…" He moved the flat palm of his hand horizontally from side to side, miming the object he was unable to name. Taking my notebook and pen, he sketched the top view of a canoe, an oblong leaf shape, and then drew perpendicular lines across it from edge to edge. Pointing at them, the canoe's transverse braces, he said, "This, Mister Dustin Leavitt, what is its name?"

"Those are the thwarts," I replied, taking the notebook from him.

"Thwarts," he repeated, and the shrinemaker, craning his neck to see the drawing for himself, silently mouthed the foreign word. "*Nguag sendeng* is performed when he put in the thwarts."

I nodded as I wrote in the margin beside his drawing.

"Finally, number four. He makes this ceremony when he put the canoe in the sea. It is called *melpas*. He says not all canoemakers perform these ceremonies. Sometimes only perform one or two, but he always perform four. He is a religious man, you see."

The next day, the "boy" Made, Ktut Kami, and I drove northeast from metropolitan Denpasar on the narrow highway that rings the oblong island toward Candidasa on its eastern end. There, the road cuts inland before bending gradually back toward the coast at Culik. Our destination was the invitingly remote stretch of precipitous coastline the highway ignored.

The countryside was planted with startling green fields of rice, the island's defining crop. Rice fields are tended communally in Bali, Ktut Kami explained, though they are divided into *sawah*, which are individually owned. Every farmer who owns a *sawah* belongs to a village association known as a *subak*, the head of which controls the supply of water upon which rice cultivation depends. The arable land of Bali is engraved with irrigation canals that not only provide water to the paddies, but for the common needs of the people, as well. Primary canals, lined with stone, ran through the villages at the road's edge, and girls in shapeless t-shirts, squatting beside them, swabbed dishes at their doorsteps beneath the bright sunshine. In the countryside, these canals became deep, wide ditches alongside the fields, where thin, shirtless farmers, standing knee deep in the brown water, unblushingly shed their bright sarongs for a morning wash.

At Kusamba, the highway descended from the open rice fields toward the wooded coast. A decade before, Adrian Horridge, in his book on Balinese watercraft, had reported trolling canoes, as well as *jukung gede*, canoes big enough to transport cattle, on Kusamba's black volcanic sand. Seeing none, we continued to Candidasa, once renowned for its wide, white, palm-lined beaches. Ironically, those very beaches had attracted entrepreneurs who mined the offshore coral reef for lime to make the cement used to construct Candidasa's tourist hotels. Deprived of the protection of the reef, the beaches soon washed away.

The highway crooked inland again through low, rolling hill country upon which the sun beat unrelentingly. Passing through Culik, a village of stone compounds

enclosing trim houses, we descended to the coast on a
dusty road, arriving just before midday in the shabby
fishing village of Amed. Its narrow crescent beach,
typical of undeveloped village beaches throughout the
South Pacific, was sparsely littered with sun-brittled
bits of plastic debris, and fresh human turds rolled in
the surf. A hopeful restaurant and bar stood by itself at
the water's edge, and its patrons, a few Western tourists
who showed every sign of having fled too far from the
busy beaches of Kuta, clustered around it in the banal
shade of striped umbrellas, stunned to silence by the
heat.

North of the restaurant, however, drawn up on
the sand, a long line of canoes, willowy booms lashed
together and canted skyward, leaned gently on their
outriggers. I hurried toward them, Ktut Kami scuttling
at my heels, his face betraying his thinly veiled exasperation as his worn black shoes filled with sand.

They were *jukung pelasan*, slender fifteen-foot trolling canoes used for fishing. Their narrow, white hulls,
rakishly prolonged by horizontal stripes at the gunwales
and waterline, drawn in vivid reds, greens, blues, and
yellows, blazed in the brilliant sunshine. Their sharply
rounded undersides, by contrast, were densely painted
in shades of blue, yellow, or red. Stout, rising timbers
called *bayungan*, the central beams of the canoes' outrigger booms, were lashed across the gunwales at bow and
stern, and talons of naturally curving wood, called *cedik*,
hooked sharply downward from them, and to their ends
were fixed the long, slender bamboo floats, one on either
side, of the canoes' twin outriggers.

Decorative wooden beaks that resembled the jaws of
a monstrous sea creature gaped from the canoes' bows,

and from their sterns fantastic tails scythed skyward, decorated with rays and flames and the images of bad-ass, gun-toting cult heroes, rampant animal icons, or political demigods.

But it was the eyes that held me: bulging, white-orbed, just behind the canoes' open jaws, their black pupils ringed with red and overarched with undulating brows. The eyes could, I believed, out-stare the challenging sea itself, which the Balinese traditionally fear, but not their destiny, about which their feelings were less than certain.

Encouraged by the presence of canoes on the beach, Ktut Kami inquired at the restaurant whether there was a canoemaker in the village, and we were directed to a small, unwalled compound down the road.

The canoe carver, in marked contrast with Ktut Kami's neatly ironed shirt and belted gray trousers, was bare-chested and wore a faded sarong, the skirt of which was pulled up between his legs and tucked into the waistband beneath his navel, transforming it into a pair of baggy pantaloons. He was painting an eye on the bow of a small canoe in the thin shade of a thorny tree when we drove up, and another man, similarly dressed, with a sparse, gray-streaked beard, assisted him. Diffident at first, if only shy, the canoemaker nevertheless invited us to rest in the shade of his small, thatched *bale*, which was constructed of rough-hewn wood, weathered by exposure to the sun and sea. Another tiny room of low-fired brick stood beside it, the sleeping quarters of the house, whose only other appointment, the kitchen, consisted of an open hearth.

When we had seated ourselves on the woven mat that covered the *bale's* elevated floorboards, the bearded man introduced himself as the village priest and added that he was also a canoemaker. Though he was obviously poor and uneducated by urban standards, Ktut Kami showed him marked deference, for he was of a highborn caste.

Ktut Kami spoke at length with the priest who, unlike his primly formal companion, was affable and relaxed. Eventually, having come to an understanding, punctuated with an exaggerated nodding of their heads, the men turned their attention to me.

"Please excuse me, Mister Dustin Leavitt, what questions would you like to ask this man?" Ktut Kami said, indicating the boat builder, who stiffened, erect and unsmiling, but attentive.

I told Ktut Kami I was interested to know the process involved in the construction of a canoe, how the work was contracted, where the timber came from. When Ktut Kami translated my questions, the men discussed the matter among themselves at length.

"When a fisherman asks him for a new canoe," Ktut Kami began, inclining his head toward the canoemaker, who stared solemnly at a point on the matting midway between us, "he sets a price..." He consulted the canoemaker briefly, who replied in a low voice. "About fifteen dollars American. The fisherman pay him half, he says, and also agrees to help make the canoe. Members of his family help, and sometimes other men from the village."

"Members of the fisherman's family?" I asked.

"Yes, just so. We call this *suka-duka*, Mister Dustin Leavitt, communal work."

I wrote the words in my notebook, the others patiently looking on.

"He then searches the mountains for a good tree,"

Ktut Kami continued when I had finished. "The tree must be big enough and wide enough for the canoe, you see. The canoe is carved from one tree only. Sometimes he must add some wood to the top, but *jukung* is always made from just one tree."

"When he adds wood to the top, does he use wooden pegs like this to hold it on?" I asked, drawing a picture in my notebook of two plank edges butted against each other with a row of round dowels inserted into matching holes between them.

Ktut Kami held the picture up for the canoemaker and the priest to see, and explained its meaning. They pointed at the picture and nodded enthusiastically at me, the canoemaker showing a double row of square, white teeth as his lips parted for the first time in a smile.

"Just so," Ktut Kami assured me, returning the notebook.

"What happens when he finds a suitable tree?"

"When he finds a tree, he must ask the priest when it is a good day to cut."

"Propitious," I said.

"Yes, Mister Dustin Leavitt! He must ask the priest when it is propitious day!" We laughed, and he went on, "Then he performs the cutting ceremony…" I looked in my notebook and provided the Balinese word, *ngebah*, which the shrinemaker had taught me the previous day. "…*ngebah*, to ask the supreme god to protect the canoe. Also to protect himself and his work. He makes an offering, called *sagi*."

"What is *sagi*?"

"*Sagi*…" Ktut Kami consulted once again with the priest and the boat builder. "*Sagi* is different here than in my village, but basically the same. The recipe is rice, coconut, sugar, water, and palm wine...palm wine can be red or white."

"Then what?"

"Then he cuts the tree. Sometimes he makes a cut in the part that is left in the ground..."

"The stump."

"...just so...and he puts a small branch from the tree in the stump. This celebrates the continue of life."

...*celebrates the continuation of life*, I wrote in my notebook, and marked it for special attention. "What happens then?"

"Then he makes the canoe. The fisherman helps him, and sometimes his family. It doesn't take a long time that way. Then he..." indicating the canoemaker, "...returns half of the money the fisherman already paid him, or if the fisherman is poor, maybe he gives all the money back to him. It's strange, yes?"

My face must have revealed my surprise at this unexpected custom, because when Ktut Kami explained it to them, the boat builder smiled and the priest's eyes grew merry. "How does that work?" I asked Ktut Kami.

He had turned his gaze toward Gunung Seraya, a mountain rising in the distance behind us, where rain clouds had begun to build.

"*Suka-duka,*" he replied. "It is the true Balinese way."

As we prepared to leave the boat builder to his work, the priest took Ktut Kami aside and spoke to him briefly. Palms pressed together, I thanked them, and as we drove away down the road, I asked Ktut Kami what the priest had said to him.

"He says the best canoemaker on this coast lives ahead. It is a long way, but we will try to find him. He told me alone because he does not want to give offense to the canoemaker of his village. He is a priest and a wise man."

The road, which had once been sealed but had now fallen into grave disrepair, climbed away from the shoreline and immediately narrowed to a stony, rutted track. This coast was relatively dry, and instead of rice, narrow terraces of beans and peanuts, which did not require irrigation, mounted the slopes above us, and isolated grape vineyards spread their dense shade over the hills below. The Java Sea lay blue and flat, and at its edge I saw a stretch of what I at first took to be pristine sand until, drawing nearer, I made out instead the white hulls of more than a hundred beached canoes. A village of tiny houses with red-tiled roofs, nestled in the shade of big, leafy trees, climbed up the hill from the small bay, and behind it, garden terraces cut into the precipitous red earth ascended and disappeared from view in the heights.

As we stopped the jeep on the verge of the road above the village, a strong, warm wind bore up to us the howls of a pig being slaughtered and the distant "*chak-a-chak-a-chak*" of men practicing the chant of Sugriwa's monkey army, with which Prince Rama battled Rawana, the King of Lanka, who had kidnapped Rama's beloved wife Sita.

Ktut Kami stood rapt. When eventually he spoke, his voice gone soft with unrequited longing, he said, "If I could, I should live here by myself, among the simple people, in a house like that one or that one. Here where it is quiet. This is the real Bali, Mister Dustin Leavitt."

Topping the rise of the headland that marked the southern end of the village's sheltering bay, we immediately found ourselves looking down the other side at yet another bay, another village, and another hundred or more canoes. I walked out along the sharp crest of the headland, looking down on the twin villages, one to my right and the other to my left. Sunlight and shadow slowly shifted across the blue surface of the sea, and out, far out held, as if in suspension, the bright orange sail of an outrigger canoe.

In the late afternoon, we arrived at the remote compound of Wayan Patra, whom the priest had called the best canoemaker on the coast. I was surprised to find him a young man. He was prosperous, tall and strong. Shirtless and dressed in a fresh sarong that clung to his narrow hips, he projected an iconic—even heroic—air. Joined by his younger brother, we sat in the low, green shade of his vineyards, conversing politely, while the canoemaker dandled his naked infant son on his knee. At a distance, among the grapes, his elderly, gray-haired mother, bare-chested in the way of very traditional Balinese women, scolded and flapped a handful of palm fronds in our direction. Unable to understand her, I asked Ktut Kami if she was upset by our presence.

"No," he said uncomfortably, "she is chasing birds from the fruit."

But his tone—and the notable absence of any birds—suggested that I had guessed correctly.

To the progressively minded governments of developing countries, who view them with disdain and embarrassment, canoes symbolize the lingering vestiges of an unwanted backwardness. They are, it is true, the most basic of boats, and they comprise the foundation of the most basic of economies, economies that have persisted at a subsistence level for generations. Which is not to say that they, or the economies they underwrite, are unsophisticated. In the profoundest sense, traditional canoes and the "canoe people" who make and use them are refined as only that which has gradually evolved in subtle compliance with the dictates of specific physical and cultural environments can be.

Nevertheless, as the world fills with people, and as their basic needs, not to mention their burgeoning desires, exponentially escalate, the physical and cultural environments that once supported them inexorably change. Stands of trees appropriate for canoe carving fall to the machinery of timber concerns, or are simply depleted by the canoe people themselves. Near shore fisheries dry up, overexploited by the industrialized fishing industries of neighboring countries that have decimated their own territorial waters. Visions of prosperity unprecedented in village life arrive from abroad and foster discontent and self-loathing among the younger generations.

Rapid adaptation, for which canoe people throughout the world are neither culturally prepared nor materially equipped, becomes for them a priority of the first magnitude, and in the absence of any means by which to achieve it, their sole recourse is to abandon what they have in favor of that which necessity thrusts upon them. It may be argued—and the argument is a valid one—that such changes are inevitable, that change and loss are indivisible, and that human beings possess, in any case, a boundless capacity for adaptation. It may also be argued that it is unwise to heedlessly throw away that which the experience of generations has given us. The capacity for self-reliance, the ability to inhabit marginal environments and to sustain rich lives in the absence of luxury and excess, are skills we may all come to require whether or not they are to our collective taste. More to the point, they are skills that are deceptively difficult to reinvent, and that may be lost through the neglect of a single generation.

The plight of canoe people nevertheless implicates us in a complex dilemma, which is further confused by the aspirations of the canoe people themselves. Many, if not most of them, have no desire to deny themselves the temptations thrust before them by the example of the industrialized world. Prosperity, in whatever form, is almost universally considered a cultural virtue. The luxury of hindsight afforded to those of us who have overindulged it, to our own chagrin, may entice us to compound our foolishness by attempting to dictate how best the canoe people may be served. However, although our own experience is undeniably meaningful, the lessons of the canoe people are not for them, who are the masters, but for us.

That evening, I walked with Ktut Kami along the shoreline of Tanjung Benoa. In a low, orange light, dozens of boats sprawled on the sand, most of them derelicts. Across the harbor, big freighters lay to the commercial docks, and in the roads modern fishing boats from Taiwan, which were relentlessly replacing the fishing canoes that had once launched from this very beach, rode at anchor.

Ktut Kami had invited me to share a "real Balinese meal" with him in his house, and later, as we consumed the meager fried fish, purchased in the marketplace with the money I had paid him, the rice and bananas and bottles of warm Coca-Cola, he spoke of the hopes he held for his younger son, who had recently married a girl of fourteen, and of his disappointment in his elder son, who was yet unmarried.

"He is making good money," he said of the older boy,

who worked as an automobile mechanic in Nusa Dua. "But he does not live at home, and he does not support his father, as he should. We do not agree about this."

He looked at me strangely. "I have no money, Mister Dustin Leavitt. I am old. What will I do?"

A sober melancholy, which had taken possession of him when Wayan Patra's old mother, "chasing birds from the fruit," shooed us from their house, had put my translator in a confessional mood. He spoke in a wandering way of his life and its trials. I was surprised to learn that his father had been a canoemaker, but that he himself had not learned the trade. He had been ambitious, he said, and had held out for the greater rewards the modern world had seemed to guarantee. Now, he worked—when he could find work, he added bitterly—as a tourist guide, showing people from other lands the shrinking vestiges of "the real Bali."

It dawned on me that he was a poor and disappointed man, and my heart broke for him, I who with the change in my pockets might have fed his growing family for a week. "What will I do?" he had pled. I thought of the canoe builder Wayan Patra's naked baby gurgling on his knee. I had no answers for him, either.

We must each make our own way to the best of our ability, and help each other when need arises, but first we must open our eyes, must plainly see what we have become. If we are capable of creating problems for ourselves or for others, then we are equally capable of correcting them. The great wheel of cause and effect grinds slowly round, its circumference unbroken by beginning or end. It turns and turns. And it is in this alone that we may discover the possibility of going on.

❧ ❧ ❧

Dustin W. Leavitt contributes articles and essays on a variety of subjects to books and periodicals. Much of his travel writing revisits Asia and the Pacific, where he has lived, worked, and wandered at various times in his life. He currently teaches at the University of Redlands, near Los Angeles.

❧ ❧ ❧

Spanish Art

Even a lousy job is not without rewards.

I PLACE THE RED *CARPETA* FILLED WITH TWENTY 60" x 40" oil paintings against the metal gate. Then I ring the doorbell.

"*Si?*" says the voice through the intercom.

"*Hola, buenas noches. Soy estudiante del Arte. Tengo pinturos de olio sobra tela. ¿Dos minutos para mirar?*"

The voice asks again: "*¿Que?*"

I clear my throat: "*Hola, buenas noches. Soy estudiante del Arte. Tengo pinturos de olio sobra tela. ¿Dos minutos para mirar?*"

The curtain from the front window reveals an old woman in a tattered blue robe, holding the front clasps of the cotton material together. She sees me from behind her gate, waving with one hand, smiling as if posing for a family picture. Then I lean forward and pull out a painting of the Eiffel tower, fore-grounded with tables spread across a cobblestone street, French people sipping coffee. When she realizes I am trying to sell her something, she waves her head from side to side, pressing her lips together as if they are chapped. She closes the curtain suddenly, disappearing into the living room.

As I pick up the *carpeta*, the duct tape-covered handle digging into the blisters on my hand, I take a breath of Spanish air. An aroma of ham with garlic potatoes and fresh bread fills my nostrils. I lick my lips as I imagine the savory meat.

I am hungry. I am cold. And it seems like it has been forever that I have been walking the suburbs of Madrid selling oil paintings with Eyal and his Israeli team. Two months ago, I answered an internet ad that said: "Are you young? In your early twenties? Want to live in Spain? We have the perfect job for you! No experience necessary." I had been living in Guam, teaching wind-surfing at a five-star resort; then in Southern China, teaching English on an academic scholarship. I loved the lifestyle of living overseas and had expected my "European adventure" to be just as fulfilling.

I arrived at the Barajas International Airport with a six-month roundtrip ticket from Chicago to Madrid, a passport, a backpack, and a small suitcase. I carried with me just a few items of clothing, a handful of English books and $500. I imagined myself selling artwork from a store, learning Spanish with ease, country-hopping by train, laughing in cafés while sipping espresso in tiny cups. Before I left, my parents said, "You are not really going. Nobody moves to a country where they don't speak the language." Then I showed them the receipt for my airplane ticket, taking great pride that I was about to do what "nobody" ever does. Now that I stand here, outside a stranger's home, trying to sell an overpriced, knock-off painting, I start to realize the legitimacy of their concerns.

First of all, I have grown skeptical of the door-to-door Israeli art selling business. In the morning, we sell to small businesses, *bancos*, *farmacias*, *panaderias*, and at night we sell in middle-class neighborhoods. We visit middle-class homes, believing that the poor cannot afford our paintings and the rich would rather go to a gallery to buy artwork. Eyal drops us off at a starting point in a rented white van with no patterns or designs along the side, briefing us beforehand on an area to cover. He drops us off far from one another to ensure that we do not accidentally visit the same place. According to Eyal, the paintings sold at 75 to 100 euros "are affordable. Spaniards love art. Trust me. You will make a lot of money." Our wages are based on 100 percent commission, which means I only make a profit if I sell a painting over 50 euros. If after two shifts of five hours, I sell one painting for 50 euros, I make no profit for that day.

To add to this, my salesman-Spanish is limited to the phrases Eyal taught me the day I had arrived: "Hello, good evening. I am a student of art. I have oil paintings on canvas. Do you have two minutes to look at them?" I don't know how to say, "Where is the bathroom?" but I can recite a list of art related descriptions: *boragon* (still life), *paisaje* (landscape), *cocos de fibre* (coconut fibers), *Michelangelo* (Michelangelo), *tres diferentes texturas* (three different textures), *solo setenta-cinco euros* (only 75 euros). Although I claim that the paintings are "originals," Eyal replaces the sold painting with an exact duplicate. One time, I walked into a graphics design office, startled to find the painting in my *carpeta,* a colorful *boragon* of a bowl of fruit, framed and hung against the wall. When the secretary asked me if she could help me, or what I assumed from her smile and open hand, I responded "*No gracias,*" excusing myself as quickly as I could from the building.

One evening, while walking through a neighborhood with high metal gates, a police car drove steadily next to me. I tried speeding up, assuming that they were on their way to a gathering of teenagers one block ahead. But after a few steps, the Spanish cops got out of the car, pistols loaded, and asked me: "What are you doing with that *carpeta?* Show me your *pasaporte.*" I pretended, which was not difficult, that I did not understand what they wanted. "These are *my* paintings," I said in English, "*I* am a student of art." After lecturing me at length with Spanish words that I did not understand, they eventually left, nodding their heads from side to side. Since then, filled with the fear of being identified, I have stopped carrying my passport during my shifts.

I walk towards the next house, leaning my weight to one side to counterbalance the heaviness of the *carpeta.* A snowflake falls from the sky, landing on my black peacoat—fading from white into a small drop of moisture. I look towards the blackened sky as a mass of white flakes float down. Single dots of whiteness land delicately onto my skin, melting into the corner of my eyes like cold tears.

Although my body craves rest, I don't envision a healthy night's sleep. At night, I lay on a bare mattress in the common room of an apartment that houses twelve other people. Most of my roommates are young

Israeli men, fresh out of completing their country's two-year military service. Eyal, their troop leader, had convinced them to move to Madrid to make some extra money. They care very little about Spanish culture, often saying: "the only reason we are in business is because Spanish people are stupid." When dinner has been eaten, the Hebrew movie turned off, the hashish smoked, I flip down the thin mattress on top of the peeling linoleum, curling up to sleep using my backpack as a pillow, my coat as a blanket. The smell of hashish lingers on my clothing and in my hair.

Tonight the weather pushes my tolerance. Normally, I would ring more bells before I found sanctuary in a café, losing myself in the novel I keep hidden inside my purse. But my fingers ache with stiffness, and the houses seem less friendly in this poorly-lit neighborhood. I look at my watch. Only four hours and forty-five minutes until the white van scoops me up. The snow floats down onto the empty street, dissolving into the wet cement.

Pulling my black hood over my head, I attempt to block the air from chilling my body. As I look around the neighborhood, I notice that there is something different about this neighborhood than the ones Eyal has dropped me off in. The street lights seem dimmed. There aren't as many cars parked along the sidewalk. Where are the people who normally walk their dogs at night? Where are the children returning home for dinner from a friend's house? Along the gate of a house with no front light, the grass tangles around the metal bars. In most Spanish homes I have seen, the yards well-manicured. But this house looks ominous, the long strands of grass neglected by the current tenants.

Walking down the damp streets, passing the unrung doorbells of possible clients, I search for a sign of light to indicate a place I could warm my body. Besides the dim street lights, the only lights I see shine through closed curtains. When I turn the corner, I notice a small neon sign lit up in orange. It doesn't say cafeteria, but it looks like a place a stranger could find shelter. When I get closer, I see a convenience store—the only commercial space for blocks, built into the first floor of a living complex.

Standing in front of the store's glass windows, the fluorescent lights allure me with their warmth. The moon overhead is a sliver of gray. The snow begins to cascade more rapidly. I open the glass door and hot air layers my skin. When my eyes adjust to the light, I study the small space. It could pass for a quaint living room. The four narrow aisles overflow with fresh bread, colorful rolls of cookies, cans of soup, jars of Spanish olives, magazines, children's toys, large plastic containers of biscuits and grains. I shake the snow from off my coat, walking towards the cookie aisle in the middle of the store. While I pretend to read the labels on a box, I eye the two people standing in the store. A woman behind the counter speaks with much energy to a customer in Spanish. She hands him a bag of eggs.

The man leaves with a plastic bag of groceries, saying, "Have a good night." As the front door of the store swings open, a draft of air circles the shop. I study the cookies more intently, crinkling the wrappers in my hands, making it obvious that I have plans to purchase an item.

Then the woman behind the counter interrupts the silence. "Can I help you?" she asks in English.

I look up from the package, surprised by the English words. A woman with dark brown hair and emerald green eyes peers back at me.

"You're not from around here," she adds.

"No," I answer, "I am American."

"A student?"

I shift my weight to one side, contemplating whether or not to tell her I am student of art. I answer, "Not quite."

"If you like you can put that thing over here." She points at the large red envelope I balance awkwardly under my right arm. "I promise nobody will take it."

In my hands, I hold twenty paintings at 50 euros each. If somebody takes them, I will owe Eyal 1,000 Euros. I have already thought of what would happen if I lost my *carpeta*. I would disappear into the Spanish landscape to a city on the southern coast—a fugitive running from the Israeli Army. I feel the soreness in my arm, the blisters in my hand, and decide that this is not the time to be scared. I'll put the paintings down but keep a close eye on them. I lean the *carpeta* against the counter.

"Much better," she comments.

I massage the palms of my hands, red and blotchy, numb from the cold air. "Thank you," I answer.

"I know whenever somebody new comes into my store. Colmenar Viejo is so very small."

Colmenar Viejo. So that is where I am. I wonder how far Colmenar Veijo is from Madrid.

"One time, last year," she continues, "a Canadian girl came in. She was a student staying with a family out here. I could tell right away that she was not Spanish."

Aware of my foreign appearance, I ask jokingly, "How did you know I am not Spanish?"

She laughs, noticing my shoulder-length black hair, oval eyes, long black coat, and unSpanish jeans. "You look Asian…maybe Japanese?"

"My parents are from Hong Kong," I respond, "but I was born in the United States."

"Chinese," she laughs. "We definitely don't see many Chinese people in Colmenar Viejo." When her eyes sparkle when she smiles, it dawns on me that this is the first time I have spoken to a Spanish person about something other then oil paintings.

"How long have you been in Spain?" she asks.

"Just two weeks."

"How do you like it so far?"

I picture the small businesses in the suburbs, the unfamiliar neighborhoods I have roamed off at and answer, "I haven't really seen much of Spain."

"Ahh, I know where you need to go." She takes out a scrap piece of paper from under the counter, a pen from a cup near the cash register and draws an outline of Spain. "You need to go here." She points her pen at the northwest region of Spain above Portugal. "This is where I am from. Galicia. It is the most beautiful part of Spain."

I lean my elbows against counter, studying the small doodle of a heart-shaped drawing that is roughly the shape of Spain.

She holds out her hand. "My name is Nila. What is yours?"

I reach across the counter, across the barrier between strangers, shaking her hand. "My name is Chellis. Nice to meet you."

Nila offers me a package of cookies of my choice, and I fill my body with sweetness and warmth. Almost immediately, I confess to her that the real reason I am in Colmenar Viejo is because I am a door-to-door salesman. But a very bad one. On a good day I sell one painting in ten hours. I spend more time in coffee shops reading a book than I do ringing doorbells. Then I tell her that this is not my real job. A month ago, I had applied to MFA programs in writing and while waiting for their response, I moved to Spain. She tells me that she went to school in the arts as well—in embroidery. She can make carpets, tablecloths, handkerchiefs, and tapestries. She tells me about life back in Galicia, about oil spills that ruin the beaches. She tells me about Spain's Arab ancestry, which is the reason why Spanish women, like her, have dark hair and green eyes. She likes to travel, too. Three years ago, she went on a week-long hike by herself, leaving her husband and son at home, traveling along the path of Saint Santiago.

As the snow continues to fall from the night sky, as customers come in intermittently to buy fruit or bread, we talk until it is time to close the shop.

Nila begins to organize the shelves, counting the cash in the register. I wander the shop, looking at a picture of Julia Roberts on the cover of a Spanish magazine, savoring the last moments of warmth before I leave.

"What will you do while I close the shop?" Nila asks, wiping down the counter with a cloth.

"I have an hour until Eyal picks me up." I look at my *carpeta*, leaning against the counter, the front flap of the folder flopping open. I dread the thought of ringing doorbells, the falling snow, the recitation of the Spanish mantra. But I say, "I'll just continue selling paintings."

She looks at me with wide eyes—the greenness like jewels. "No, I insist, if you are not too uncomfortable, to

join me at my house for dinner. My house is small, and
it is messy, but I have some food if you are hungry. Have
you tried *jamon Serrano* or Spanish wine?"

I don't hesitate with my answer: "That would be
great." I have peered inside many Spanish homes, even
walked into one while trying to make a sale, but otherwise I have never been inside one. While Nila packs up
her stuff, I think that in a typical situation this could be
dangerous: going home with a woman I have just met
in an unfamiliar, suspiciously dark neighborhood. I hear
my mother's voice in my head: "Never trust a person
who is being nice to you. You never know what they
may want."

"Are you ready?" asks Nila, carrying a box of food
with bread and fruit. "This is for my mother. She lives
down the street. She always calls me to bring her leftover
food."

"Yes, I am ready," I say, nodding, balancing my *carpeta* under my arm. As we leave the store, a chill runs
through my body. Although it has been snowing for
three hours, none of the snow has collected along the
sidewalk. When it reaches the cement, it dissolves almost
immediately, as if a mere figment of my imagination.

"My car is right here," she points, then laughs. "Hold
on. It's very messy." Pulling out a broken piece of furniture from the passenger seat, she shoves it into the
backseat. "I like to repair tables." She moves some dirt-
smeared cloths the car floor and adds: "My son was just
at the park and his shoes were dirty." Then she opens
the trunk and says: "You can put your *carpeta* in here."
The space crammed with boxes, books, old clothes has
just a tiny opening for my *carpeta*. A car with bright
headlights passes on the road. As the two narrow beams

of light shine directly into my eyes, I begin to have my doubts that I should follow this strange woman into her home.

"Chellis?" Nila interrupts. "Your *carpeta*?" She reaches out her hand to help me, the same hand I had shaken just three hours ago. I look at her milky white hand with slender fingers, a dark mole on the top of her skin, and remember my mother's words: "Never trust a person who is being nice to you. You never know what they may want."

I look down the dark road; the neighborhood seems colder, even darker then what I had remembered just three hours before. I was once invited into a Spanish home during a night shift, by a person I could not even see. All I heard were a few sentences in Spanish over the intercom and the sound of his gate buzzing to let me in. Certainly, going to Nila's house would be safer than walking into a complete stranger's home. I help Nila cram the *carpeta* into the small space. She slams the trunk shut and adds, "See, a perfect fit."

After I settle into the passenger seat, rubbing my hands together for warmth, Nila turns on the car and the heater blasts with warm air. I do not know if it is from the weather or from the way Europeans drive, but when Nila zips through the neighborhood twisting and turning down the narrow, curvy road, I tighten my grip along the handle of the car door. Holding on in this way is the only way I can prevent my head from knocking against the window. We enter an unfamiliar part of the village. Then she stops along the side of the road in a sudden screech, as I relax my body into my seat. The snow continues to fall from the sky, disappearing onto the hood of the car.

"I need to drop off this box of food for my mother," Nila explains. I unfasten my seat belt as she stops me, "No, don't worry. I'll be back shortly." She leaves the car, opening the trunk to take out the box. Then she slams the trunk shut, shaking the entire car, leaving me in complete silence. I tuck my legs into my chest, resting my chin against my knee, listening to the beating of my heart. The windows begin to fog up, making the evening's scenery hazier, more ambiguous. This is what it would be like if I were sitting in nothingness, a black hole, a windowless room where my eyes never learn to adjust. I am an anonymous person with no place to go, no money, no form of identification. Even if I were to leave this car right now, grab my *carpeta* and walk down the street, I don't know where to go. Nila drove for five minutes, twisting and turning down streets I have never seen. I could retrace my steps to the pick-up point but I would have no idea if I were going in the right direction. There are no taxis passing along this road at this hour, in this obscure neighborhood, in this Spanish village. But even if there is one taxi that happens to come along this road, I don't have the street name of the place I am supposed to be picked up by Eyal in one hour. I could always go back to Eyal's apartment in Alcobendas. But it took us an hour in the white van on the freeway from Alcobendes to Colmenar. A cab ride back to Eyal's place would cost me 60 to 100 euros. Let's just say a cab happens to drive by at this exact moment, on this exact street, in this obscure neighborhood; let's just say, I happen to have 60 to 100 euros; let's just say, I happen to get a taxi driver to take me all the way to Alcobendas, I don't have the street address to Eyal's apartment. I would be circling the suburb of Alcobendas at midnight, looking for a familiar landmark, for a white apartment tucked in a narrow alleyway on the second floor.

Nila opens the car door as I jump up, bumping my knee against the glove compartment—my heart racing.

"Sorry that took me so long," she says, turning on the car. "Are you hungry?"

With short breaths, my hand pressed against my chest, I answer: "Actually, I am."

She speeds off down the road, twisting through narrow streets, up and down hills, through a village that looks quaint, even in this darkness. She parks the car along the sidewalk in front of a line of connected houses, across from an automobile factory. "Here we are," she announces, turning off the ignition. "Don't worry about the *carpeta* in the car. I'll drop you off when it is time to go."

We walk towards a gate, past doorbells that I should be ringing. As she unlocks the gate with a key, I think that this is not a line I often cross—the one between the gate and the customer's home. I have seen so many houses through gates like this one, picturing what the people inside are eating for dinner, picturing the kind of artwork that hangs on their walls, picturing the feel of clean sheets that they tuck in to sleep at night.

"Well, come on, Chellis," pleads Nila, "do not be shy."

I follow her past the gate, down the short walkway and into her home. When she shuts the front door, a tall balding man with a friendly grin walks into the hallway. Nila leans forward and gives him a kiss on the lips.

"Chellis, meet my husband Juan. He's an animal doctor." Juan looks at me with a peculiar look as Nila turns to him and explains something rapidly in Spanish. A little boy with rosy cheeks comes barreling down the stairs.

"And this is my son Iago." She leans down and gives him a peck on the cheek. "He is ten years old this year." She turns to Iago and explains more things in rapid Spanish. This triggers him to step towards me, shake my hand and utter in a soft voice: "*Hola*, Chellis."

I spend the next hour engulfed in Nila's home, surrounded by the furniture and tapestries hand-embroidered by Nila. She takes me for a tour of her three-story home, pointing out the tiles she had picked herself, the view from her top balcony, pictures of Iago as a baby. We sit down to a meal of Spanish cheese, *jamon Serrano*, white asparagus, sampling Spanish wine until my face flushes red. I teach Iago how to say my name in Chinese: "Ying Sang-Fun," which he says perfectly in the correct tones, repeating my name every five or ten minutes while the three of us roar with laughter. I listen to Juan explain in his limited English his line of work: "I like sheep. I like sheep very very much." Nila explains to me that he is one of Spain's best sheep doctors. She tells me a story about how when she was my age she lived in England as an au pair, which is why she can speak English. She has never been to the United States but she would like to if she had the chance. When it is nearly 10, I say my good-byes to Iago and Juan as Nila and I leave her home, returning to her small, over-packed car. While driving me to Eyal's pick up point, she is in the middle of a story about a Spanish festival that only happens in the spring.

"Turn here," I direct, interrupting Nila's story—passing her unlit store where we first met just hours before. When we reach the empty corner, she pulls to the side of the road and turns off her car. We sit in her two-door car, our breaths fogging the cold windows.

She continues: "So, you must go to Segovia. It is only an hour's drive from here. Segovia is famous for their tall Roman archways, called *acueductos* that were once used to carry mountain water to the city. The stones fit perfectly together like a puzzle piece," she puts one hand on top of the other stacking imaginary bricks, "there is no cement to hold the stones together."

"How high are they?" I ask.

"Oh, very tall. Taller than most buildings. You can drive under them. They are very very amazing."

In the distance, I see two bright headlights. When the lights face the side, I recognize Eyal's, white van. The van stops at the corner—right on time: 10:00 P.M. A puff of smoke gathers behind the exhaust pipe.

"Nila, that's my ride."

"Oh, already?" She digs her hands into her armpits, warming them for heat. "Well, let's get your *carpeta* out of the car."

We get out of the car, prying the *carpeta* from the trunk. I tuck the large red envelope of paintings against my side—feeling the familiar weight in my arms. Nila leans forward and gives me a hug, which I return with my one free arm.

Pressing her hands into her coat pocket, she says: "Chellis, I had such a wonderful evening talking to you. I wish you all the luck in Spain. If you need anything, a place to stay, questions on Spanish culture, please call me." She hands me a slip of paper with two numbers—one for her home and one for the shop. It is the same scrap piece of paper with the drawing of Spain and Galicia mapped out.

I smile back to her and say: "Thank you so much for tonight Nila. I promise you that I'll call you when I am more settled in." I want to thank her for introducing me to her family, trusting me inside her home. But I hold my tongue unable to express the words in an articulate way. I walk towards the van, waving to her over my shoulder. She waves back with one hand, the other in her pocket, shivering as the snow melts into her dark hair.

Eyal opens the doors to the van's back door. He heaves my *carpeta* on top of a stack of other *carpetas*. He asks: "So did you sell any paintings tonight?"

My cheeks turn warm, maybe from the wine, maybe from the fact that I had barely opened my *carpeta,* and I smile. "No, I didn't sell any paintings tonight. But I had the best shift of my life." I turn to Eyal while he is closing the van's door and ask him: "Have you ever tasted Spanish ham?"

The first time I had *jamon Serrano* was in Nila's home that snowy night working for Eyal, selling oil paintings. The next time I did was five months later in the same place with Juan, Iago, Nila, and my parents. My mother always said, "Never trust a person who is being nice to you. You never know what they may want." She sat at Nila's table laughing over a meal of grilled eggplant with olive oil, baked *pescado* with garlic, fresh bread with Spanish cheese and *jamon Serrano*. Nila explained to her the origins of Catholicism, the birth of Jesus Christ, the history of gothic architecture, how to make homemade butter. At that time, my mother turned to me and asked: "Chellis, how do you know Nila?" Nila and I made eye contact—her emerald eyes locking into mine—and I answered: "Mom, I met her through work. Remember when I told you that I was once an art dealer?" I looked back at Nila, who chuckled underneath her breath. "I

tried to show her an oil painting, but instead she showed
me Spain."

≫ ≫ ≫

*Chellis Ying is studying for an MFA in writing at the University
of San Francisco and a big fan of the* Iron Chef. *She has traveled
to China, South Korea, Japan, Thailand, Malaysia, Singapore,
Guam, Saipan, and various European countries. She lives in San
Francisco.*

JANE MARSHALL

❧   ❧   ❧

Trigger Happy in Cambodia

The shadow of evil reaches into the present.

COILS OF BARBED WIRE UPON CONCRETE WALLS
surrounded the compound, though the guards
who had once flanked its perimeter were now only ghosts
and shadows. The woman who asked me for money in
broken English and the pamphlets and books that she
sold looked gaudy and out of place, even disrespectful
considering their home. I was inside Security-21, a school
turned torture chamber, and now a tourist attraction for
those with strong stomachs. My eyes fell upon a building
and my legs carried me to it. From the outside it was a
typical school building, long, two-storied with numerous
small rooms, but as I looked inside I saw what no children should see. The rectangular room held nothing but
a metal bed frame with unknown devices strewn along
its springs, and a photograph strung up on the wall. The

picture described what the room no longer could; a man lay on the same bed with shackles on his arms and legs, his fat and muscle eaten by time and grief. His hair was thin and dirty and his eyes...my eyes fell to the floor for reprieve but they were met with decades-old bloodstains and I backed away. This was the interrogation building.

I grew up in Canada in a comfortable home, without threat of war, free from the fear of having my body explode from land-mine contact, and far removed from threats such as the Pol Pot regime, an extreme communist movement that was responsible for some 2 million deaths in less than five years. I did not have to worry about being arrested and executed in a place like S-21. Before entering Cambodia I had spent months sunning myself on Thailand's beaches, thinking of nothing more challenging than accidentally ordering squid rather than chicken for my lunch by the sea. From Thailand, Cambodia sounded intriguing, like tough travel. I knew nothing. My understanding of Cambodia encompassed little more than the vague knowledge of land mines, and that Phnom Penh, the capital city, was fairly dangerous. Who put those nasty land mines in the fields? I could not have told you. And I could not understand why my hands would shake at the end of each day I spent there, as I washed my supper of rice down with Angkor beer, or why I felt dizzy each morning when I opened my eyes and found myself looking through the guesthouse's barred window in downtown Phnom Penh. We knew that place was risky, yet it was so easy to get our visas.

Luckily my feelings of unease did not inhibit me from exploring the city, despite the guesthouse clerk who warned us, "No walk at night. You take cab to restaurant and bar, take cab home. I sleep here, let you in."

And he did. He slept inside the iron bars that held out beggars and other unwanteds on a dirty little couch or the floor with his body curled in a position that made his bony knees flare out and accentuated his joints. We woke him each night to get into the guesthouse and he never seemed to mind. One morning, I convinced my friend Krystyna to explore S-21, or Tuol Sleng, the war museum. How else was I going to learn to feel comfortable, to feel less like an ignorant idiot, blind to why Phnom Penh was so poor and sad? I ached to know why so many beggars were picking through the remains of the market that was set up each night behind our guesthouse, eating rotting litchi and crushed bananas, and why when friends in the street stopped laughing together their eyes would cloud over and their faces would close. So we set off.

Without thinking, I approached another tourist who stood behind me at S-21's interrogation room.

"Are photographs allowed?" I inquired. She looked at me with disgusted, judgmental eyes and answered my question without words. She was crying. Quickly, I left the interrogation wing and moved on to the next building to escape her and the image she held of me: a disrespectful tourist with a fetish for gore. She did not know that I was just stupid.

A feeling of displacement washed over me as I walked to the next building where the long-term prisoners had been held. The day was bright and hot, but the aura was dark. Clouds should have been casting shadows and brimming with drops that needed to spill, but instead the hot Cambodian sun blazed hard on the concrete schoolyard and scorched the shadows that lurked in my imagination. The only reprieve was under the palm fronds that lined the compound, or in the deteriorating buildings.

A sign of scrolling Cambodian script that was translated into English was posted to remind prisoners of the rules:

1. Do not be a fool for you are a chap who dares to thwart the revolution.
2. You must immediately answer my questions without wasting time to reflect.
3. While getting lashes or electrification you must not cry at all.

If you do not follow all of the above rules, you shall get many lashes of electric wire.

This holding section was identical to the interrogation building but was filled with brick cells that measured less than two square meters. People lived here, sometimes for months, with their legs shackled to iron bars as though the tiny cell was not confining enough. They reminded me of kennels, but with the constant recognition of school floor tiles, those ones from the 1940s and 1950s that look like grocery store floors, and I could not forget reality. Humans were held here. The museum's pamphlet explained that iron buckets or empty ammunition containers were placed in each cage for defecation and urination. Imagine feeling the urgency of a certain pressure on the bladder and then being forced to ask permission before relieving it. They could not move their bowels without asking or they would be beaten severely. What would I do if I had no control over my own bodily functions? Would I still feel human?

Krystyna looked dazed and I knew it was not from the heat. "Let's keep moving," she whispered.

In the third building, faces, some almost smiling, others trampled and emaciated, stared at us from the walls. Back in the late 1970s the prison guards had taken pictures of each prisoner at S-21. They took accurate records—photographs, interviews, documents—the process was calculated. I walked in slow circles, drawn sporadically to the hundreds of faces that were beaten and banished from this world, women with shiny brown eyes, children with tousled hair, men lying on the ground half dead, all crystallized in time. We quickly left and their eyes followed.

From the second story I looked through barbed wire into the compound. Though now rusting, it was strung meticulously across the balcony to prevent prisoners from jumping to their deaths. I imagined watching soldiers in the compound and seeing the children who had been trained to torture. Apparently their young age at training allowed them to achieve what was beyond the cruel ability of the adults. Playground equipment was set up in the center and used to hang prisoners upside-down while their faces were forced into containers of excrement. Childhood had a different meaning and I tried to block out mine because it made me feel guilty.

Pol Pot, the general of the communist Khmer Rouge movement that was responsible for approximately 2 million deaths between 1975 and 1979, was a name I had never heard before. Since my return from Cambodia I have learned that his army trained children to torture and murder Cambodians. If they did not follow orders, their short lives would be ended. Over twenty thousand humans were tortured at S-21 in the name of the Khmer Rouge revolution. How does a country move beyond such a past when over two-thirds of its people suffer from post-traumatic stress syndrome? Many of its citizens had to choose plastic arms and legs from storerooms in Thai refugee camps because the Khmer Rouge had hacked theirs off. Looking back I hope I can understand why Cambodia seemed edgy and dark, even on its sunny days, and why there were so many begging on the streets and picking through the trash because of their loss of land, livelihood, and appendages.

The next image to fill my view was a photograph of a woman. She was seated with her back against some kind of machine and its metallic arms reached out to her temples. She had beautiful long black hair, though matted and dirty, but her eyes held nothing in them. The sockets dared not look down, because worse than torture is the torture of loved ones. Her baby rested on her lap. The machine was designed to send powerful electrical impulses through the body, to punish those who would not talk or opposed the Khmer Rouge revolution. This last building was filled with artifacts of torture and paintings that depicted the methods used. I will never forget the last painting I saw before leaving the building, and I understood why my boyfriend Mike had decided not to come to this place.

A painting hung near the exit door and when I saw it I laughed out loud. It felt similar to having the urge to laugh at a funeral, when the mind takes a break from reality and tries to find some reprieve. Through the sun that streaked in the open door I saw soldiers with bayonettes, poised upwards to the sky, ready to take aim at their target. They were in a forest, and women were poised on the verge of...I do not know what. I cannot imagine what they were thinking. Their babies had been ripped from their arms and the soldiers were throwing them high into the air and shooting them. They were shooting babies. How can a mother survive? I guess those ones did not.

Krystyna looked at the painting briefly and we left the compound, hopped on a moped, and watched in awe as images skittered across the available space left in our minds. People sold rice from their stands, drove by in Mercedes, begged with arms or stumps, and tried to sell us Pomellos when we reached red lights. They all seemed different to me now.

After a cold shower and some water we went for dinner with Mike and his friend Dan and found a restaurant that was brimming with people, their drunken joyous faces bubbling with laughter and their cheeks plump with rice. The contrast of this exuberant group to my mood was welcome, and we sat at a large plastic table in some bright red chairs and ordered beer. Mike and Dan's experience revealed Cambodia's bizarre transition from past to present. They had found a shooting ground and paid $20 (American currency of course) to fire thirty rounds of ammunition from a machine gun.

Apparently the building was a large brick bunker with a standard patio door entrance. Sitting on one side of the door was a large pot filled with local flowers, and inside was a large cushion for resting on while releasing bullets.

"The guy held my shoulder from behind, and I unloaded thirty rounds from an AK-47!" Mike exclaimed. "It happens so fast, all of a sudden thirty rounds are gone from the gun. You can shoot that in less than two seconds."

Danny laughed and said, "Yeah, and guess what else you can do there? You can have a live chicken for a target! Not only that, but for $200 they let a cow out into the field and you can blow it up with a rocket launcher."

I was laughing hard by this point. "Who in the hell would want to blow up a cow?" I asked.

"Oh, I think it would be cool," Danny replied. And with that I realized how Cambodia is going to come out of its slump. With its lack of rules and the ability to let imaginative tourists spend hoards of money to try their hands at destruction, Cambodia will make money and begin to rebuild itself. The average yearly income in Cambodia is approximately $230 U.S., so to let a "rich" foreigner pay 87 percent of an annual income for kicks seems like a good way to make money. I had to admit, there was a certain appeal to Mike and Dan's story, and I wondered what it would feel like as I spat out the bullets at top speed from a cold, heavy machine. So why not provide tourists with thrills that they cannot find in Canada or America? Who has ever heard of going to a carnival and paying to shoot a live chicken? If you hit it, would you win a stuffed animal?

One morning in Siem Reap, a small town in Cambodia, Krystyna, Mike, and I walked to a local outdoor food stand for breakfast. We ordered the standard breakfast food of fried rice and stared at the river. It sounds lovely, but the river was brimming with bits of colorful refuse. As we ate under the canopy, four boys aged four to eight walked toward us and stopped at the edge of the shade. They were homeless children, covered in dirt, dressed in bright mismatched cotton clothes and holding plastic bags. The store owners did not seem to be upset when the boys held the bags to their mouths and began to sniff the fumes inside. My fork stopped on its way to my mouth and I stared as they got high from the glue. They wanted our attention, and one boy stared at me with his round brown eyes that had now clouded over, the spirit within them on a distant planet where hunger could not affect it. I was disgusted. They stood with their heads falling backwards and their mouths hanging open, so high they could not speak, and in a moment I hated them. I hated that a four-year-old needed to huff glue, and that the restaurant owners did not seem to care. I could not eat. I hated them and loved them at the same time; part of me wanted to hold them and scrub them clean of all the dirtiness that surrounded them, and the other part wanted to yell at them and kick them out of my perception of reality. As we left, they came at us and begged for money, which we did not give them, and then they finished our food, grabbing handfuls of the rice and shoving it into their mouths before the restaurant owners could throw them out. They were starving; I felt empty, too.

Cambodia surprised and frightened me. Before 1975 it was a growing, productive, prosperous country like Canada, but four years of communist terror shook its foundations to the core. Chickens snacked on people's corpses and pregnant women were speared with bayonets, all in the name of a cause. Today, Cambodia's people are still recovering from the horror they witnessed and are picking up their lives. The remnants, the limbless beggars who cannot work, the children sniffing glue, and the rampant rise of prostitution fueled by tourists are offset by the sparks of hope seen in busy restaurants and the vendors working to sell their wares. I saw things I did not know were real in this world, or possible, and I saw how humans cope and move on.

Back home in Canada, I remember how lucky I am to be able to sleep in a bed without the fear of a soldier coming to the door to steal me away, but I also remember that life can so easily change.

≈ ≈ ≈

Jane Marshall is a graduate of the University of Alberta with a major in English. She lives in Alberta, Canada, with her husband and young son.

MARK HAWTHORNE

❧ ❧ ❧

Peak Experience

The author gets a taste of enlightenment.

FROM THE BASE OF THE HILL, IT LOOKED LIKE A long climb. I had been in Ladakh, high in the Himalayas of India, for a month when I finally visited Tsemo Gompa, a tiny, fifteenth-century monastery on Namgyal Peak overlooking Leh. "Go to the *gompa* today," Yangchen, my Ladakhi landlady, had told me. "It is an easy walk."

Once part of Tibet's westernmost region, Ladakh has maintained a close relationship with its neighbor. Since 1950, when Chinese Communists invaded Tibet and outlawed most religion, Ladakh has become one of the world's last strongholds for Tibetan Buddhism. To see Ladakh is to see what Tibet once was—a Himalayan wonderland where Tibetan Buddhism permeates every aspect of life.

The path to the *gompa* was a dusty, rocky trail that countless visitors had formed for the likes of me to climb, and halfway up the hill I took a moment to enjoy the view. The city of Leh, Ladakh's capital and once part of the Silk Route, spread out from the ancient palace to a narrow ribbon of highway, with dozens of low, flat-roofed buildings in between. Barley fields in neat, asymmetrical shapes carpeted the valley floor. Punctuating the landscape were Buddhist *chortens*, their whiteness a stark contrast to the surrounding earth tones. Looking like giant chess pieces set against the barren mountain scenery, the *chortens* each house a Buddhist relic and are believed to have been first built during Emperor Ashoka's reign 200 years before Christ. As I sat on a rock catching my breath, I watched a coil of ceremonial smoke rising from amid the poplars and tamarisk trees near a temple in town.

I resumed my trek and climbed closer to the small, stoic maroon monastery near the top of the hill. Tsemo Gompa ("red monastery") is the focus of reverence and respect for the Buddhists in Leh, who are as devout as they are cheerful. I had come to the region to experience as much of the culture as possible, so it was curiosity as much as respect for the Buddha that led me up Namgyal Peak.

Another dozen yards and I turned to find a lone hiker just beginning to make the climb; I assumed it was just another curious pilgrim. But when he quickly managed to catch up with me, I knew he had to be Ladakhi. His light-brown pants and blue pullover sweater looked too clean to have come up the hill with him.

"*Julé*," I said, greeting him with the Ladakhi word for hello, goodbye, and thank you.

"*Julé*," he said. "American?"

"Yes," I answered, a bit embarrassed that it was so obvious. He balanced a set of keys in one hand and a wine bottle in the other, yet he scaled that steep trail with the skill of a mountain goat. I, in contrast, scrambled up slowly—often on my hands and knees—trying to gain purchase on the jagged earth. Within moments he and his unsullied clothes had outdistanced me.

When at last I met him at the summit, he was unlocking the monastery door. He showed me into one of the temples—a dark chamber festooned with colorful paper garlands. Sandalwood incense barely masked the musty odor of a room that was too long kept secret. An altar in the center of the room held a small *chorten*, on either side of which stood a Tantric Buddhist statue. The statues' heads and multiple arms reflected the dim light from a score of votive lamps on the floor, adding a dramatic highlight to the scene. A few green apples and a bowl of rice rested at the foot of the altar—an offering to the gods.

My guide bowed and filled the lamps with clarified butter from his wine bottle, lit the few that had burned out, and then ushered me outside. He locked the door and disappeared around the corner.

Left on my own, I wandered farther uphill to the rear of the monastery, which overlooked another valley. I was atop a peak bisecting two worlds—one a wide plateau filled with human activity and vegetation, the other a pristine valley bereft of man-made structures.

Long lines of Buddhist prayer flags hung from ropes tied between the *gompa* and several rocky points nearby. The small flags were made from cloth in the five holy colors: red, blue, white, green, and yellow. Each was

inscribed with a prayer and hung by a devotee to disintegrate in the elements, carrying its message of peace
into the winds. As I sat facing Leh under a rainbow of
the wildly flapping flags, a woman and a young boy approached from the opposite side of the hill. They each
tied a red, freshly printed flag over an old one that had
long ago been bleached a pale pink in the Himalayan
sun. They paused long enough to show their respect for
the *gompa*, then retreated down the hill.

I sat and stared across the Indus Valley to the mountains. The jagged peaks, some reaching heights above
20,000 feet, are often home to ascetic monks who find
the isolated locale ideal for meditation. I wondered if
perhaps a monk could be sitting on a lofty perch that
very moment, looking across the valley toward this sacred site.

About halfway down the hill stood Leh Palace, inspired—says the legend—by the Potala, the Dalai Lama's
erstwhile winter palace in Lhasa. As I sat watching the
shadow of the *gompa* stretch behind me, the rarefied air
became cool and still, as if heralding a great awakening,
and I was overcome by a sense of belonging—something
I had never felt in any other country.

The sound of copper horns interrupted my contemplation. These long, richly decorated instruments, called
rag-dum, are played by monks and emit a loud, haunting tone. The sound seemed to be coming from the
Jo-khang Buddhist temple in Leh, where a thin column
of smoke still rose. Sitting alone outside the monastery,
enjoying the Himalayan scenery and the monks' music,
I became overwhelmed with the peaceful spirit that
permeated the land. Indeed, life itself felt dramatically
richer and purposeful.

Suddenly, my focus both narrowed and widened. While I lost peripheral vision, I gained an inner perspective that was both exhilarating and startling. I felt my spirit testing the boundaries of my body, making me seem at once larger and smaller than my physical form. For a moment I understood all of life's mysteries, as though some cosmic voice was telling me simply, "It is." Oddly enough, it made perfect sense to me. I saw myself as a vital component of the universe and completely understood my place in it. In an instant I understood the realm of the afterlife, the complex dualities in physics, the common truth in all religions, and the very origins of life itself.

The moment of awakening passed all too quickly— too quickly to grasp all the answers that had echoed within me. But I was left with a lingering taste of clarity; I had retained just enough understanding to give me profound peace. Without consciously seeking it, I suddenly understood the Oneness of Everything and how, as the Hindus teach, the *Atman* (individual soul) and *Brahman* (universal soul) are actually one. I also realized I would never be able to adequately describe my sense of complete joy, serenity, and comprehension. Motionless and content, I was ready to sit there for days, foregoing food and sleep, just to feast on that feeling of wonder and excitement.

Every sense felt sharpened as I walked back to my guesthouse in neighboring Changspa. I took a renewed interest in the sights, sounds, and smells of Ladakh. Many families in the village were busily winnowing in the fields, separating the chaff from the barley grain. Before the winnowing, the crop had been spread out in a large circle and beasts of burden were guided over it, threshing the grain. I watched three family members in one of the circles, gracefully scooping up the harvested crop with large wooden forks and pitching it into the air. The breeze blew away the chaff, leaving the heavier grain to fall to Earth. Content and spiritual, they sang a prayer while working, which translates as:

> Oh, pure Goddess of the Winds!
> Oh, beautiful Goddess of the Winds!
> Carry away the chaff!
> *Ongsla skyot*!
> Separate the chaff from the grain!
> Where there is no human help,
> May the gods help us!
> Oh, beautiful goddess,
> *Ongsla skyot*!

The slow song had a chant-like quality, and the strong voices, in easy rhythm with the pitching and flying barley, filled me with admiration for this culture. Everything has a purpose in Ladakh. Even singing.

And nothing is wasted. Ladakhis can little afford to allow such resources as food, water, or animal and even human waste to go unused in their delicately balanced environment. Animal dung is particularly precious, for it provides fuel for cooking and warmth. Women carry large baskets made from sticks on their backs and wander throughout their village, collecting the brown pies deposited by cows, yaks, horses, and donkeys. They pick them up with bare hands—a tactile communion with the land—and adroitly toss them into the basket. The dung is then set on stone walls at home where it dries in the sun.

Each morning I would pass a few of these tireless Ladakhis, who scanned the ground in search of fuel. "*Julé!*" they would say happily upon noticing me, proudly chucking a fresh patty over one shoulder.

"*Julé!*" I would reply. Hello, goodbye, and thank you.

❧ ❧ ❧

A California-based writer, Mark Hawthorne works in marketing and contributes to Hinduism Today *magazine. He won the 2003 Mona Schreiber Prize for Humorous Fiction and Non-Fiction.*

PATRICK FITZHUGH

≈ ≈ ≈

The Redemption of Odysseus

Literature has a strange way of coming alive.

S OMEWHERE IN A DARK ATTIC CLOSET IN THE HOUSE of my father, among the cobwebs and the shadows, a copy of *The Odyssey* sits gathering dust. I remember that book. My father tried to read it to me once, long ago, his voice as wise as old Homer himself. He spoke of a cunning Greek warrior and a sea-god's curse, of a long journey home, and of one-eyed giants and sex-crazed women...and always...always he spoke of the wine-dark sea. I snuggled in under the blankets next to my father, burrowing like a mole into that great plain of pillows and comfort. He sat upright, half-moon spectacles balanced on the precipice of his nose. My younger brother sat on the other side of him, and together we listened in silence, transported to a land three thousand years before, just as fathers and sons have done for centuries, for millennia, listening to *The Odyssey*—the most enduring tale of the Western world.

Odysseus had the perfect life. He had it all at one point—king of the island paradise of Ithaka, married to the most enchanting woman in the region. She had just brought their first child into the world, a beautiful baby boy. He ruled with strength and mercy. A good guy, this Odysseus. But then his world fell apart.

He was summoned to a war a thousand miles away, where honor and obligation bade him fight a war he didn't care about. Ten years the war kept him—ten years of inhaling dirt and dust and watching friends die in agony. He yearned for news of his wife, Penelope, and his infant son. Many a night found a battle-weary Odysseus among his slumbering brother warriors, sitting and staring at the quiet canopy of night, whispering words to the stars.

But this was all pretext to the story—for *The Odyssey*, I soon learned, was not about the Trojan War. It was about a poor bastard trying to get home. Odysseus had to be the unluckiest guy I'd ever heard of. Those ten years on the battlefield were bad; but the nine years sailing home were worse. A hell of a lot worse.

My father was fond of old Odysseus—he would sometimes break from the reading and look up, and comment on what long odds that guy faced but kept on fighting, fighting, fighting, against whatever terrible challenge reared its head. Even when the whole ocean stood against him, Odysseus fought back.

My father felt a kinship with Odysseus. I think, somewhere deep down, he thought he *was* Odysseus, fighting against the unfair odds the world was continually throwing at him, doing his best to emerge with his honor and his family intact.

Odysseus wasn't the strongest guy, or the fastest, or the best-looking—all accounts of him make that quite clear. In fact, he's described as red-headed, fair-skinned, stocky, and as walking with a slight limp—a reminder of a hunting accident in which he took a boar's tusk in the thigh. But Odysseus was smart. And more than that, he could endure more than anyone. He could carry the world on his back and he'd refuse to buckle—I think that's what my father identified with the most about Odysseus.

Odysseus's nine-year journey can be traced back to a single incident. He and his crew happened to set camp on an island inhabited by a race of one-eyed ogres: the Cyclops. One especially foul-tempered Cyclops named Polyphemus trapped Odysseus and his men in a cave and announced his intentions to devour them all. Slick Odysseus, however, managed to get Big Unibrow stone-cold drunk on Thracian wine. As the Cyclops lay in a blissful stupor, Odysseus snatched a giant timber from the fire and plunged it into the single eye of Polyphemus. As Odysseus and his men dashed back to their ship, they looked back to see the surreal image of the great Cyclops staggering out of his cave, caressing the hole in his head. The beast called to his father, Poseidon, god of the sea:

> "Father, may Odysseus never get to his home in Ithaka. But if he must, let him arrive late, in evil plight, and all his comrades dead."
>
> (IX, 588-592).

And so it was that Odysseus managed to piss off Poseidon, not the divinity you want mad when you're sailing home. Poseidon made the next nine years of Odysseus's life among the most miserable any man has ever faced. He summoned the most savage seas and the foulest winds and sent them to destroy our hero. He never did succeed in killing poor Odysseus, but he delayed his homecoming for nine terrible years; and this journey of agony and washing ashore on fantastic, treacherous lands, this is the fabric of *The Odyssey*.

My brother and I listened to the trials and feats of Odysseus, of his sly tricks, of his wily ways, of his cool confidence, how he sidestepped death when it seemed most inevitable. In fact, Athena, goddess of wisdom, describes his as "a many-colored mind ever framing some new craftiness." He was the intellectual hero, the antithesis of meatheads like Hercules; after all, it was he who came up with the most famous ruse of all time: the Trojan Horse.

But every hero has his weakness.

As my father continued reading, that of Odysseus started to reveal itself, becoming more and more apparent as we traveled on: Odysseus had a rather lofty opinion of himself.

Yes, times were different three thousand years ago. But my brother and I would listen and with each battle or beast from which Odysseus emerged victorious, my brother and I would peer around the hulking form of my father, where our skeptical gazes would meet, and we would simultaneously roll our eyes. (And we weren't the only ones who felt that way: Dante relegates Odysseus, in the *Inferno*, to the Eighth Circle of Hell. Dante was not impressed with Odysseus's Trojan Horse idea, which allowed him to trick the unwitting Trojans and slaughter them in their sleep.)

No wonder this red-headed warrior ran into so many problems. No wonder Poseidon threw a fit and vowed to torture Odysseus after he maimed his son: Odysseus actually had the audacity to taunt poor Polyphemus as he sailed away. Even Odysseus's own men begged him to stop, fearing his words would come back to haunt them:

> So they begged me to stop
> but they couldn't bring my fighting spirit round.
> I called back with another burst of anger, "Cyclops—
> if any man on the face of the earth should ask you
> who blinded you, who shamed you so—say Odysseus,
> raider of cities, say that *he* gouged out your eye!....
> No one will ever heal your terrible eye, not even your
>   earthquake father god himself!"
>
> (IX, 556-561, 582-583)

When Odysseus humiliated the Cyclops with those poison words, when Odysseus expanded his taunts to include even the gods, were we really supposed to pity him when Poseidon whipped up terrible sea-tempests as a consequence? It seemed that during those uncertain times, when monsters and giants walked the earth, the one thing you could count on was Odysseus beating his own chest like a lowland gorilla and proclaiming his own greatness. Later in the story, as the hero and his men sail toward the Siren coast, where terrible enchantresses sing songs that lure men to their doom, Odysseus rallies his troops' morale in typical fashion:

> "Friends, we've seen worse danger than *this* before!
> Remember when Cyclops vaulted us in his cave? My
> courage, my presence of mind saved us all!"
>
> (XII, 228-230)

That was it. My brother and I were willing to grant Odysseus a generous pardon for his inflated ego in light of the extraordinary circumstances that he faced. But he kept at it with such fervor, with such unrelenting ferocity, that we had reached the breaking point. My brother and I could stand it no longer.

"Dad," my brother interrupted, "Why does Odysseus think he's so great?"

My father looked perplexed. "What? What do you mean?"

"He brags a lot."

I agreed.

My father was taken aback.

My younger brother then used three words to dismiss three millennia of tradition and storytelling, diagnosing precisely this Greek hero's malady.

"Odysseus is conceited."

My father tried valiantly to continue the epic over the next few nights, but we would have none of it: our verdict was final. Three thousand years of Western literary tradition be damned! As far as I was concerned, Odysseus was a stupid, stupid man. He wasn't heroic; he was annoying.

At the root of much of his braggadocio lay one fundamental problem. Odysseus spoke of Poseidon sending sea-shaking storms and towering waves; but I knew there were no such storms where he sailed. Odysseus, you see, had a basic credibility problem. After our occasional complaints became outraged cries of protest against the rampant egotism and hyperbole of perhaps the Western world's greatest hero, it came down to one final incident—the one that broke the camel's back. Odysseus, as he always seemed to do, used an inexcusably generous heaping of poetic license in describing a storm sent by Poseidon:

A towering thunderhead mounted over our small
    ship…
All of a sudden killer squalls attacked us, screaming
    out of the west,
and a murderous blast toppled the mast backward.
The mast went crashing into the stern,
    it struck the helmsman's head and crushed his skull to
    pulp…
Round the ship spun,
    reeling under the impact of thunder and lightning…
my shipmates pitching out of her—
and the gods cut short their journey home.
But I went lurching along our battered hulk until…
I lashed the mast and keel together, made them one,
riding my makeshift raft
as the wretched galewinds bore me on and on.

                         (XII, 437-459)

"I don't believe any of this," I snorted. "Why is it so
hard to sail home? It's not like he's in a real ocean like the
Atlantic or Pacific…I mean, he's in the *Mediterranean*."

I dismissed it all as hyperbole. I know the North
Atlantic can turn into a monster, when the depths of winter descend upon those icy, blackened waters. The poison
winds that scream down from the Arctic transform the
ocean into a thing of terror. But Odysseus was not in the
wild expanse of the Atlantic. He was in the Mediterranean,
and I had seen pictures of the Mediterranean. And from
all I had seen, it did not look scary. On the contrary, it
looked entirely benign. European people in Speedos and
lots of gel in their hair sipping drinks on a sandy beach.
Umbrellas in the sand. Sun. Folks taking their tans very
seriously. Turquoise water that whispers "plish…plash."
No savage sea; a bathtub. This was the Mediterranean!

My father turned the page and revealed a two-page, full color illustration—an artist's conception of the storm that destroyed Odysseus's ship. Wind howled and swells swirled, and pieces of his boat were littered about like splinters. In the bottom right corner of the depiction, my brother and I noticed something: a little human head, bobbing up and down in the furious gale, with little human arms clinging madly to a plank of the wrecked ship. The head had red curly hair and a beard. It was Odysseus, desperately fighting for his survival, teetering upon the very edge of death.

My brother and I looked at poor Odysseus. And then we laughed.

My father stopped reading and paused for a suspenseful moment...he looked at each of us with stern, deep-set eyes. Then he slammed the book shut and threw it across the room. Thus my father's quest to provide his children with a deep appreciation of classical literature concluded with a single epithet of resignation: "The hell with it."

And then, understandably, he left the room.

Now, years later, somewhere in a dark attic closet in the house of my father, among the cobwebs and shadows, a copy of *The Odyssey* sits gathering dust...

Not long ago, I went to Italy. I was studying in Florence, the birthplace of the Renaissance, the cradle of human achievement. But after a while, I found myself eager to escape—to flee from the beautiful accomplishments of man. I was surrounded by the world's finest art, by the masterpieces of Giotto, Ghiberti, and Caravaggio. But I yearned to see good old nature: rugged, wild, indomitable. The author Henry Beston once proclaimed,

"The world is sick to its soul for lack of elemental things," and I had all the symptoms. I wanted rocks and sea and cliffs. I wanted the cry of seagulls and the roar of surf. I wanted to run from the sophisticated world by which I was now enveloped, and to sprint and shout along the edge of the sea!

After a twelve-hour train ride, a two-hour bus, and procuring a room in the village of Atrani, I wandered north along the Amalfi coast. I had come to witness her legendary terrain, and I had come to see what the local tourist board had dubbed "the eighth natural wonder of the world": the Emerald Grotto. It was a sea-cave that, when the sun shines in, transforms the entire cavern into a brilliant azure cathedral. Somehow, after a week spent analyzing ten different paintings all called *The Annunciation*, this sounded just right.

The thin ribbon-strip of road hugged the cliff, curving and bending a thousand feet above the sea. I walked, surrounded by a staggering opera of natural beauty, its plunging stone cliffs reverberating with baritone power, and a vast, lapis-colored sea singing an alto aria far, far below.

I could see Hephaestus, the divine craftsman, in a foundry on Olympus, sweating with labor and forging this elemental dreamworld of rock and cliff. I could see James Bond zipping along this coastal road in a blazing red Ferrari, accompanied by a heartbreaking Venus whose hair billowed in the breeze, a woman who had stepped straight from Botticelli's canvas to Bond's front seat.

Buses were strangely common on that precariously perched road. A madly revving motor would signal a hasty downshift, and the lumbering vehicle would whip around the blind corner, the passengers entrusting the driver beyond my comprehension. I would step aside and the elephant would rumble past, the cement shuddering beneath my feet. I held my breath, half-expecting to feel a rainfall of pebbles, followed by a dreadful crumbling of cliff, and an interminable, sickening free fall . . . and then a splash into the cobalt cradle of the Mediterranean.

This was a landscape at which I could only shake my head. Reason prevented me from believing what I saw, that such sharp beauty existed not simply in the times of Homer, but continues to exist right now.

This was my first venture to that sacred sea: the Mediterranean! This body of water possessed some mysterious trait that caused great civilizations to bloom. So wondrous was the ancient Mediterranean that five of the seven ancient wonders of the world stood upon her shores: only the pyramids at Giza and the hanging gardens of Babylon did not hear the lapping of the Mediterranean at their doors.

I had hiked a healthy few miles out of town now, and soon I came to a gateway on the side of the road. It stood before the staircase that led down the cliff to the mouth of the Emerald Grotto. The gates, however, were shut. And locked. My heart sank as I noticed a handwritten sign: "Emerald Grotto closed today."

Outrage gripped me as it grips anyone who journeys a great distance, only to find their destination closed on the whim of a lazy local who was, most likely, sleeping off a hangover.

I glared at the sign, grinding my teeth. How can a grotto be closed? How does a natural wonder take the day off? I was indignant. I had taken an overnight train, a bus, and a two-hour walk from my hotel to see this so-called grotto. As I stood there, hands on hips, a few motorists pulled up, glanced at the sign, and were grossly ignorant of the good fortune they had in being able to shrug in mild disappointment, throw the car into reverse, and speed away.

I hated Italians. Good-for-nothings.

Dejection made the walk back all the longer. I started in low spirits, cursing with every footstep...but then I stopped. I stood at the side of the road, next to the stone wall, all that separated drivers from a plunge into the abyss.

I held the cold stone tight and leaned over the edge. A stampede of butterflies fluttered in my stomach: a thousand feet below, the sea crashed upon the rocks.

I happened to glance a quarter mile up the road, where I could see that the sheer cliff transformed to steep hillside, and anyone with a few ounces of agility and an abundance of bitterness toward the gatekeeper of the Emerald Grotto could easily descend to the shoreline and make an unsanctioned visit to this dazzling wonder of nature.

After fifteen minutes of tripping over agave plants and scrambling downhill, I stumbled onto a lovely and welcome surprise: a graceful stone staircase gliding to the bottom of the hill. It was the very staircase to which I, and all other comers that day, had been denied entrance by that lazy Italian.

I followed the steps to their end near the shore: to the left, the vertical cliff rocketed skyward; to the right, the lapis-colored Mediterranean danced; and directly ahead lay a narrow walkway that ran fifty feet along the ocean edge. On the other side of the walkway, stone steps were carved into the cliff. They rose to a height of ten feet, stopping suddenly at an ominous black cave—the mouth of the Emerald Grotto.

It was then that something caught my attention.

The Mediterranean Sea was angry. Very, very angry.

From a thousand feet above, this sea was the soothing blue of a blueberry slush-puppy, the glamorous, postcard sea of Amalfi, a well-behaved and mild-mannered aqua beauty.

From twenty feet away, the sea was a killer.

The sea was rage manifest. The sea was not lapis-colored; it was the color of power, the color of violence, the color of quick moving currents flecked with specks of seaweed and froth. I never knew the Mediterranean could roar.

Ancient mariners would tremble as they neared the lairs of Scylla, a hideous tentacled beast, and Charybdis, a monster on the sea floor that would suck down entire ships. Here, the sea was indeed churning with gargantuan beasts. Scylla and Charybdis were alive again, gnashing and thrashing once more.

Chaos-colored swells were rumbling from the deep, long lines paralleling the shore, feathering at their crests, readying their shoreward assault. The crash of wave on rock was an artillery explosion, echoing off the surrounding granite amphitheater. Sea spray shot skyward and rained down like clumps of earth on a battlefield.

The walkway to the grotto was the most dangerous place of all. Every few seconds, I watched that fifty-foot path drown. Most days, I'm sure, the gentle sea would tickle the platform edge, glistening like lapis, like an Amalfi postcard under the Mediterranean sun. But now the waves were slamming the small seawall and screaming onto the platform. One moment the walkway appeared safe and dry; a moment later, it was buried under ten feet of sea. Any human standing there would be crushed by the wave against the cliff. Then the wave would recede, drag you away, and feed you to the tentacled monsters.

I realized why the Emerald Grotto was closed: the sea would murder any soul that crossed that walkway.

I looked at the violence around me. Those tales...those tales of old Odysseus...of sea storms and Poseidon's rage that kept him from Ithaka for nine years. It all came racing back: Odysseus and his battles with the sea, and my unabashed skepticism of it all.

> The boom of a heavy surf on jagged reefs—
> roaring breakers crashing down on an ironbound coast,
> exploding in fury—
> the whole sea shrouded—
> sheets of spray—
> Odysseus's knees quaked and the heart inside him
>   sank;
> He spoke to his fighting spirit, desperate: "There's no
>   way out of the boiling surf—I see no way!
> If I clamber out, some big swell will hoist me,
> Dash me against that cliff!
> If I keep swimming down the coast...
> a dark power will loose some monster at me,
> rearing out of the waves!"
>
> (V, 418-423)

So the Mediterranean *was* capable of such wrath. I had long doubted old Odysseus, the veracity of his tall tales, which had seemed to me nothing but poorly crafted excuses for his lack of seamanship. No, no, no. The nine years of suffering on the sea and strange lands, trying to return to his family. It wasn't a lie. Odysseus had told the truth!

As I looked out at the heaving sea, my boyhood came flying back to me. Eight years old, lying next to my father. He was reading to my brother and me. My father was raised in the hills of remote Appalachia; now he was trying to give a Classical education to his boys. He was teaching us about every man's odyssey. He was preparing us for the trials and hardships that we would face one day. He had spent twelve hours at work—just like every other day. And he walked out of his office, exhausted, and into our bedroom to escape the vulgar world and share his beloved *Odyssey* with sons. And I showed my appreciation by scoffing and shaking my head.

I was a grown man now, standing alone on a storm-lashed coast. The sea tossed and boiled. I was thinking of Odysseus, suffering somewhere out there on the turbulent sea, trying to make his way back home. I was thinking of my father, suffering somewhere out there in the turbulent world.

I apologized to Odysseus. And I apologized to my father.

I turned my gaze to the mouth of the Emerald Grotto. It was beckoning just fifty feet past this gauntlet of vicious sea. I had come to see this grotto. I had traveled 500 miles and descended a cliff; all this to be turned away fifty feet from the door. Would Odysseus have turned around?

I watched the waves. I studied them. I timed them. I was going to cross that fifty-foot gauntlet. I stepped to the bottom of the staircase. Breathed deeply. Shook my legs. Waited for a lull in the onslaught of surf.

Lightning flash...white-tailed comets...fleet-footed Hermes...the whistling west wind...blind, desperate speed...the sprinters of the First Olympiad.

I charged.

My eyes saw one thing: the steps on the other side of the walkway, stepping up the cliff toward the grotto, up from the walkway and away from the raging surf. Those steps were solace. They were safety.

They were all I saw until I was halfway there; then some instinct begged me to turn my head and look toward the open Mediterranean. A great wave was hurtling toward me, speeding in like a blue-robed gladiator to slam me against the cliff.

As the wave screamed over the seawall and onto the walkway, I leaped up the stone steps of the Emerald Grotto. The thousand white tongues of seafoam licked at my heels like hungry snakes.

Safe.

The black mouth of the grotto opened wide before me. It was barred, however, by an old, rusted gate, guarding the entrance like rotting teeth. Locked. There was no going in. I gripped the cold iron and peered into the darkness, this black hole for which I had fled the Renaissance.

At first, all was black. The cave was a vacuum—immune to light, sealed from sound. Human senses were useless here. But then, beneath the constant roar of sea, a tiny, delicate sound was born, and began to grow. It was the chiming of tiny bells, coming from some mysterious source. It was the water within the cave, chiming against the stone walls and echoing like an elfin symphony.

My eyes began to adjust, and slowly shapes began to take form. This was no emerald grotto. No azure prisms glittered on the walls. This place, on this day, was the loneliest place on earth. The cave was veiled in gloom. Stalagmites rose eerily from the black water. Through the shadows, an object floated softly upon the water. I struggled to focus, when a current sent it drifting toward me. I peered through the metal gate, and was confronted by a disquieting image: hovering in the midnight gloom was a lone and ghostly dory, empty of rider.

Its hull glowed opal, tethered to a jutting spire of granite by a rope draped in seaweed. Two oars rested side by side on the boat's bottom. My imagination began to run wild.

There seemed something sinister about this place of shadows, and I tried to identify what unsettled me. And then it occurred to me: this dreary place was no simple cave! I had traveled faraway to an abandoned shore, and here before me lay the lost entrance to the Underworld!

The Greeks and Romans had always believed the souls of the dead would make this inevitable pilgrimage, to the mouth of a mystical cave. Here they would walk the stone steps, pass through the mouth of the grotto, and step into the lonely boat below. Charon the boatman would be waiting for them, and he would ferry them across the River Styx to the land of the dead.

It was all fun and games as I pretended to spook myself with tales of the ancient dead. But as I stood there, wonderment running rampant over reason, a strange thing began to happen. Slowly I became more aware of my precarious position: I stood atop a stone staircase carved into the thousand-foot cliff; the fearsome sea heaved behind me, and it began to take on the characteristics of a conscious and terrifying being. Its rage grew, the waves coming faster and fiercer, as though the sea was remembering who it was and what it could do here in this ancient place. The yoke of modernity was thrown off and, it seemed, the great sea-god Poseidon had risen from his ancient slumber, slammed his knife-pronged trident upon the quaking ocean floor, and he ruled this sea once more!

Before me lay the River Styx. And there was the empty boat of Charon, and any minute he would appear from the darkness, hunched over, hooded, and he would step into the dory and raise a bony hand in my direction, and slowly he would beckon me to enter.

No one knows where Odysseus really sailed. Scholars and sailors have hotly debated this topic for thousands of years. But something about this place screamed *The Odyssey*. The granite blades of cliff, the sparse vegetation of the shore, even the shape of the clouds overhead; it all evoked a clear image of that ancient story. Why? Why should this arbitrary spot of earth suddenly inspire such visions of something I had so quickly dismissed as a boy?

Odysseus, the story goes, actually did visit the Underworld on his journey. A witch named Circe told him one of the ghosts there could tell him how to get home. But Odysseus was terrified. He had seen warfare and bloodshed, but nothing could prepare him for the Land of the Dead.

As I remembered his experience there, I stared into the cave with growing unease: he had said the entrance to the Underworld was a foreboding cave next to the sea. He never went inside, but stood at the mouth of the darkness, just as I was now doing. And as he stood there, like a nightmare, shadows began to emerge from the depths,

> ...up out of the darkness they came,
> flocking toward me, the ghosts of the dead and gone...
> Brides and unwed youths and old men who had
> suffered much

and girls with their hearts freshly scarred by sorrow
and great armies of battle dead, stabbed by bronze
    spears,
men of war still wrapped in bloody armor.

(XI, 41-46)

It is here that transpires one of the most poignant scenes in all literature. As souls of the dead emerge from the darkness, float past, and disappear once more, Odysseus recognizes a familiar face. It is the face of his beloved mother, Anticleia:

But look, the ghost
Of my mother came! My mother, dead and gone now.
Whom I had left alive when I sailed for sacred Troy.
I broke into tears to see her here.
She knew me at once and wailed out in grief
"Oh my son—what brings you down to the world
of death and darkness?"

(XI, 94-105)

The great warrior begins to crack. Struggling to hold himself together, tears pouring down his face, he searches for some shred of comfort. He asks his mother about his wife and boy, almost afraid to hear the answer. Nearly twenty years have passed since he has seen them.

"Please tell me about my wife, her thoughts...still
    standing fast beside our son,
still guarding our great estates?
Or has she wed some other countryman at last?"

(XI, 201-204)

His mother replies:

> "She's still waiting there in your halls, poor woman,
> suffering so, her life an endless hardship like your own…
> weeping away the days."
>
> (XI, 205-209)

Odysseus, shaking with grief, asks what caused her to die. Did she suffer an accident while he was away these many years? A sickness, perhaps?

> "No, it was my longing for *you*, my shining Odysseus—
> you and your quickness, you and your gentle ways—
> that tore away my life that had been so sweet."

And here Odysseus, the man of the iron will, he who could endure hardship and heartbreak beyond all other men, here we see the mighty King of Ithaka buckle.

> And I, my mind in turmoil, how I longed
> To embrace my mother's spirit, dead as she was!
> Three times I rushed toward her, desperate to hold her,
> Three times she fluttered through my fingers, sifting
>   away
> Like a shadow, dissolved like a dream.
> I cried out to her, words winging into the darkness:
> "Mother—why not wait for me? How I long to hold
>   you!"
> My noble mother answered me at once:
> "My son, my son, the unluckiest man alive!
> This is no deception…this is just the way of mortals
>   when we die."
>
> (XI, 230-256)

Years later I read *The Odyssey* again, and I stopped when I came to this passage. My father had never said much about his own mother. My brother and I had never even seen her. We never asked, either.

Only recently I learned that she died when my father was a boy. He never really recovered. Even as an old man, he would have dreams that she had come back. They would sit down and talk, and he would tell her how much he missed her. How he loved her. Then dawn would come, and my father would wake up—and his mother would disappear. He was alone.

I could see my father, like Odysseus, trying desperately to embrace his mother's ghost.

The British scholar Ernle Bradford was a lifelong student of Homer and *The Odyssey*. He attempted to locate the real places the Greek warrior sailed—including the Underworld. He spent years tracing the Mediterranean coast in his sailboat, armed with hordes of ancient charts and a copy of *The Odyssey*. His adventure, *Ulysses Found*, (Ulysses was the Roman name for Odysseus), is a classic. And it speaks of the ancient Underworld as a real place:

> Not all Homeric commentators have been content to dismiss Odysseus's visit to the Underworld without attempting to locate it geographically. The French archaeologist Victor Bérard would have sited the entrance to Hades near the Gulf of Naples, and it is certainly true there were several places in the ancient world which were believed to lead down to the grey kingdom of the dead.

My eyes widened when I came across this excerpt. The Emerald Grotto—the cave that filled me with such dread—was indeed near the Gulf of Naples. In fact, as I read on, I learned with amazement that many students of the Odyssey—both ancient and modern—place the home of the witch Circe on Capo Circeo, in central Italy.

It was from here that Odysseus set out on his voyage to the Land of the Dead.

I found a map and looked up Capo Circeo. I couldn't believe it. It lay just fifty miles north of the Emerald Grotto.

I shook my head. Did Odysseus set sail from Capo Circeo and venture fifty miles south to this sea-cave? Was this grotto where the warrior tried to embrace his dead mother?

It was a brisk, windy day. Standing at the mouth of the cave, I found myself continually looking over my shoulder. I was afraid to turn around.

Just then, a puff of wind blew from the grotto, from somewhere deep within, as though wafting past the countless tormented inhabitants of that underground realm, whispering of laboring men hammering stones and shoveling ditches, and somewhere deep within, the giant god Hades sat upon his marble throne, content to be god and tyrant over all the dead.

It was an unexpected puff of wind—warm, heavy, like a haunting human breath

It brushed my cheek and blew the hair from my face. And then another breath emerged. And another. What was this unnerving respiration? What were these breezes blowing from Hades, through the Underworld, rippling the surface of the River Styx, and whispering as they departed the grotto? My heartbeat quickened, though I told myself it was nothing, and I couldn't help but wonder what on earth was happening. The eeriness of the breath from the cave was unbearable. I looked behind me and glanced at the pounding surf against the cliff, still surging over the walkway. I was surrounded by the nightmares of Odysseus, by the screaming monster-infested sea on one side, and by the shades of the dead on the other! I had to leave that place. I looked once more into the cave of night, at this point fully terrified that some specter was about to emerge from the darkness.

> I held fast before the cave, hoping that others might
>   still come,
> shades of famous heroes, men who died in the old days
> and ghosts of an even older age I longed to see...
> But before I could, the dead came surging round me,
> Hordes of them, thousands raising unearthly cries,
> And blind terror gripped me—panicked now that the
>   depths of hell
> Might send up from Death some monstrous head,
> Some Demon's staring face!
> I rushed back to my ship, shouting to all hands
> To take to the decks and cast off quickly.
>
>   (XI, 719-728)

Odysseus would have gone mad if he stayed at the Gates of the Dead. And I, too, needed to sprint away from that cavern, timing my escape to charge once more past the surging seas. The scholar J.E. Harrison said, "It is rash to tarry too long in Hades, lest the dim uncertain twilight baffle and daze us, and we behold no longer clearly the light of the upper world."

Odysseus was a man who was very tired of pain. He was sick of the vulgar, violent world, and he wanted, ultimately, simply to go home. His infant son had become a strong man in his absence—Odysseus longed to go home and meet this young man. At home in Ithaka, peace was waiting for him. At home in Ithaka, his dogs were waiting for him. His vineyards and fields were waiting for him. And Penelope, his gentle, pure-hearted wife, had been waiting for him faithfully for nearly twenty long years.

An hour after I had fled the doorway to the Emerald Grotto, I was back upon the spaghetti strand of road, walking back to the village of Atrani. Tour buses and Ferraris motored past, tourists oohing and aahing and madly snapping photographs of this Italy—which so stunningly matched the travel agency posters! I looked out at the unending sea. From here, from a thousand feet above, the sea appeared calm and postcard-perfect, cloaked once more in a lapis-colored mask.

Far off, close to the horizon and a thousand feet below, I saw a dark speck floating upon the cobalt Mediterranean. It appeared to be a boat. I looked closer, squinting my eyes, focusing on that lonely vessel.

I wondered who was out there. It was probably some old fishing trawler, coming home with the day's catch. But something about this place, about this ancient, wild coast, triggered the thought in my mind: that was no fishing boat out there. It was old Odysseus, the tired and homesick warrior, upon his creaking ship, worn weary by a recent battle and unwittingly drifting toward another, and all the while, floating before him, leading him on, was the dream of all that awaited him in Ithaka. His wife, Penelope. His grown son. And his long-lost companion, Peace.

I had once mocked that poor soul out there. I had dismissed the stories about his life and its hardships. But now I had seen them firsthand and I had witnessed the tempests he sailed through.

I took it all back. Everything I had ever said about him. In my eyes, Odysseus had been redeemed.

Though I couldn't see all the way out there, in that moment, as he drifted along in the distance, searching for respite from the daily battle, that bearded Greek warrior looked just like my father, when he read *The Odyssey* aloud, so many years ago, to my younger brother and me.

⚘ ⚘ ⚘

Patrick Fitzhugh is the founder of Audissey Guides, audio tours that allow cities to tell their wildest tales. Importantly, the tours point out all the taverns along the way. Sample the moonshine and see the latest destination guides at www.AudisseyGuides.com.

DONALD A. RANARD

❧ ❧ ❧

The Accidental Hotel

It was there all the time, obscure, disheveled,
but bearing the riches of a bygone era.

How had I missed the Atlanta? There it had
been, all those years, in a city I knew as well as
any, just the kind of place I liked—or used to like. I'd
long ago assumed that hotels like the Atlanta didn't exist
anymore.

I stumbled upon the Atlanta in Vientiane, a small,
dusty town that anywhere else in Asia would be the capital of a backward province but in Laos was the capital of
the country. One morning, after a fire had closed down
my usual breakfast place—a no-name hole-in-the-wall
where the city's dwindling population of pedicab drivers gathered over Vietnamese drip coffee and Chinese
doughnuts—I found myself in a small, stylish café overlooking the Mekong. Sipping coffee and munching on a

croissant, I noticed a guidebook to Bangkok somebody
had left open and face down on a chair next to me. I'm
not in the habit of reading guides to Bangkok, after
twenty-five years of visiting that city, but I did this time,
and there it was, the first thing I read, a two-paragraph
reference to a low-budget hotel I'd never heard of, the
"historic Atlanta." Historic? I thought the only hotel in
Bangkok that could claim that label was the flawlessly
refurbished Oriental, with its old-world elegance and
its new-world prices. After the Oriental, the choices in
Bangkok were pretty much indistinguishable from what
you found in most Asian capitals nowadays: There were
the 5-star chains, at one end of the spectrum, and the $5
backpacker dives, at the other. And between the anonymous luxury of one and the anonymous squalor of the
other, there were the mid-range businessman's hotels,
clean, efficient, and charmless—downmarket, sidestreet
editions of the luxury hotels that lined the city's main
thoroughfares.

But the Atlanta didn't fit those categories—or any
other that I knew. Its prices put it in the backpacker category, but whoever heard of a backpacker place with a
swimming pool (the first hotel pool in Thailand, according to the guide), a lobby used as a backdrop for fashion
shoots, and a restaurant that once catered to royalty and
diplomats? I jotted down the address and telephone
number.

Back in Bangkok, the mystery deepened when no one
I talked to, not even my old Thai friends, could tell me
anything about the Atlanta. In fact, no had even heard of
the place, and when my taxi pulled up in front of the hotel
one muggy evening, I began to see why. Housed in a dirty
gray concrete mid-rise, tucked away at the end of a nonde-

script side street, the Atlanta was easy to miss even when you were there. From the outside, it looked like another one of Bangkok's Vietnam War-era R&R hotels turned low-budget dives, the kind of place that had all the mod cons—and none of them worked. But no matter how bad it turned out to be, I'd already made up my mind: I was going to spend the night. Nothing was going to get me back out into the city today. Bangkok is a dysfunctional L.A., a sprawling, disorienting place, without center or discernible design, perpetually gridlocked, and on the brink of breakdown. It took us an hour to travel a distance I could have walked in twenty minutes.

The cab driver stared at the hotel glumly. I knew what he was thinking: Anyone staying at this dump wasn't going to tip. But I did, surprising him, then stepped out of the cab and into the hotel, and it was *my* turn to be surprised.

I did what everybody does entering the Atlanta for the first time. I put down my bag, and looked around in wonder. What *was* this place? I'd stepped back into another era, but which one? With its red leatherette circular sofa in the middle of the room, polished terrazzo floor, and wide, winding staircase that seemed to float in space, the lobby evoked a sleek modern grace, the '50s with hints of the Deco '20s. But it bumped up against an older aesthetic, Europe in the Gilded Age, in the room's ornate chandelier and faux gold-leafed mirrors. Facing the entrance on either side of the lobby were two pedestaled bronze dachshunds, ridiculously elongated, someone's private joke, a kitschy counterpoint to the rest of the elegantly appointed room.

I crossed the lobby to the front desk, bracing for disappointment. I knew what you got for 250 baht in

Bangkok, and it didn't look anything like this. But the girl at the front desk confirmed the guidebook prices: 250 for a single with a fan, twice that amount for a big room with air con. My room, a single, would be ready in a few minutes. She was young, eighteen, maybe nineteen, with too much makeup, inexpertly applied, and in her black, pleated schoolgirl's skirt and tight, white blouse she looked like a dirty old man's fantasy, a naughty coed in a blue film. She handed me a mango drink garnished with a purple orchid. "Would I also like to see a 500 baht room?" she wondered. One had unexpectedly opened up. "I would," I said, and drink in hand, wandered off to get a better look at my new digs.

The Western Union Travel Section, consisting of a couple of desks and a high table stacked with laminated travel maps, occupied one side of the lobby. Tucked away on the other side was a small sitting area with an over-stuffed sofa and armchair and a writing desk stocked with hotel stationery ("In residence at the Atlanta," the letterhead said) that brought to mind a nineteenth-century London hotel for gentlemen bachelors.

Time and place shifted again, as I stepped outside the lobby, past a small tropical garden, to the swimming pool. On the other side of the pool, jazzy geometric designs in cheery '50s colors ran alongside a wall. The sound system played Sinatra, then Ella. Except for the peeling paint on the wooden deck chairs and the cloudy water in the pool, it might have been an upscale American motel, circa 1957. All that was needed to complete the picture was a blonde in a one-piece sipping a daiquiri. Instead—back to modern times—a young woman in a buzz cut, peasant dress, and combat boots sat under an umbrella, hand-rolling a cigarette.

The bellhop, a friendly androgyne, beckoned to me; my room was ready. As we walked up the winding staircase, the hotel transmogrified itself again, this time into its opposite. If the downstairs was an unclassifiable mix, there was no mystery about the upstairs. *Now* I know where I am, I thought, as I followed the bellhop inside a fourth-floor single. It was the kind of featureless, functionally furnished affair—basic amenities, but nothing more—that I'd stayed in twenty-five years ago when I'd backpacked across Asia, from Kathmandu to Kuta Beach. It was good value for the price, but I was disappointed; the downstairs had prepared me for something different, something out of the ordinary. My spirits lifted, a few minutes later, when I saw the more expensive room. It had the same threadbare, mismatched furnishings, but it was spacious and had a sitting room with a sofa and coffee table. Embassy Suites furnished by Salvation Army.

I took out a bottle of Mekong whiskey and an aluminum cup from my pack, poured myself a drink, and tried to puzzle out the place. I'd gotten to the point in my travels where I could tell at a glance what to expect from a hotel. But so far the Atlanta had confounded me every step of the way.

What *was* this place?

Fifty years ago the Atlanta was the top hotel in Bangkok—so I learned the next day from Charles Henn, whose father, Dr. Max Henn, had built the hotel. A neat, slight figure in khakis and a polo shirt, Charles was half-German, half-Thai, and all English, a graduate of Oxford and Cambridge, and when he wasn't at the Atlanta, keeping an eye on things for his ninety-one-year-old father, he was in England, teaching international law and advising big business on Asia.

Charles, who grew up at the Atlanta in the '60s, was too young to remember much about the hotel's glory days, but, having seen the scrapbooks and heard the stories, he was an expert guide to the era. In its heyday, the Atlanta had been more than a hotel, he told me one morning in the course of a two-hour tour. It had been the center of social life for the city's Thai and expatriate elite, a place where foreign diplomats and businessmen rubbed shoulders with local movie stars and royalty. The hotel had the two best Western restaurants in town: the Rheinterrassen, the terrace on the Rhine, the country's first German restaurant, modeled after a German hunting lodge, with a German cook and a Swiss baker, and the Continental, with teak-paneled walls and deep-rose velvet curtains, where, every Wednesday evening, the Queen of Thailand dined. There were fashion shows in the lobby and parties by the pool, with live music and the latest American movies on a cinemascope screen. Henn built three yachts, the first privately owned yachts in the country, and took his friends on island-hopping trips off the southern coast fifty years before the area would become the latest backpacker falling-off place and the locale for the book and the movie *The Beach*. Henn established the country's first scuba-diving club, its first travel agency (The Trans-Global Flying Club), and cofounded the Thai Hotel Association.

By the late '60s, the tourist industry that Henn had almost single-handedly launched was transforming backwater Bangkok—and bringing an end to the Atlanta's reign. Bigger, more luxurious chain hotels eclipsed the Atlanta, and as the hotel's fortunes faded, so did Max

Henn's interest. He began to pay less attention to the
Atlanta, leaving it in the hands of his staff, mostly distant relatives and old family retainers of his well-born
Thai wife. The Atlanta was on the verge of falling off
the map altogether when it was discovered by globetrotting backpackers, drawn to its air of ruined glory.

"They were the early hippies, the flower power
people," said Charles. "They smoked dope, but they
were nice. Father got on with them well. They all came
here through India, and Father had lived for years in
India—he was the original globetrotter. They stayed
here for next to nothing. Some even stayed free. Father
felt sorry for them."

For Charles it was a happy time that would seem
unusual only years later, in retrospect. "My chauffeur
would take me to school everyday," he said. "And then
I would come back home and spend the afternoon with
the hippies. They used to help me with my homework.
We did Shakespeare together. They explained Blake to
me."

With no one at the helm, the Atlanta continued on
its downward spiral, and in the mid-'80s, when Charles
returned to Thailand from his studies at Cambridge,
the hotel was no longer the charming, ramshackle place
he remembered. The place had deteriorated badly, and
not just physically: Hard-core drug users and prostitutes
had replaced the pot-smoking flower children from
Charles's childhood. In the '50s, the Atlanta had been a
regular feature in the society pages of the local English
language newspapers; now when the hotel made it into
the newspaper, it was under the headline, "Drug Bust
at the Atlanta" or "Foreigner Arrested with Underage
Thai Schoolgirl." The Atlanta was so rundown and

seedy that even the Lonely Planet—the guidebook for shoestring travelers—was warning its readers away.

Charles found himself in a quandary. The Atlanta was on the brink of ruin, it was clear. And it was just as clear that he was the only one with the interest and know-how to save it. But Charles was an academic, a Ph.D.; he hadn't spent all those years at Oxford and Cambridge to end up running a broken-down hotel in Bangkok. He worked out a compromise: He would oversee the renovation of the Atlanta, but leave the day-to-day operation to the staff, freeing him to spend half the year abroad, pursuing his professional interests.

Charles began with a modest goal: to halt the hotel's decline. He painted the place, fixed what was broken, and replaced the badly damaged teak beds and desks in the rooms with iron furniture he made himself, having learned welding as a boy from his yacht-building father. He instituted and enforced new hotel rules—no drugs, no prostitutes, no loud music, no porn videos. He put together a guide for guests on the dos and don'ts of travel in Thailand. (Charles on clothing: "Whatever going native may mean in the latter part of the twentieth century, it does not mean a freakish or slovenly experience.")

But what began as a rescue operation eventually became something else. Under Charles, the luxury resort turned place of last resort began to carve out yet another identity for itself. Precisely *what* was hard to say. Even now, after more than a decade under Charles, the Atlanta remained a work in progress, though its future might be glimpsed in its restaurant.

It was the same restaurant, the Continental, where half a century ago, the Queen used to dine, but there was almost nothing left from that era. It was a simple place, or seemed so at first glance. A long and narrow room, with red leatherette banquettes and formica tables, a newspaper rack, stocked with American, French, and German periodicals, and a shelf of travel books, it looked to be a cross between an American diner and the faculty reading room of a small liberal-arts college. But there was more to the restaurant than first met the eye; each day I discovered something new to like. The sound system played classical music in the morning, jazz standards in the afternoon, and every night after dinner a video from Charles's private collection of film classics was shown on an overhead TV screen. There were stylish, off-hand references to Thailand, so low-key you didn't notice them at first. On the wall, black-and-white photos showed scenes from turn-of-the-century Siam, poised between its Thai past and its Western future, and at noon everyday there was an hour of gently swinging jazz by Thailand's clarinet-playing king. Among the mainstream newsmagazines was a scholarly journal on Southeast Asian studies from Amsterdam, and Charles's video library included every Western movie set in Thailand, from the 1926 *Chang*, the first Western film about Thailand, to *The Bridge Over the River Kwai*.

One thing you did notice, as soon as you ordered your first meal, was the menu—not the food on the menu, but the menu itself, a ten-page mini-disquisition on Thai food, complete with title (*Thai Food: What It Is, How to Order It, and How to Eat It*), text, and footnotes. The text explicated each dish with scholarly seriousness, but the footnotes were a random meander: Ketchup, the all-American staple, got its name from the Chinese *koe chup*, you learned on one page; in ancient Indonesia, lemon grass was cut by young girls, "as their purity would bring out the best in the plant's fragrance," you learned on another. There were quotes from nineteenth-century travelers to Siam, including this one from Edwin Young, an Englishman, on native eating customs: "Whenever the voice of hunger makes itself heard, its appeal is promptly responded to, and consequently, great irregularity prevails in the times of meal."

The quote could stand as a motto for the restaurant, where there was a waitress ready to take your order from early in the morning until late at night, whenever the voice of hunger—or thirst—made itself heard. It was the kind of place travelers were always looking for, a combination restaurant, café, and bistro, where you could get a good, inexpensive meal, linger for hours over coffee, or while away a hot afternoon over beer. It was a natural gathering place, and what was best about the restaurant was what was best about the hotel that housed it: the mix of people. In an age of niche marketing, the Atlanta was an anomaly; it cut across the usual, segregating categories of age, class, and lifestyle. There were has-been hippies and would-be hipsters, clean-cut college students and backpacking grandmothers, budget-minded families and middle-aged men on a Bangkok debauch, German scholars of Thai Buddhism, Swedish relief workers on R&R from Cambodia, blue-collar Brits, freelance writers, one or two indigents, and on the sidelines, quietly studying the show, a contingent of local day-trippers that included, every Sunday at noon, a small group of Thai Baptists from a neighborhood church.

The restaurant became my favorite place; when I was in the hotel and not sleeping, I was there, planning my day over coffee in the morning, reviewing it over beer in the afternoon. For someone like me, who at times likes to be with people and at other times just likes to be around them, it was perfect. It had what Ray Oldenburg, in an essay on the enduring appeal of French cafés, called the "unique blending of the public and the private." People were there if you wanted company, but there was no pressure to interact; conversations ended as easily as they began.

One day I met a middle-aged Canadian radio journalist launching a new life as a Bangkok-based freelancer, on another day, a six-foot-tall waitress from Amsterdam who had just traveled solo down the Mekong River from China to Laos, and on a third, a sixty-something guidebook editor, a tough, classy lady from New England, Katherine Hepburn with a backpack.

He was there everyday, a small, elderly gentleman in a bush suit, sitting at a desk to the side of the travel section, quietly working his way through a newspaper. "Who's *that*?" I wondered the first time I saw him. But after a while I stopped noticing him. He faded into the background, becoming part of the ambience, the atmosphere of the room.

Then one day I realized with a small start who he was, that he was Max Henn, the man who had built the Atlanta. "I do not like journalists," he snapped when I approached him for an interview. But when he found out that I'd spent the last three years in Sri Lanka, he softened. He'd been there years ago, when it was Ceylon and belonged to the British. What was my analysis of the war? He wanted to know. He listened intently to my less-than-articulate response, then delivered his own cogent analysis, in precise, German-accented English.

He was ninety-one, as old as the century, and nearly as experienced. Wherever you'd been, whatever you'd done, he'd been there, done that—and probably before you were born. He was a man of strong opinions and firm will, which made it all the more odd the way his life had unfolded, by quirk, luck, and happenstance. The hotel was full of would-be adventurers, wannabe Indiana Joneses, but Max Henn had had more adventure by accident than all of them put together would ever have by design.

He came to Thailand in 1948, by way of the subcontinent where he'd worked for British Intelligence and the Maharajah of Bikaner, in remote Rajasthan in northwestern India, and before that, Germany, where he'd grown up in World War I Berlin in a Prussian Jewish family of some prominence; a favorite uncle had built some of Germany's most famous warships. His Ph.D. thesis on TNT had earned him a coveted government job, testing explosives, and in another era he might have spent his life quietly working his way to the top of the civil service, but this was the time of the Third Reich. One day he received a warning from a high government official, an old family friend: It was no longer safe for him, a half-Jew, in Germany. He should leave at once.

He bummed around Europe for a year, worked as an explosives expert with an anti-Franco group in Belgium with links to British Intelligence, and, then, after Germany tried to extradite him, fled by boat to North Africa. With papers provided by the British, he traveled by car from Morocco to India, crossing Algeria, Libya, Egypt, Saudi Arabia, and Iran.

When he arrived in Bangkok in 1948, he was only passing through, on his way to the other side of the

world, to the Dominican Republic, to take a job as
the industrial adviser to President Rafael Trujillo. But
Thailand, lovely and languid, the surface texture of life
so full of ease and grace, captivated Henn. And there
were opportunities for people like him, practical men of
science. Henn ditched his Dominican plans and settled
down in Bangkok, marrying a Thai woman from an
old Bangkok family. One morning, years later, he would
pick up the newspaper and read that the Latin American
dictator he'd almost worked for had been assassinated.

The hotel came to Henn only after his first business,
the Atlanta Pharmaceutical Company, failed to get off
the ground. There were just a few international hotels
in Bangkok then, none of them very good—the Oriental
was badly delapidated—and, when a team of American
cartographers needed a place to stay, Henn converted
the top floor of his laboratory into rooms. After the
Americans, Henn put up a group of displaced Dutch
from recently decolonized Indonesia. Opening a hotel
was the next logical step, but one that Henn resisted at
first. He was a scientist, he told his friend the American
ambassador, not an innkeeper.

He was not a diplomat either, but in the late '60s, with
Indochina engulfed in war, he became one. As a state-
less businessman with high-level contacts on both sides
of the war, Henn was perfect for the role of unofficial
go-between. He practiced his own shuttle diplomacy,
meeting with General Giap in Hanoi, Prince Sihanouk
in Phnom Penh, Prime Minister Souvanna Phouma in
Vientiane. Though his sympathies were pro-American,
Henn came to believe the war—or at least the way
America was fighting it—was a terrible mistake. "Make
war or make business," he told General Westmoreland,

who had moved his family into the Atlanta in the mid-'60s. Henn began a correspondence with Senator William Fulbright, the anti-war senator from Arkansas. "Your letters are wonderful," Fulbright wrote back, "but your English is a little Germanized."

In 1970, with the hotel—and his own marriage— foundering, Henn left Bangkok to take a job as an agent with the U.S. Drug Enforcement Agency in Vientiane, Laos. In the remote, hill tribe regions of Indochina, opium had long been used as a painkiller by the old and the sick; now it was being manufactured into heroin and shipped to Saigon, where it was sold to homesick GIs. It was a hugely profitable business involving Chinese drug lords, Corsican gangsters, renegade CIA agents, local businessmen, and high government officials. Henn saw the work as a chance to finally do something socially useful, to fight an unequivocal evil. Instead, he walked into a morally murky world of smoke and mirrors. He lasted three years. "I didn't like the people I worked with and I didn't like their behavior," he said. "Most of all, I didn't like what they told me: 'Dr. Henn, remember whatever you do, don't embarrass our organization. If you deal with generals, admirals, or people in high political office, don't touch them. Refer your knowledge to New York and don't talk about it.'" Back in Bangkok, in the crumbling world of the Atlanta, he wrote long, anonymous letters to the English language newspapers, detailing the dirt of the drug trade. He signed the letters "Mephisto."

He delivered his story in one seamless monologue, and now, with hardly a pause, he was off on another topic: the collapse of the Thai economy. I let him go on; I was curious to hear what a Western businessman with a half century's experience in Thailand would have to say about the biggest story in the region since the fall of Saigon. He rounded up the usual suspects—corrupt politicians, crony capitalists—but then took off in a startling direction. The root cause of Thailand's problems wasn't too little democracy, as most critics had it, but too much: Democracy had ruined Thailand, turning upside down the natural order of things, the proper relationship between ruler and ruled, husband and wife, father and child. His criticism wasn't new, it was as old as democracy itself, but it was startling to hear it today, at the end of the twentieth century, when everyone at least paid lip service to the century's reigning ideology. He reached into his desk, took out a stack of postcards, and handed me one. "A Warning From Isis," it said. It called for a "higher knowledge of nature" to avoid "a cataclysm of total destruction."

He settled back in his chair. He was finished. "Do you have a question?" he asked. *Did I have a question?* Yes, I had a question. I had 50 questions, maybe 100, but I didn't know where to begin—I was overwhelmed by the material, the sheer improbability of his story, the elusive character of the man, and now the strange turn the conversation had taken. Who *was* this person, this globetrotting, German-Prussian-Jewish refugee turned spy-innkeeper-diplomat-DEA agent, this engineer who issued warnings of apocalypse from Egyptian goddesses, this businessman who had helped bring the modern world to Thailand and now railed against it? I probed, politely, his political affiliation. I needn't have been polite. He told me forthrightly that the only political party he had joined, back in Berlin in his university days, had supported the return of the monarchy. Of course! A monarchist! I'd been wondering where he fell on the political spectrum, and now it turned out he didn't fall on the spectrum at all, not the twentieth-century spectrum, at any rate.

Later on that day, I bumped into Charles in the lobby. I told him about my interview with his father.

"I'm a bit surprised Father talked to you," Charles said. "He doesn't talk to many people, especially journalists. Did he tell you how he got out of Germany?"

"Some government official warned him. "

"Did he tell you who?"

"No."

"It was Hermann Goering—you know, Hitler's right-hand man. Goering not only warned Father; he helped him get out. He made all the arrangements."

"Goering! How did your father know *him*?"

"He was a family friend, through his mother."

"And how did *she* know him."

"Now, that's a story in itself. Goering got into a car accident in Berlin. Grandmother happened to be there at the time, and came to his assistance. They became good friends after that."

It was Christmas morning. I was in the sitting room of my Salvation Army suite, on the threadbare sofa, tying my shoe laces, when I noticed a piece of paper under the door. I read it twice before it sank in I was being invited to a party. *Dear Guests*, it began in an elegantly cursive script. *Christmas is a time when hotels and restaurants double or triple their prices. Here at The Atlanta, we have a different tradition. Here at The Atlanta, we offer guests a complimentary Christmas buffet, and you are of course warmly invited to join the party tonight.*

The music in the restaurant that evening was mid-century American; the food, served buffet-style, was traditional English, with a nod to Germany. As Mel Tormé crooned his way through a medley of Christmas standards, guests helped themselves to roast turkey and stuffing, English sausage, mashed potatoes, cranberries, and stollen, German Christmas cake. On the door a marquee announced the evening's video. It was—what else?—*White Christmas*.

Halfway into the evening, Dr. Henn and Charles entered the restaurant. They slowly made their way through the room, greeting people, wishing everyone a Merry Christmas. Father and son were dressed in their usual outfits, the father in a pearl-gray, Thai-silk bush suit, the son in slacks, polo shirt, and loafers, and if they were even a little disappointed that the guests had come to this special, once-a-year dinner in shorts and t-shirts, they didn't let on.

Charles paused in front of a guest who was tucking into his food as if it were his last meal. Which just might have been the case: The day before I'd heard him on the long-distance phone in the lobby pleading for money. He was an American, in his late thirties, a solitary figure, tall and gaunt and unkempt, with a limp and the smell of bad mental health about him. He was the kind of lost soul who washed up in Bangkok all the time, and to Charles he must have been a reminder of the bad old days, when the Atlanta had been full of people just like him. But the suave and gracious host didn't miss a beat: "How's the food? Good? Great. Be sure to go back for more—there's plenty."

When I first met Charles, he seemed out of place in his own hotel. Whatever the Atlanta had been in the past and whatever it might become in the future, it was still a low-budget hotel; for the past week, I'd been trying without success to get the cheerfully incompetent cleaning crew to do something about the grime on my bathroom floor. With his impeccable British English, his smart casual clothes, his perfect taste carefully concealed behind an Oxbridge insouciance, Charles seemed to belong somewhere else. ("Oh, I don't know much about music," he'd said after being complimented on the Haydn, Mozart, and Bach that played quietly in the restaurant each morning, each piece seguing seamlessly into the next. "I just follow the BBC policy—nothing after the nineteenth century before nine.") It was easy to picture Charles in a small bed-and-breakfast in the English countryside, sipping a brandy in front of a fire with the guests, harder to picture him here, in a little-known budget hotel in a city that was Asia's best example of development gone amok. But not tonight. Tonight Charles didn't seem out of place at all. Tonight, as the old Atlanta briefly came back to life, offering a glimpse of a gentler and more genteel Bangkok, he was right at home. It was the guests who seemed out of place.

Postscript

Since this article was written, Max Henn, the Atlanta's founder, has died. Charles Henn, Max's son, continues to make improvements in the hotel, without altering the Atlanta's essential character. Rooms have been renovated, the swimming pool has been retiled, and a small writing room, with old roll-top desks, has been added to one corner of the lobby. Room rates, however, have been left largely untouched.

❧ ❧ ❧

Donald A. Ranard is a writer and editor in Tegucigalpa, Honduras, and the Washington, D.C. area. The son of diplomat parents, he grew up in Japan, Malaya, and Korea. He has lived, studied, and worked in Taiwan, Laos, Thailand, Hong Kong, the Philippines, Sri Lanka, and Honduras. His articles have appeared in The Atlantic Monthly, The Washington Post, *and the* Los Angeles Times, *among other publications.*

LEILANI MARIE LABONG

❧ ❧ ❧

Refining the Vegetable

Beware the Japanese Way.

THE VIEW FROM ALBUQUERQUE, NEW MEXICO WAS
golden, if you looked east; and if your gaze could
somehow burrow a hole through the Sandia Mountains,
and then stretch across the Midwestern plains, out
through the toe of Florida, and over the European continent, you would eventually—and through sheer imagination—reach Japan. But then again, even a marshy
swamp would give off that pretty, joyful glint if one was
looking at it through eyes rheumy with boredom and
disillusion. Fifteen years in a small city is likely to induce
a kind of cabin fever in the tormented youth, in myself
especially, since I perceived the city limits of Albuquerque
to be marked with electrical fences to keep the herd from
straying into the savage world beyond. Albuquerque's
isolation was disturbing to me, as if its inhabitants were

a forgotten tribe of strip mall-dependent people in a *Twilight Zone* episode, and I existed somewhere in the gray static.

From my perch high atop the red rock formations on a plateau of high-altitude desert, I could see the glimmer of overcrowded Japanese cities lit with enough neon to be seen from the moon, and the sweet promises of anonymity and unfamiliarity which emanated from them. To be able to turn down a tiny back alley and *not* know what I would find, *not* know if there was going to be a sweet shop or an old run-down theater with a burnt-out marquee, or better yet, *nothing at all*, was electrifying and made the hair on my arms rise.

If I squinted for better focus, I could see technology so advanced and abundant that I imagined I could detect the blue electromagnetic waves surging from cellular phones to TV/wristwatches to itty-bitty spy cameras and back to cellular phones again. And I was comforted by the Japanese practice of Zen meditation, and how it acted as the organic counterpart to this buzzing blue energy, keeping their society balanced, so that if I sat zazen in a temple for hours on end or raked labyrinthine meandering lines through their rock gardens, I could revive my dead inspiration.

One July day a few years ago I boarded a Japan Airlines flight to Osaka, with a signed contract to teach English in the Kyoto public school system tucked safely into my passport, and my trunk of Colgate, Oil of Olay, and Woolite weighing down the belly of the plane. These were the only ties with America I would not cut—material luxuries which made my life easier, kept my clothes from fading, my teeth from rotting away (I read that Japanese toothpaste did not contain fluoride), my skin

from drying out. Basic necessities for molting. Or emerging. I gripped my pink government-issued handbook on
Japanese workplace conduct and my *Culture Shock! Japan*
guidebook while the plane taxied, having carried them
on board to cram for my new life, and unintentionally let
them slip from my fingers as soon as my stomach leapt
away, signaling that we were airborne.

I should have seized them to my chest, welded them
to my hands, held on to them for dear life.

"Beware the Japanese Way."

It was a phrase mentioned in passing, murmured into
the hot summer wind, in the hopes that it would find my
hearing. Who said it, I don't know, perhaps expatriates
whose tolerance for disenchantment had reached their
limits, and who moved back to America to recalibrate;
or perhaps it was a nagging little thing called instinct.

I didn't know that the "entity" I sensed encroaching
upon the honeymoon of my new life was in fact the
Japanese Way reaching its hundreds of tiny feelers in my
direction. That while I was busy Googling items on my
cute little *keitai denwa* (a miniature cellular phone), my
fingers aching from pressing buttons and my eyes red
with fascination, the Japanese Way was trying to sense
me, trying to navigate my landscape. And it distracted me
with its delectable *ichigo daifuku* (strawberries wrapped
in mochi), which I popped into my mouth incessantly
as I strolled the red-lanterned Pontocho Street trying to
catch glimpses of the mysterious geisha emerging from
the tea houses. The entity tried to discern the texture
of my personality: the jagged peaks of my intolerances,
the quiet valleys of my sympathies, the pliability of my
boundaries. Could it latch on and then simulate itself
through me? It's true that my first impression of Japan,

garnered as I wandered Kyoto Station lugging my trunk
of American vanity behind me, was that the Japanese
worker bees moved in sleepwalking droves, from one
train to the next, as if the momentum of monotony was
the beat to which they lived their lives.

I was willing to eat fried fish for breakfast and pay
a huge sum for a single Fuji apple; I was prepared to
compromise the integrity of my posture for the constant
bowing, and even prepared to live the life of an illiter-
ate, the sharp strokes and smooth curves of the Japanese
characters never fully making sense to me. And even
in light of these concessions, still I felt something was
slightly askew, like the metallic tinge of tap water. I
filled my pockets with jingling *omamori*—good luck
charms for such things as love, earthquake protection,
car trouble—to ward off any impending catastrophe.

But it was there with me in the back seat of my boss's
car on our way home from a welcome luncheon soon after
my arrival. It lounged on the empty seat space, *tsk-tsking*
the mistake I made two hours before when I climbed
into the front seat, not knowing that it was inappropriate
for a guest of honor to sit with the driver. "*Sonoseki wa
tokubetsuna seki desu*," my boss politely corrected me later,
explaining that the back seat was the seat of privilege in
the Japanese society. So I settled there, and tried to have a
conversation in broken English with her eyes in the rearview mirror while the entity prodded at me, mockingly.

At dinner with friends one evening, I tried in vain
to order exactly what I craved after a day of pushing
my way through the crowds in Osaka: salmon and rice
with a glass of iced tea. The waiter nodded and scribbled
something down on his notepad, and then in an odd
twist, began to breathe heavily and sweat.

"Are you all right?" I asked him, a little stunned.

"I'm sorry, miss, but iced tea is not available with the *miso yaki* salmon." He wiped his brow.

"*Demo, asoko no hito tsumetai ocha nondeiru*" (But that person over there is drinking iced tea), I argued. The people at my table stopped their conversations to watch me take on the Japanese Way, which was akin to rubbernecking at a bad traffic accident.

"*Kare wa yaki soba tabeirukara,*" (Because he's eating fried noodles), the waiter replied, further explaining that my particular meal came with either Orange Fanta, Melon Fanta, hot tea, or coffee, none of which seemed particularly well-paired with a grilled salmon steak. The eyes of my peers on me, I wanted to plow on for all foreigners in Japan—I would be their Joan of Arc—I would raise my fists in the name of all that is sensible and sound in this world. But alas, my idealism would not win over my hunger and fatigue. I breathed in deeply and said through my gritted teeth that Orange Fanta would be fine, thank you very much.

Still I clenched my *omamori* in a palm moist from anxiety, hoping that a tighter grip could squeeze out some protection from the Japanese Way, but the pesky thing followed me to the grocery store, where I could not find whole wheat bread, only thick slabs of white bread sold in loaves of six or eight slices. And where the beauty aisle was stacked with whitening products designed to rob skin of its healthy glow and replace it instead with a pinkish, porcelain glaze. You could find eye glue in the same aisle, used by my female high school students to prop their eyelids open with the intent of giving their exotic, Eastern eyes a more Western shape, perhaps to match their dyed Western hair, streaks of blond or chestnut disrupting their raven tresses. Teachers would stand at the school gate on certain unannounced mornings and scrutinize the students as they passed through to make sure their shirts were tucked in and their ribbons in place, that their skirts were knee-length, and their hair black. If it wasn't black, it was spray-painted.

Conveniences I took for granted in America were sources of frustration in Japan. I had to manually fill my desperately antiquated washing machine with a garden hose only to subject my clothes to a turbulent cold water wash cycle, and then lift them out, threads dangling, into the neighboring compartment for the equally violent spin cycle. Oceans of Woolite could not have saved my clothes; they simply could not be revived.

Since the Japanese did not install central heating into their buildings, my thirty students huddled around a single kerosene heater for warmth during the winter months. "*Seitotachi wo gaman doyoku surutame ni*" (To strengthen the students), a teacher clarified one day when my impatience had reached near boiling. I wore a thick fleece and muffler in my own home just to move from the kitchen to the bathroom. It baffled me that I could stand on the peak of Mount Fuji and e-mail my friends from my cellular phone which weighed mere ounces, but nearly die on my own futon during the harsh winter night due to hypothermia. It crossed my mind that my neighbors would find me dead, or maybe just freeze-dried for posterity, in my freshly laundered, shredded bed clothes.

In the summers, the school buildings would be virtual ovens, and though the classrooms did not have swamp coolers, the teachers' lounge did, and I remember thanking the Mother of God on my first day of work when

I saw those glorious machines perched in the window sills. But a scant survey of the scene revealed dozing teachers with beads of sweat trickling down their faces, and wet saddlebags underneath their armpits.

"Can we turn on the swamp coolers?" I asked my supervisor, an English-speaking woman. She raised the handkerchief square in her hand to her nose and giggled. I wasn't particularly amused—no, I think irritated would be more accurate—but I returned a laugh as a gesture of goodwill.

"Yes, of course. But not until August first," she said quite matter-of-factly.

"But everyone is too hot." In case it wasn't obvious enough, I waved my hand over the room to reveal the misery, like Vanna White revealing a set of prizes in the final round of *Wheel of Fortune*.

"Please be patient," she said as she covered her nose again and walked away. I could not believe that there was an official day to turn on the air conditioner—an official day to begin basic comfort.

I tried to equalize my negativity by seeking out the things I appreciated about Japan so that I wouldn't be tempted to pack my bags in defeat. I ate *ichigo daifuku* by the carton, wiping the dribbling strawberry juice off my chin with the back of my hand. I combed through the community postings for tea ceremony exhibitions because I was captivated by its grace and its calm—watching the slow movements of the hostesses dressed in kimonos masterfully changing water into a froth of bitter green tea was a cultural repose that re-tuned me. The sounds of *chadou* are gentle, good for quiet reflection, or, if that is even too much to endeavor, the sounds can also clear any thought from your mind, and before you know it you're meditat-

ing. *Chadou* is a silent ceremony, with the exception of the
eurhythmic swish of kimono sweeping the tatami mats as
the women move about the room on their folded legs, the
hot water rippling into the ceramic drinking bowls, and
the bamboo whisk whipping, in figure eights, the pow-
dery *matcha* into a smooth lathery concoction.

I visited the temples during their spring and autumn
light-ups, night-time illuminations of their gardens.
The soft spotlights betrayed the innocence of the cherry
blossoms or the mischief brewing within the fiery red
maple leaves. Incredibly, the beauty that these temples
possessed in their elaborate gilded roofs and altars
abundant with offerings of shiny, curvaceous fruit and
crisp paper money, was mediocre compared to nature's
simple turning phases. These light-ups were popular
with lovers, and it was refreshing for me to see that the
rigid Japanese did indeed celebrate love with lingering
touches and neck nuzzles, inspired by a backdrop of
petal perfection, if only twice a year.

Also, I prayed. On my way to work, on my way
home, on my way to shop at the Gap on the corner of
Kawaramachi and Shijo I stopped by tiny shrines and did
the ceremonial hand-clapping and bell-chiming before I
bowed my head in prayer. I appreciated this methodol-
ogy which seemed so unrestrained by religion, free to
be adopted by anyone who believes that the spiritual
connection is strengthened by every clap and every ring,
and even just by entering under the red *torii* to view the
sacred space, ornamented with fat, gilded Buddhas and
cauldrons of burning incense, the thin streams of fragrant
smoke helixing around chains of origami cranes.

I prayed for Japan to find its niche within me, or
vice versa, because I found myself cursing its backward

ways. It was as if I had relocated from one *Twilight Zone* episode to another, this one about a cult that worshipped protocol and pretense.

Despairing, I dredged up my high school world history lessons and blamed Japan's younger generations for the horrific war crimes their grandfathers were responsible for, namely the rape and massacre of hundreds of thousands of Chinese during World War II by Japanese soldiers with a skewed sense of patriotism. I was desperate for something to hang my disappointment on, and if these people were capable of such atrocities, how could I expect them to be logical enough to install heat into their classrooms so that my students didn't have to spend their English lessons blowing hot air onto their fingers to ward off frostbite? I found it completely absurd that I could order an entrée of choice, but not a beverage. I didn't understand their obsession with all things white—white bread, white rice, white faces, white people, or their need to mimic the Caucasian hair color, skin color, eye shape. So I prayed. Every day. For understanding. For the glittery promise I saw in the distance from my perch on the red rocks to reveal itself quickly because I had already wasted enough time and energy on culture shock.

Hence I was not surprised when the holy disclosure I was seeking found me between the bread aisle and the dairy case of my local grocery, in the form of a can of Kagome Vegetable Juice, where, in tiny letters above the distinguished Kagome name was the phrase, "Refining the Vegetable." In that instant, like a flash of bright light so fleeting had I flinched I would have missed it, the Japanese Way had funneled its menacing self into a single point of resolution. I looked at the shelves of six-slice loaves of white bread and sighed. Ah, of course, how could I have not seen it before? The Japanese Way existed for purposes of refinement. Faces slathered in whitening creams, spray-painted hair, the August 1ST swamp cooler launch, and an unwanted Orange Fanta were all manifestations of the need for order, purity, and accord. (I am certain that the people of Nanking, China—the descendents of the victims—would agree.) I stood dumbfounded in the aisle, a bag of white bread dangling from one hand and the can of vegetable juice clutched in the other, shaking my head.

Every second Tuesday I team-taught English Comprehension with a Japanese instructor, Miyako-sensei, who asked me every second Monday to devise a lesson plan for the class. This is the model of the five-second conversation we would have three minutes before each class. X and Y are variables representing different lesson plans:

Leilani: Sensei, today I have prepared materials for X. It's a game that has been successful in my other classes. The students will enjoy this new way of learning how to use conversational English.

Miyako-sensei: *Gokurosamadeshita.* (Thank you for your hard work.) Today the students will do Y.

Leilani: O.K. Shall we go to class now to prepare your lesson?

When this happened the first time I was furious, having stayed up half the night with my ear pressed to my stereo speaker trying to find the clearest words that the students could recognize in the mumbling sea of an Elvis ballad. Not a difficult exercise—a mere filling-in-the-blanks with the carefully omitted words as they grooved

to "Are You Lonesome Tonight?"—but fun and culturally relevant since the Japanese love Americana, and who
could be more representative than the King of Rock 'n'
Roll? Instead the students read silently a boring story
from their text about twin baby boys who had an iron de-
ficiency and began to gnaw on their wooden crib and put
handfuls of dirt in their mouths to compensate for it. Due
at the end of class were the written answers to the story's
comprehension questions. *When did the mother notice
the twins' strange behavior? How was their sickness cured?*
Always, each class was conducted in complete silence.

This constant disregard of my contributions to a class is
supported—coddled, rather, like a swaddled newborn—by
the two live-and-die-by tenets of the Japanese Way: *honne*
and *tatemae*, the personal truth and the social norm.

Tatemae demands that I be satisfied with Miyako-
sensei's effort to ask for my input, even though she had
already planned the class. In her mind, she had spared
my feelings by having the same pithy little conversation
with me before each class. Miyako-sensei did not worry
that her obvious indifference to my ideas and the trans-
parency of her effort might have offended me.

The Japanese teacher was also obligated to ask me to
prepare a lesson simply because I was to be considered a
"colleague," appointed by the ruling powers to act, at the
very least, as a cultural liaison to the school, even if all I do is
stand next to the blackboard as the token non-Japanese person, handing chalk to Miyako-sensei whenever she needed
it. Hiring forty-five new foreign teachers every school year,
the Kyoto Board of Education can claim that it makes ardent strides toward globalization, and should be considered
by the rest of the world to be multicultural. *Tatemae* is the
Ministry of Tourism's Full-Color-Pamphlet-Truth.

However, the fact that Miyako-sensei never used my lesson plans comes straight from the heart of *honne*—the Dear Diary Truth. I am certain that in a pink Hello Kitty diary with a heart-shaped lock, she confessed her resentment toward the token foreigner who was dropped from the sky armed with sharp irregularly-shaped traditions—ones that allow her to teach English using films such as *The Breakfast Club* (Dear Diary: What is meant by the word *poontangers?*) and songs by Elvis (Dear Diary: Is it possible to be *nothing but a hound dog?*). There were textbooks that mapped out the reading, speaking, and comprehension exercises for every level, so, Dear Diary, why this need to *create?*

Just as one would not freely broadcast the contents of her diary to the general public, it is an unspoken rule—one that is communicated through knowing glances and other common avoidance measures ("selective hearing" and "changing the subject" among them)—that one's *honne* shall never find its way beyond the heart-shaped lock and onto uttered breath.

"I'm sorry. Maybe I misunderstood. You said we're going to teach the story about the Beaver Twins?" I argued, placing my lyrics worksheet and Elvis CD down on my desk with an annoyed thud.

"Yes. Today the students will read from the text," chirped Miyako-sensei. I kept my gaze locked on the worry furrow crinkling between her brows. She was looking at a broken light fixture behind me that kept blinking on and off in Morse code rhythms. C-O-M-P-O-S-U-R-E. I saw the pattern reflected in her glasses.

"I see. Didn't you ask me to prepare a lesson?"

"Please save it for the next class," she hissed, obviously irritated at my naïveté, my spoken *honne*.

Two weeks later, during the next class, the students read a story about how yawning is contagious. *Name one reason people yawn.*

Boredom.

One exceptionally frosty morning, I tunneled through a mountain of blankets to slap a hand on my buzzing six A.M. alarm. I ached with dread. The renewal contracts were due that day, so if I wanted to stay another year, I would have to put pen to paper to prove it.

The school I taught at was built on the site of an ancient Edo-period castle. The school gates are the original castle gates—very beautiful with heavy wooden doors and iron hinges—much more majestic than the chain-link fences of the other schools I visited. Every time I climbed the hill and those wooden doors came into view, I was reminded that the Japanese Way is just as enduring, a practice thousands of years old, like the tea ceremony I love so much, and not likely to disintegrate just because one foreigner happened to beat her head against the wall whenever she wanted to eat ham and cheese on whole wheat, or wanted her English Comprehension class to fill in the words *heart* and *come back* into *Is your _____ filled with pain/Shall I ____ again?*

Thanks for your concern, Elvis, because my heart was filled with pain. Would I come back again? The Board of Education needed to know. Could I survive another year of suppressing my *honne*? In America, our *honne* glistens like gold, and is worth just as much. It's the First Amendment to the Bill of Rights, for heaven's sake. Not the Second or the Third or even the Fourth. It's why we televise war coverage, why we have community access channels, why we can rally together to support this cause or that. The media, politicians, movie stars, and American ESL teachers bow down at its altar. It carries all of the fervor such revolutionary ideas tend to generate. But here in Japan, that's a fire that gets snuffed, or isn't even lit in the first place.

I could feel my personal boundaries softening in order to allow other ideas and beliefs to exist. The ultimate contradiction was that culture shock served to make room for ideas that are firm and rigid, and at times unforgiving. *Tatemae*, for all the fakery it allows, is as solid as my own belief that such an attempt at refinement could never survive, since it is based on dishonesty. Or could it be that *tatemae* is merely the heavy copper lid placed over a simmering cauldron of opinions and resentments, a fragrant *honne* brew? Perhaps the actual mystery of the Japanese Way is whether or not the truth is taken into consideration when the Japanese make their private judgments. In her Hello Kitty diary did Miyako-sensei write, "I feel bad because I am misleading Leilani," or did she write, "I feel bad for Leilani because she does not understand *tatemae*"? Did she rely on *tatemae* to alleviate her guilt without even a split-second thought as to how her actions affected me? Hopefully the Japanese do not just avert their eyes and change the subject because they are on autopilot. In another thousand years my presence here will be forgotten, and the Japanese Way will live on, snickering at those who try to keep it at bay.

Dear Diary:

Today was strange. I found a small sweet poised in the center of my desk—an *omiyage* (memento). Miyako-sensei returned from a business trip and brought it back for me. I suspect she wants to be friends. I'll think about it. But I did smile at her and bow my gratitude.

For lunch I pulled the tab on a ready-to-heat can of pumpkin soup, and instead of using a spoon, I sipped it from the rim of its bowl, in the same way I would drink miso soup. I had the revelation that a spoon would only be an impediment to my satisfaction.

But what happened in the ladies' room surprised me most: I flushed before I peed. There was a woman in the stall next to mine and I didn't want to embarrass either of us, so I masked the sound. And then another woman came in after me and did the same thing. It was like a symphony of flushing toilets. Beethoven would not be amused. I washed my hands quickly and dashed out so that I didn't have to see the other women.

As I sat in my parlor this afternoon with the renewal contract on my lap and my bowl of soup poised at my lips, I thought that if I left I would sorely miss my *manjuu* (sweets) store across the street where the tiny *oba-chan* (grandmother) pulls out two *ichigo daifuku* for me even before I reach her window. I love her two-teeth smile.

I would miss the frogs croaking in the rice paddies, the jingling *omamori* hooked onto belt loops and key rings throughout Japan, and the clapping that sends prayers to heaven: Oh Buddha, please grant me some tolerance.

Culture shock is a stern and steadfast teacher with a will greater than mine. An entire culture is more likely to have an affect on me than me on it, so what if I conceded? What if I packed up my American imperialism and shipped it home to New Mexico? Would I spontaneously combust without my heavy royal cloak? I guess not. Mature? Maybe.

It was a decision I made after I'd counted to three and grabbed from the air the first thought I had, which was of the flushing concerto in the ladies' room this morning. As a chuckle escaped from my lips, a drop of pumpkin splattered onto the renewal contract, right on the X.

❧ ❧ ❧

Upon returning to America after a four-year stint in Asia, Leilani Marie Labong promptly forgot her backpacking survival skills and slipped back into her habits of royalty. She currently lives in San Francisco, where she avoids public restrooms at all costs, insists on drinking Pellegrino daily, and works as the research editor at a local lifestyle magazine, 7x7.

BILL SHERWONIT

~*~ ~*~ ~*~

Journey to the Night Sky

An ancient envoy connects the physical and spiritual worlds.

"If the stars should appear one night in a thousand years, how would men believe and adore, and preserve for many generations the remembrance of the city of God!"   —Ralph Waldo Emerson

Late evening in the Peters Hills. The September sun has been swallowed by the Alaska Range, and only a thin, faint purplish glow now marks its passing. As day gives way to night, I stand on a northwest-facing ridge and search the landscape for lights. In the distance are a few scattered cabins and a mining camp, barely visible in the deepening dark.

Higher on this ridgeline, I could look east and see the Parks Highway, with its lights of cars and lodges. Or, turning south, I would see the faraway urban glow of Anchorage. But where I'm camped, the surrounding hills shield me from highway and city. Here, in the far western corner of Denali State Park, I've serendipitously chosen a site where artificial lights won't disturb my wilderness nights.

Above me, wispy clouds have moved in from the southwest, and no stars are visible as I crawl into my tent. Several hours later, feeling chilled, I awake; it's much colder than my first night in these hills. I add another layer of clothes and then, sensing that the temperature drop reflects clearing skies, I open the tent door—and am greeted by the universe. Never have I seen such an Alaskan sky. No moon, no aurora, and no city glare. Thousands of brilliant stars sparkling in deep blackness. How to describe such an unexpected and overpowering sight?

I'm reminded of a wonderful story I read many years ago, the 1941 science-fiction classic *Nightfall*. Using the words of Emerson quoted above to begin his tale, Isaac Asimov explored how humans might react if they witnessed darkness and stars only once every 2,000 years. Would we experience spiritual rhapsody? Or go insane?

On this September night, the heavens hold promise, not danger. Lured skyward, I'm pulled from my drowsiness and out of the tent. Still in my sleeping bag—and no longer chilled—I lay my head on the frosted tundra and face the night sky. So many stars. Such immense, unfathomable distances. A taste of infinity, an escape from ego.

In Anchorage, I seldom gaze for long at Alaska's nighttime sky, except to watch sunset afterglows, northern lights, meteor showers, or, perhaps, a full moon hanging low over the mountains. Hidden by clouds and summer's late-night sun, or dimmed in winter by urban glare, the stars hold little allure. Not enough, certainly, to draw me out of the house and into the cold.

Tonight is different. I wander in a dreamlike trance among the Milky Way, the Big and Little dippers, the Gemini twins, and the seven sisters of the Pleiades. I wish I recognized more of the constellations. I want to know their ancient names, their legends, their origins. What is the story of Orion, the giant hunter? Or Taurus, the bull? And where are they hiding? So many stars fill the sky that I have difficulty seeing shapes and forms. Perhaps if I'm patient enough, ancient patterns will reveal themselves. As author and human ecologist Paul Shepherd explains it, "the spectacle of stars seems at first formless and chaotic. But it is far too large a part of the world to accept as randomly structured.... We discern or make there organic figures."

More than anything, humans have used animal forms to shape their universe and give it meaning. I like the idea of mythic creatures inhabiting the sky above this wilderness landscape. The constellation I know best is the Big Dipper. Yet it is part of a much grander figure, one I wasn't taught to recognize as a boy: Ursa Major, the Great Bear. In *Secrets of the Night Sky*, stargazer Bob Berman suggests "It's odd, to say the least, that so many ancient civilizations discerned the shape of a bear in this region of the sky.... A bear is stretching it, and yet that is exactly what Native Americans, ancient Greeks, the Germanic tribes of middle Europe, and others saw in this formation. Why such disparate civilizations should all project the same unlikely bruin onto these northern stars remains a mystery." I like that, too: the fact that modern scientists can't figure out why several cultures, widely separated by time or distance, identified essentially the same Great Bear in the heavens. What could they see—or imagine—that we can't now?

The myths explaining the origins of Ursa Major vary greatly, yet those of many North American Native groups are similar in that the bear is "born" in the heavens and later becomes an envoy connecting the physical and spiritual worlds. It seems the perfect story for a magical night spent in grizzly country.

While most cultures have reveled in the images, stories, and meaning apparent in the night sky, ours has largely blocked it out with city lights and, consequently, learned to ignore it. This seems a paradox, given our nation's great interest in space exploration. While the masses watch *Star Trek* and *Star Wars*, the heavens themselves have become the domain of astronomers, physicists, and other scientists who, with their high-tech instruments, probe, dissect, and analyze the universe as they "figure out" the universe's mysteries. In the process, something has been lost. As with so many things nowadays, there's too much science and analysis, too little myth and magic. Too much arrogance, too little humility. Too much separation from the rest of creation, too little connection.

Here in the Peters Hills, on a starry Alaskan night like no other I've known, I reconnect with the wonder I felt as a boy, while gazing at Connecticut skies. I shrink in size to an insignificant speck, yet I'm part of the glorious enormity that this extraordinary spectacle reveals. My imagination stirs, takes flight among faraway blazing suns and the power they reveal. Gradually I realize it was no accident I chose this place to camp.

I have no idea how long I'm caught up in this reverie. Maybe ten minutes, maybe an hour. When I finally
check my watch it's nearly 4 A.M. Already, the stars'
brightness has begun to fade, and a pale glow lights the
eastern horizon. I drift back to sleep, my spirit cleansed
by starlight.

❧ ❧ ❧

*Bill Sherwonit is a nature writer and the author of many books on
Alaska, including* Alaska's Accessible Wilderness. *He is also a
co-editor of* Travelers' Tales Alaska, *and lives in Anchorage. For
more information, go to www.billsherwonit.alaskawriters.com.*

ACKNOWLEDGMENTS

We have received so much support from so many people on our publishing odyssey that it would be an exercise in futility to thank everyone properly. Our sincerest gratitude goes out to all the writers who've contributed to our books, all readers who've read and enjoyed them, all critics who've taken the time to review us, and all travelers whose dreams were encouraged in one way or another through the sharing of these many travelers' tales. And of course we thank our families, friends, and staff, especially Susan Brady, without whom nothing would be possible. Finally, a special thanks to co-founder Tim O'Reilly for his inspiration, generosity, and patience, and to the great people at his company, O'Reilly & Associates (now O'Reilly Media), who years ago gave us the best and most wholehearted launch anyone could wish for.

"Cause for Alarm" by Deborah Fryer published with permission from the author. Copyright © 2005 by Deborah Fryer.

"Part Lao, Part *Falang*" by Kathryn Kefauver published with permission from the author. Copyright © 2005 by Kathryn Kefauver.

"The Concorde, R.I.P." by Bruno Maddox reprinted from the October 2003 issue of *Travel & Leisure*. Copyright © 2003 by American Express Publishing Corporation. All rights reserved.

"The Passenger" by Rick Carroll excerpted from Madame Pele: True Encounters with Hawai'i's Fire Goddess by Rick Carroll. Copyright © 2003 by Rick Carroll. Reprinted by permission of Bess Press and Rick Carroll.

"Just Chicken" by Kathleen Comstock published with permission from the author. Copyright © 2005 by Kathleen Comstock.

About the Editors

James O'Reilly, president and publisher of Travelers' Tales, was born in England and Raised in San Francisco. He graduated from Dartmouth College in 1975 and wrote mystery serials before becoming a travel writer in the early 1980s. He's visited more than forty countries, along the way meditating with monks in Tibet, participating in West African voodoo rituals, living in the French Alps, and hanging out the laundry with nuns in Florence. He travels extensively with his wife, Wenda, and their three daughters. They live in Palo Alto, California, where they also publish art games and books for children at Birdcage Press (www.birdcagepress.com).

Larry Habegger, executive editor of Travelers' Tales, has been writing about travel since 1980. He has visited almost fifty countries and six of the seven continents, traveling from the frozen Arctic to equatorial rain forest, the high Himalayas to the Dead Sea. In the early 1980s he co-authored mystery serials for the San Francisco Examiner with James O'Reilly, and since 1985 their syndicated column, "World Travel Watch," has appeared in newspapers in five countries and on WorldTravelWatch.com. As series editors of Travelers' Tales, they have worked on some eighty titles, winning many awards for excellence. Habegger regularly teaches the craft of travel writing at workshops and writers conferences, and he lives with his family on Telegraph Hill in San Francisco.

Sean O'Reilly is a former seminarian, stockbroker, and prison instructor who lives in Virginia with his wife Brenda and their six children. He's had a life-long interest in philosophy, theology, and travel, and recently published the controversial book, How to Manage Your DICK: Redirect Sexual Energy and Discover Your More Spiritually Enlightened, Evolved Self (www.dickmanagement. com). His most recent travels took him on a month-long journey through China, Indonesia, Thailand, and Ireland. He is editor-at-large and the director of special sales for Travelers' Tales.

TRAVELERS' TALES
THE POWER OF A GOOD STORY

New Releases

THE BEST TRAVEL WRITING 2005 $16.95
True Stories from Around the World
Edited by James O'Reilly, Larry Habegger & Sean O'Reilly
The second in a new annual series presenting fresh, lively storytelling
and compelling narrative to make the reader laugh, weep, and buy a
plane ticket.

IT'S A DOG'S WORLD $14.95
True Stories of Travel with Man's Best Friend
Edited by Christine Hunsicker
Introduction by Maria Goodavage
Hilarious and heart warming stories of traveling with canine companions.

A SENSE OF PLACE $18.95
**Great Travel Writers Talk About Their Craft, Lives,
and Inspiration**
By Michael Shapiro
A stunning collection of interviews with the world's leading travel writers,
including: Isabel Allende, Bill Bryson, Tim Cahill, Arthur Frommer, Pico Iyer,
Peter Matthiessen, Frances Mayes, Jan Morris, Redmond O'Hanlon, Jonathan
Raban, Paul Theroux, Simon Winchester, and many more.

WHOSE PANTIES ARE THESE? $14.95
More Misadventures from Funny Women on the Road
Edited by Jennifer L. Leo
Following on the high heels of the award-winning bestseller *Sand in My
Bra and other Misadventures* comes another collection of hilarious travel
stories by women.

SAFETY AND SECURITY FOR WOMEN
WHO TRAVEL
(SECOND EDITION) $14.95
By Sheila Swan & Peter Laufer
"A cache of valuable advice."   *—The Christian Science Monitor*

A WOMAN'S PASSION FOR TRAVEL $17.95
True Stories of World Wanderlust
Edited by Marybeth Bond & Pamela Michael
"A diverse and gripping series of stories!"   —Arlene Blum, author of
Annapurna: A Woman's Place

THE GIFT OF TRAVEL $14.95
Inspiring Stories from Around the World
Edited by Larry Habegger, James O'Reilly & Sean O'Reilly
"Like gourmet chefs in a French market, the editors of Travelers' Tales pick, sift,
and prod their way through the weighty shelves of contemporary travel writing,
creaming off the very best."   —William Dalrymple, author of *City of Djinns*

Women's Travel

A WOMAN'S EUROPE $17.95
True Stories
Edited by Marybeth Bond
An exhilarating collection of inspirational, adventurous, and entertaining stories by women exploring the romantic continent of Europe. From the bestselling author Marybeth Bond.

WOMEN IN THE WILD $17.95
True Stories of Adventure and Connection
Edited by Lucy McCauley
"A spiritual, moving, and totally female book to take you around the world and back."
—*Mademoiselle*

A MOTHER'S WORLD $14.95
Journeys of the Heart
Edited by Marybeth Bond & Pamela Michael
"These stories remind us that motherhood is one of the great unifying forces in the world."
—*San Francisco Examiner*

A WOMAN'S PATH $16.95
Women's Best Spiritual Travel Writing
Edited by Lucy McCauley, Amy G. Carlson & Jennifer Leo
"A sensitive exploration of women's lives that have been unexpectedly and spiritually touched by travel experiences.... Highly recommended." —*Library Journal*

A WOMAN'S WORLD $18.95
True Stories of World Travel
Edited by Marybeth Bond
Introduction by Dervla Murphy

— ★ ★ ★ —
**Lowell Thomas Award
—Best Travel Book**

A WOMAN'S PASSION $17.95
FOR TRAVEL
True Stories of World Wanderlust
Edited by Marybeth Bond & Pamela Michael
"A diverse and gripping series of stories!"
—Arlene Blum, author of
Annapurna: A Woman's Place

Food

ADVENTURES IN WINE $17.95
True Stories of Vineyards and Vintages around the World
Edited by Thom Elkjer
Humanity, community, and brotherhood compose the marvelous virtues of the wine world. This collection toasts the warmth and wonders of this large extended family in stories by travelers who are wine novices and experts alike.

HER FORK IN $16.95
THE ROAD
Women Celebrate Food and Travel
Edited by Lisa Bach
A savory sampling of stories by the best writers in and out of the food and travel fields.

FOOD $18.95
A Taste of the Road
Edited by Richard Sterling
Introduction by Margo True

— ★ ★ ★ —
**Silver Medal Winner of the
Lowell Thomas Award
—Best Travel Book**

THE ADVENTURE $17.95
OF FOOD
True Stories of Eating Everything
Edited by Richard Sterling
"Bound to whet appetites for more than food." —*Publishers Weekly*

HOW TO EAT AROUND THE WORLD $12.95
Tips and Wisdom
By Richard Sterling
Combines practical advice on foodstuffs, habits, and etiquette, with hilarious accounts of others' eating adventures.

Travel Humor

SAND IN MY BRA AND $14.95
OTHER MISADVENTURES
Funny Women Write from the Road
Edited by Jennifer L. Leo
"A collection of ridiculous and sublime travel
experiences."
       —*San Francisco Chronicle*

HYENAS LAUGHED AT ME $14.95
AND NOW I KNOW WHY
The Best of Travel Humor and Misadventure
*Edited by Sean O'Reilly, Larry Habegger & James
O'Reilly*
Hilarious, outrageous and reluctant voyagers indulge
us with the best misadventures around the world.

LAST TROUT IN VENICE $14.95
**The Far-Flung Escapades of an
Accidental Adventurer**
By Doug Lansky
"Traveling with Doug Lansky might result in
a considerably shortened life expectancy…but
what a way to go."
   —Tony Wheeler, Lonely Planet Publications

NOT SO FUNNY WHEN $12.95
IT HAPPENED
**The Best of Travel Humor and
Misadventure**
Edited by Tim Cahill
Laugh with Bill Bryson, Dave Barry, Anne
Lamott, Adair Lara, and many more.

THERE'S NO TOILET PAPER $12.95
ON THE ROAD LESS TRAVELED
**The Best of Travel Humor and
Misadventure**
Edited by Doug Lansky   —— ★*★*★ ——

—— ★*★*★ ——   *ForeWord Gold Medal
Winner— Humor
Book of the Year*
*Humor Book of the Year
Independent Publisher's
Book Award*

WHOSE PANTIES ARE $14.95
THESE?
**More Misadventures from Funny Women
on the Road**
Edited by Jennifer L. Leo
Following on the high heels of the award-
winning bestseller *Sand in My Bra and other
Misadventures* comes another collection of
hilarious travel stories by women.

Travelers' Tales Classics

COAST TO COAST $16.95
A Journey Across 1950s America
By Jan Morris
After reporting on the first Everest ascent in
1953, Morris spent a year journeying across
the United States. In brilliant prose, Morris
records with exuberance and curiosity a time
of innocence in the U.S.

TRADER HORN $16.95
**A Young Man's Astounding Adventures
in 19th Century Equatorial Africa**
By Alfred Aloysius Horn
Here is the stuff of legends—thrills and
danger, wild beasts, serpents, and savages.
An unforgettable and vivid portrait of a
vanished Africa.

THE ROYAL ROAD $14.95
TO ROMANCE
By Richard Halliburton
"Laughing at hardships, dreaming of beauty,
ardent for adventure, Halliburton has managed
to sing into the pages of this glorious book his
own exultant spirit of youth and freedom."
       —*Chicago Post*

UNBEATEN TRACKS $14.95
IN JAPAN
By Isabella L. Bird
Isabella Bird was one of the most adventurous
women travelers of the 19th century with
journeys to Tibet, Canada, Korea, Turkey,
Hawaii, and Japan. A fascinating read.

THE RIVERS RAN EAST $16.95
By Leonard Clark
Clark is the original Indiana Jones, telling the breathtaking story of his search for the legendary El
Dorado gold in the Amazon.

Spiritual Travel

THE SPIRITUAL GIFTS $16.95
OF TRAVEL
The Best of Travelers' Tales
Edited by James O'Reilly & Sean O'Reilly
Favorite stories of transformation on the road
that show the myriad ways travel indelibly
alters our inner landscapes.

PILGRIMAGE $16.95
Adventures of the Spirit
Edited by Sean O'Reilly & James O'Reilly
Introduction by Phil Cousineau

ForeWord Silver Medal Winner
— Travel Book of the Year

THE ROAD WITHIN $18.95
True Stories of Transformation
and the Soul
Edited by Sean O'Reilly, James O'Reilly &
Tim O'Reilly

Independent Publisher's Book Award
—Best Travel Book

THE WAY OF $14.95
THE WANDERER
Discover Your True Self Through Travel
By David Yeadon
Experience transformation through travel
with this delightful, illustrated collection by
award-winning author David Yeadon.

A WOMAN'S PATH $16.95
Women's Best Spiritual Travel Writing
Edited by Lucy McCauley, Amy G. Carlson &
Jennifer Leo
"A sensitive exploration of women's lives
that have been unexpectedly and spiritually
touched by travel experiences.... Highly
recommended."
— Library Journal

THE ULTIMATE JOURNEY $17.95
Inspiring Stories of Living and Dying
James O'Reilly, Sean O'Reilly & Richard
Sterling
"A glorious collection of writings about the
ultimate adventure. A book to keep by one's
bedside—and close to one's heart."
—Philip Zaleski, editor,
The Best Spiritual Writing series

Special Interest

THE BEST $16.95
TRAVELERS' TALES 2004
True Stories from Around the World
Edited by James O'Reilly, Larry Habegger &
Sean O'Reilly
"This book will grace my bedside for years
to come."
—Simon Winchester, from the Introduction

TESTOSTERONE PLANET $17.95
True Stories from a Man's World
Edited by Sean O'Reilly, Larry Habegger &
James O'Reilly
Thrills and laughter with some of today's best
writers, including Sebastian Junger, Tim Cahill,
Bill Bryson, and Jon Krakauer.

THE GIFT OF TRAVEL $14.95
Inspiring Stories from Around the World
Edited by Larry Habegger, James O'Reilly
& Sean O'Reilly
"Like gourmet chefs in a French market, the
editors of Travelers' Tales pick, sift, and prod
their way through the weighty shelves of
contemporary travel writing, creaming off the
very best."
—William Dalrymple, author of *City of Djinns*

DANGER! $17.95
True Stories of Trouble and Survival
Edited by James O'Reilly, Larry Habegger &
Sean O'Reilly
"Exciting...for those who enjoy living on the
edge or prefer to read the survival stories of
others, this is a good pick."
— Library Journal

365 TRAVEL   **$14.95**
A Daily Book of Journeys, Meditations, and Adventures
Edited by Lisa Bach
An illuminating collection of travel wisdom and adventures that reminds us all of the lessons we learn while on the road.

THE GIFT OF RIVERS   **$14.95**
True Stories of Life on the Water
Edited by Pamela Michael
Introduction by Robert Hass
"...a soulful compendium of wonderful stories that illuminate, educate, inspire, and delight."
—David Brower,
Chairman of Earth Island Institute

FAMILY TRAVEL   **$17.95**
The Farther You Go, the Closer You Get
Edited by Laura Manske
"This is family travel at its finest."
—*Working Mother*

LOVE & ROMANCE   **$17.95**
True Stories of Passion on the Road
Edited by Judith Babcock Wylie
"A wonderful book to read by a crackling fire."   —*Romantic Traveling*

THE GIFT OF BIRDS   **$17.95**
True Encounters with Avian Spirits
Edited by Larry Habegger & Amy G. Carlson
"These are all wonderful, entertaining stories offering a *bird's-eye view!* of our avian friends."
—*Booklist*

IT'S A DOG'S WORLD   **$14.95**
True Stories of Travel with Man's Best Friend
Edited by Christine Hunsicker
Introduction by Maria Goodavage
Hilarious and heart warming stories of traveling with canine companions.

Travel Advice

THE PENNY PINCHER'S PASSPORT TO LUXURY TRAVEL   **$14.95**
(2ND EDITION)
The Art of Cultivating Preferred Customer Status
By Joel L. Widzer
Completely updated and revised, this 2nd edition of the popular guide to traveling like the rich and famous without being either describes, both philosophically and in practical terms, how to obtain luxurious travel benefits by building relationships with airlines and other travel companies.

SAFETY AND SECURITY   **$14.95**
FOR WOMEN WHO TRAVEL
(2ND EDITION)
By Sheila Swan & Peter Laufer
"A cache of valuable advice."
—*The Christian Science Monitor*

THE FEARLESS SHOPPER   **$14.95**
How to Get the Best Deals on the Planet
By Kathy Borrus
"Anyone who reads *The Fearless Shopper* will come away a smarter, more responsible shopper and a more curious, culturally attuned traveler."
—Jo Mancuso, *The Shopologist*

SHITTING PRETTY   **$12.95**
How to Stay Clean and Healthy While Traveling
By Dr. Jane Wilson-Howarth
A light-hearted book about a serious subject for millions of travelers— staying healthy on the road—written by international health expert, Dr. Jane Wilson-Howarth.

GUTSY WOMEN   **$12.95**
(2ND EDITION)
More Travel Tips and Wisdom for the Road
By Marybeth Bond
Packed with funny, instructive, and inspiring advice for women heading out to see the world.

GUTSY MAMAS   **$7.95**
Travel Tips and Wisdom for Mothers on the Road
By Marybeth Bond
A delightful guide for mothers traveling with their children—or without them!

Destination Titles

ALASKA	$18.95
Edited by Bill Sherwonit, Andromeda Romano-Lax, & Ellen Bielawski	
AMERICA	$19.95
Edited by Fred Setterberg	
AMERICAN SOUTHWEST	$17.95
Edited by Sean O'Reilly & James O'Reilly	
AUSTRALIA	$18.95
Edited by Larry Habegger	
BRAZIL	$18.95
Edited by Annette Haddad & Scott Doggett	
Introduction by Alex Shoumatoff	
CENTRAL AMERICA	$17.95
Edited by Larry Habegger & Natanya Pearlman	
CHINA	$18.95
Edited by Sean O'Reilly, James O'Reilly & Larry Habegger	
CUBA	$18.95
Edited by Tom Miller	
FRANCE	$18.95
Edited by James O'Reilly, Larry Habegger & Sean O'Reilly	
GRAND CANYON	$17.95
Edited by Sean O'Reilly, James O'Reilly & Larry Habegger	
GREECE	$18.95
Edited by Larry Habegger, Sean O'Reilly & Brian Alexander	
HAWAI'I	$17.95
Edited by Rick & Marcie Carroll	
HONG KONG	$17.95
Edited by James O'Reilly, Larry Habegger & Sean O'Reilly	
INDIA	$19.95
Edited by James O'Reilly & Larry Habegger	
IRELAND	$18.95
Edited by James O'Reilly, Larry Habegger & Sean O'Reilly	

ITALY $18.95
Edited by Anne Calcagno
Introduction by Jan Morris

JAPAN $17.95
Edited by Donald W. George & Amy G. Carlson

MEXICO $17.95
Edited by James O'Reilly & Larry Habegger

NEPAL $17.95
Edited by Rajendra S. Khadka

PARIS $18.95
Edited by James O'Reilly, Larry Habegger & Sean O'Reilly

PROVENCE $16.95
Edited by James O'Reilly & Tara Austen Weaver

SAN FRANCISCO $18.95
Edited by James O'Reilly, Larry Habegger & Sean O'Reilly

SPAIN $19.95
Edited by Lucy McCauley

THAILAND $18.95
Edited by James O'Reilly & Larry Habegger

TIBET $18.95
Edited by James O'Reilly & Larry Habegger

TURKEY $18.95
Edited by James Villers Jr.

TUSCANY $16.95
Edited by James O'Reilly & Tara Austen Weaver
Introduction by Anne Calcagno

Footsteps Series

THE FIRE NEVER DIES $14.95
**One Man's Raucous Romp Down the Road of Food,
Passion, and Adventure**
By Richard Sterling
"Sterling's writing is like spitfire, foursquare and jazzy with
crackle...."   *—Kirkus Reviews*

ONE YEAR OFF $14.95
**Leaving It All Behind for a Round-the-World Journey
with Our Children**
By David Elliot Cohen
A once-in-a-lifetime adventure generously shared, from the
author/editor of *America 24/7* and *A Day in the Life of Africa*

THE WAY OF THE WANDERER $14.95
Discover Your True Self Through Travel
By David Yeadon
Experience transformation through travel with this delightful,
illustrated collection by award-winning author David Yeadon.

TAKE ME WITH YOU $24.00
A Round-the-World Journey to Invite a Stranger Home
By Brad Newsham
"Newsham is an ideal guide. His journey, at heart, is into
humanity."   *—Pico Iyer, author of* The Global Soul

KITE STRINGS OF THE SOUTHERN CROSS $14.95
A Woman's Travel Odyssey
By Laurie Gough
Short-listed for the prestigious Thomas Cook Award, this is an
exquisite rendering of a young woman's search for meaning.

*ForeWord Silver Medal Winner
— Travel Book of the Year*

—— ★ ★ ★ ——

THE SWORD OF HEAVEN $24.00
A Five Continent Odyssey to Save the World
By Mikkel Aaland
"Few books capture the soul of the road like The *Sword of
Heaven,* a sharp-edged, beautifully rendered memoir that will
inspire anyone."
                    —Phil Cousineau, author of The Art of Pilgrimage

STORM $24.00
**A Motorcycle Journey of Love, Endurance,
and Transformation**
By Allen Noren
"Beautiful, tumultuous, deeply engaging and very satisfying.
Anyone who looks for truth in travel will find it here."
                    —Ted Simon, author of Jupiter's Travels

*ForeWord Gold Medal Winner
— Travel Book of the Year*

—— ★ ★ ★ ——